Contents

Illustrations

The Born Exile

GILLIAN TINDALL

The Born Exile

GEORGE GISSING

TEMPLE SMITH · LONDON

First published in Great Britain 1974 by
Maurice Temple Smith Ltd
37 Great Russell Street, London WC1

© 1974 GILLIAN TINDALL
ISBN 0 8511 7051 X

Printed in Great Britain by
Clarke, Doble & Brendon Ltd, Plymouth

I believe a novelist would make the best biographer: I wish I had someone's life to try my hand upon.

George Gissing
in a letter to Clara Collet
November 1895

The art of fiction has this great ethical importance, that it enables one to tell the truth about human beings in a way which is impossible in actual life.

Commonplace Book

One puts into literary form hopes which are not very likely to be realized.

Gissing to a bookseller friend

Digest Biography

This is intended for the majority of readers who are probably not familiar with the details of Gissing's life. Those who are will perhaps wish to go straight on to the Introduction.

George Gissing was born on 22 November 1857 in Wakefield, Yorkshire. He was the eldest son of a chemist and amateur botanist, Thomas Waller Gissing, who had recently come from East Anglia and who kept a shop in Westgate in the centre of the town.* Subsequently two more boys were born, Will (who was to die in early manhood) and Algernon, who also became a writer, prolific if undistinguished, specializing in books on the English countryside. Then came two girls, Margaret (Madge) and Ellen (Nellie) neither of whom married. They spent their lives in or near Wakefield and for some years in the 1890s and 1900s ran a school there. On them eventually devolved the responsibility of bringing up Gissing's two sons by his second wife.

George, as the eldest son and obviously 'bookish' and intelligent, early became the focus for his family's social aspirations. He was sent first to a small school in Back Lane, Wakefield (still standing) connected with the Unitarian Church.† When Gissing was thirteen his father died: the following year, through the good offices of Quaker friends of his father's who had sat with him on the Town Council and who wished to help the bereaved family, George was sent to a small boarding school at Alderley Edge,

---

* The shop, Number 30, still stands and was, till recently, a small branch of Boots the chain chemists.

† The teacher's name was Harrison, one which was to dog Gissing throughout his life—Helen (Nell) Harrison was the name of the girl he first married, and Frederic Harrison was an early benefactor to him in London. There was, of course, no family connection between the three.

Lindow Grove, Cheshire, run by James Wood.* From Wood, Gissing learnt the exaggerated respect for the classics which was the mark of the educated Englishman of the period. He also acquired a reputation for being 'a glutton for work' and for throwing himself whole-heartedly into plays and recitations. He was an extremely apt pupil, and at fourteen and a half was awarded three years' free tuition at Owens College, Manchester (which later became Manchester University) as a reward for coming top over all England in what was then called the Junior Oxford examination. During most of these years he continued to board at Alderley Edge, going into Manchester daily, and also acted as a pupil-teacher in the school. In 1875, by then living in Manchester, he took the matriculation examination for the University of London, and won exhibitions in Latin and English. Prizes and awards had characterized his school life, and he seemed set fair for a distinguished academic career.

However in the spring of 1876, when Gissing was eighteen and a half and might have expected to go to London University the following autumn, it came to the notice of the authorities at Owens that money had been disappearing from the cloakroom. A trap was set, and it became evident that Gissing was the culprit. At a special meeting of the Senate all his awards were removed from him and he was summarily dismissed. The excuse that he had stolen in order to provide money for a girl, Nell Harrison, who would otherwise 'take to the streets' did not improve his case in the eyes of the authorities. He was also taken before the magistrate and condemned to one month's hard labour in gaol, which he served.

Gissing's immediate movements on coming out of gaol are not clear, but it is thought that he worked for a while in the offices of a shipping clerk before deciding to ship himself to the New World. By the autumn he was in Boston; in early 1877 he taught for several months in the High School at Waltham, Massachusetts, where he was incorrectly believed to be a graduate. He seemed to be getting on well, but he left his job without warning one day and spent that summer wandering the States. He reached Chicago, where he managed to sell some short stories

---

* The building still stands: it is now called 'College flats' and is on the main road from Manchester to Stoke-on-Trent, now no longer rural in character.

to a local newspaper. Later, he moved back East to Troy, New York State, believing that he might have a market for his work there. His hopes proved unfounded, and, destitute, he kept himself alive for several days on handfuls of peanuts from a street seller. He subsequently found work, possibly with a travelling photographer, possibly with a plumber. Between September and October he returned to England, having borrowed money from his brother Algernon in order to pay the steerage passage. On his return or shortly after he sought out Nell Harrison again. By the autumn of 1878, if not before, she had joined him in London, where he was paying six shillings and sixpence a week for one room in a house in Gower Place* and working as a clerk at St John's hospital for skin diseases in Leicester Square.

In 1879 he was writing *Workers in the Dawn* and attempting a domestic life with Nell in extremely modest circumstances. At the beginning of this year he met, through an advertisement, Bertz, a German intellectual who became a lifelong friend though, after 1884, a pen-friend only—Gissing was a voluminous letter-writer. Otherwise at this period his contacts with social and intellectual equals were almost non-existent. His school and college friends were in the north and he had in any case broken with most of them after the shameful episode in Manchester. The only one with whom he seems later to have resumed contact was Morley Roberts, who was not always in England. He made attempts to find companionship in the Radical working-class movement, lecturing for a brief period to a Working Men's Club in Paddington, but soon became disenchanted with this. He finally married Nell in October 1879—they had by that time moved to Colville Place, near Goodge Street.† It was similar and nearby to the Charlotte Place figuring in *Workers*, which was published that November. Gissing himself paid for the publication out of the remains of a small sum left in trust for him by his father.

The book was an almost total failure, but it was read some eight months later by one influential person—Frederic Harrison, a journalist by trade and a Positivist by conviction; Harrison described himself as 'a humble follower of Comte, Mill, Spencer and Darwin'. He invited the young writer to dinner and, learn-

* Since demolished.
† Much of this alley still stands.

ing that he was having a struggle to live, wrote on his behalf
to a number of literary men including John Morley, the editor
of the *Pall Mall Gazette*, and recommended him to a number
of acquaintances as a private tutor. Gissing had by this time left
the hospital job, and was attempting to support himself and Nell
by giving lessons, frequently going short of food in order to
buy books from secondhand stalls. This period is evoked in *The
Private Papers of Henry Ryecroft*. He did not at first, or for
some time, mention Nell's existence to the Harrisons. Towards the
end of 1880, when he and Nell were by then living in Islington,
he was engaged to tutor Harrison's two small sons, and it seems
probable that he never again suffered real want, but his brief
experience of absolute poverty had bitten deep and he remained,
for the rest of his life, fearful to the point of paranoia on the
subject.

John Morley was of the opinion that Gissing had considerable
journalistic gifts but the only journalistic enterprise in which
he persisted for any length of time was the contribution of
articles to a review run by Turgenev, the Russian novelist, whose
books he admired and whose influence is apparent in some of
his own work. In February 1881 he and Nell moved to three
rooms in Westbourne Park, a more genteel district near the
Harrisons, to whom he had now confided his past and present
troubles, and for a short while that year he dated his letters,
Harrison-style, according to the Positivist calendar. Life with the
disturbed, alcoholic Nell was becoming more and more difficult.
Gissing—or someone—later ripped the relevant pages from his
diary, but his letters to Algernon for that period gradually
abandon the pretence of domestic unity and tell, either overtly
or by implication, a tale of quarrels, problems, recrimina-
tions, trial separations and trial reunions. Perhaps in order
to provide for Nell away from himself, Gissing moved back
to Gower Place, and throughout the latter part of 1881
and 1882 Nell was several times admitted to hospital and
at other times boarded with assorted acquaintances or
keepers. Meanwhile, Gissing was working on the never-
published *Mrs Grundy's Enemies*. In mid-1883 he was still tutoring the Harrisons, and others, working on *The Unclassed* and
urging Algernon (a law student) to read more philosophy. By
September of that year his association with Nell was apparently

all but ended, except that he still paid money for her support. It was then that he was visited by a police sergeant, who intimated that Nell was a common prostitute and wondered why Gissing did not try to get a divorce. Gissing considered the matter but then abandoned it, fearing further problems. At this period he was living, more or less comfortably for the first time, with a family in Oakley Crescent, Chelsea. In May 1884 he moved to Milton Street, Regent's Park. In June *The Unclassed* was published: at this point Gissing had already made the acquaintance of George Meredith, who was the publisher's reader. Later that year came his first experience of staying in an upper class household—the Gaussens, whom he had met through the Harrisons. Almost immediately after his return to London he started the first draft of *Isabel Clarendon*, making use of the new setting. He also moved for the first time to a proper flat, 7K Cornwall Mansions, Marylebone (the block still stands) which became his base for the next six years; his life was gradually taking on a more middle-class colouring, though he still lacked sufficient contacts with people who shared his interests.

Through 1885 he was living at 7K and writing *Isabel Clarendon*, *A Life's Morning** and *Demos*, the first book to bring him any real success. For part of that year a young Gaussen son was boarding with him, and he also continued to tutor other pupils. Towards the end of that year Algernon, who had perennial difficulty finding a settled occupation (a difficulty that was to be his for years), came to live with him for a while, and it was now George Gissing's turn to offer his brother loans. In March 1886 *Demos* was finished, and later that year, while Algernon was still with him, he wrote *Thyrza*. The following year Algernon got married; Gissing was alone again and seems to have suffered a good deal from loneliness and depression. He tended to avoid earlier friends such as the Harrisons. Little creative work was produced during 1887, only a never-published novel *Clement Dorricott*.

In January 1888, while he was on holiday at Eastbourne, he was called back to London by the news of Nell's death: for four years he had not seen her. Although this freed him to marry again, he seems to have experienced no great sense of re-

* Actually published after *Demos*, but written before, while Chapman the publisher was havering about taking *Isabel Clarendon*.

lief, but at any rate the financial burden of Nell was removed from him. Later that year he wrote *The Nether World*, his last 'low life' novel, and then, in September, made his first lengthy trip to Europe: he stayed first in Paris, then went on to Rome, Florence, Naples and Venice. He returned only in March 1889 and at once started the book which was to become *The Emancipated*, making immediate use of the Italian experiences.

He spent much of the summer in Wakefield with his family, and in August went to the Channel Islands with his sister Madge. In the autumn he was back again in London, seeing various new acquaintances. He was also interesting himself in the New Woman. In November he set off on his travels again, going to Italy and then on to Greece, a long-cherished dream ever since the days of his classical education. Early in 1890 he was staying in Calabria, in southern Italy, where he was ill with a condition diagnosed, for the first time, as 'a touch of congestion in the right lung'. He travelled home via Naples. He arrived home in March but must still have been in funds, for in April he set off again for Paris with both his sisters.* He spent much of that summer, again, in Wakefield, making abortive starts on several books, one of which was eventually to become *New Grub Street*.

He had calculated that he had enough in the bank to last him till September. When that month arrived, and he was back in London, he still had not got any new novel properly underway, and was beginning to feel hounded by the idea that he must, in order to be at peace with himself, find a wife. It was on the 22nd of that month that he appears to have picked up, in Oxford Street, Edith Underwood, the daughter of a monumental mason, who was destined to become the second Mrs Gissing and almost as unsuitable a choice as the first. At once he got to work, and by Christmas *New Grub Street* was finished. In February 1891, at the age of thirty-three, he married Edith, apparently against both his own better judgement and hers, and took her to live in lodgings in Exeter.

That year, isolated in the West Country from even such intellectual companionship as London had offered him, he wrote *Born in Exile*, followed by *Denzil Quarrier*, the only one of his novels he claimed to have written easily. At the end of the year his eldest son, Walter, was born, and shortly afterwards sent to a

* Foreign travel was relatively cheap at the period.

foster mother because of supposed difficulties in caring for him at home (the Gissings had by this time rented a house in Exeter). By April 1892 the baby was back again; Gissing found himself having to stop work to prepare Walter's feeds and was already thoroughly disillusioned with Edith. It was during this period that *The Odd Women* was written. By the end of the year such was the state of tension in the household that Gissing was renting a room away from home in which to work.

In the summer of 1893 he paid a short visit to London, with its libraries and other amenities, and this seems to have decided him to move back there. It was probably then that he first met Clara Collet, an educated young woman who was to become his confidante and loyal friend. By September he, Edith and the child were settled in Brixton, which was to become the locale for his next novel, *In the Year of Jubilee*, written between January and April 1894. By the end of June he had finished his first one-volume novel, *Eve's Ransom*. In September the family moved again, to 'Everleigh', Worple Road, Epsom (still standing), which was to be their home till the break-up of this marriage three years later. Already Gissing was stating in his diary that only the existence of the child, who had become dear to him, prevented him from leaving home. That autumn he met, through his publishers, Miss Orme, a somewhat eccentric and 'advanced' woman who several years later was to take charge of Edith for him. He ended his diary for that year with the note that in the course of it, his expenses had been only £239 6s. 9d. while his earnings had been £453 12s. 5d.: whatever the disaster of his private life, his career was prospering. *New Grub Street*, in particular, had made him far better known, and he was now also writing and publishing short stories and trying his hand at one-volume novellas.

The following year, 1895, he earned over £500. He also began for the first time to have a circle of literary acquaintances. Through a new friend, the banker Edward Clodd, he met Grant Allen (the author of the succès de scandale *The Woman Who Did*) and also met and stayed with Thomas Hardy. He also re-met his old friend from Wakefield and Manchester days, Henry Hick, now a doctor, who became a close friend during his last years. In January 1886 a second son, Alfred, was born, and the following April Gissing took Walter, by then four years old, to Wakefield

and left him there in the care of his sisters to get him away
from the household of quarrels and scenes, but the removal
hardly helped his relationship with his wife. During this year he
wrote *The Whirlpool*, and met J. M. Barrie and H. G. Wells: the
latter became a close friend.

Early in 1897 relations between Gissing and his wife deteriorated
still further. In February he left her suddenly, and sought refuge
with the Hick family in Kent, but in the next few months Miss
Orme and Miss Collet between them seem to have encouraged the
couple to try to patch up their relationship again. Gissing retreated for a while to Budleigh Salterton; then, in August, he
and Edith tried a holiday together in Yorkshire with the children,
but it was not a success. Meanwhile the state of Gissing's lungs
was causing anxiety; he was approaching forty and was beginning
to be preoccupied with his physical condition and with the
possibility that he might die soon if he did not take care of himself. It seemed a good idea that he should winter in Italy. He left
for Siena, then Calabria, and by December was in Rome working
on his book on Charles Dickens. Edith and Alfred, then rising
two, went to live with Miss Orme at Tulse Hill. In the February
of 1898 Gissing was ill in Rome with what was described as 'flu.
In the spring the Wellses visited him there; on his way back home
Gissing visited Potsdam and saw Bertz, whom he had not seen
since 1884. Back in England he rented a house in Dorking, Surrey,
where he more or less went into hiding, having developed a horror
that Edith might discover where he was.

Towards the end of this summer he met Gabrielle Fleury,
who was to be the third woman in his life. She was French, and
wrote to ask him if she could translate *New Grub Street*. He
invited her to visit him and subsequently the relationship
flourished by correspondence. It was immediately after meeting her that he began *The Crown of Life*. He and Gabrielle
continued to write enthusiastic letters to one another throughout
the winter, which Gissing spent in Dorking and in poor health.
In the course of this time it was decided between them that they
should set up together in France in a common-law marriage—
which meant, in effect, that Gabrielle's relatives should think she
was really married, while most of Gissing's English acquaintances
should not know of her existence. In April 1899 Gissing, who
had by now, to his distress, lost sight of the exact whereabouts

of Edith and Alfred, paid a brief visit to Walter in Yorkshire, and then departed for a new life in France.

He and Gabrielle spent that summer partly in Italy and Switzerland and returned to Paris in the autumn, to a flat shared with Gabrielle's widowed mother at 13 rue de Siam, 16è.* They spent the winter there, and Gissing wrote *Our Friend the Charlatan* and a never-published book called *Among the Prophets*. In April 1900 he paid a visit to England; his health seemed to be temporarily better. He and Gabrielle spent that summer in the Nièvre, in central France, and he began work on *The Private Papers of Henry Ryecroft*, the supposed autobiography of a writer. They returned to Paris for the winter. Gissing was worried about money again: his most recent publishers, Lawrence & Bullen,† had gone bankrupt, he felt that his brief period of success was over and was wondering if he could reduce his weekly payment of £2 to Edith. The Parisian winter depressed him and he became homesick. Early in 1901 things improved somewhat, with a publisher planning a sumptuous edition of his travel book *By the Ionian Sea*. In May, again worried about his lungs, he visited a French specialist, who diagnosed bad emphysema and chronic bronchitis. He then went to England and saw an English specialist who recommended different treatment, taking in particular the view that another winter in Paris would mean death for Gissing. Encouraged by the Wellses Gissing entered an English sanatorium for the summer at Nayland, Suffolk, much against Gabrielle's wishes. He returned to France, but the following winter (1901–2) was spent by him in a boarding-house for invalids at Arcachon in South West France while Gabrielle remained in Paris with her mother. Here he wrote *Will Warburton*, his last complete novel. It was while he was there that he received news that Alfred, then six, had finally been removed from Edith's care, and that Edith had been confined in an asylum for the insane.

In May 1902 he and the Fleurys took a house at Ciboure, a suburb of St Jean de Luz on the Basque coast. It was believed that the climate there would do his illness good. The rest of the

---

* A plaque now marks it.

† His relations with his numerous publishers were never happy or secure, his attitude to each in turn tending to progress rapidly from fervent enthusiasm to utter condemnation.

year was passed 'in ailing idleness'. However, he studied Spanish and made a few friends among the English colony in the small town. The following spring, having decided that, after all, it would be better for him to be farther inland, he and the Fleurys moved to a house in Ispoure, a tiny village just outside the walls of St Jean Pied de Port, the little medieval town at the foot of a pass through the Pyrenees, an old route of the pilgrims and of Charlemagne. The house, the Chalet Elgué, still stands. Here he began *Veranilda*, his long-planned historical romance, but was never to finish it. Shortly before Christmas 1903, he went on a day's trip to the mountains with some visiting Fleury relatives and caught a cold which rapidly became pneumonia, accompanied by myocarditis. He died a few days later, in a high fever and delirium. During his last days Wells, summoned by Gabrielle, was at his bedside. So was Cooper, the English clergyman of the area, who was misled by his ravings into believing that this life-long atheist had died a convert to Christianity. Roberts, the other friend who was summoned, had been ill himself, and reached St Jean Pied de Port only on 29 December to learn that Gissing had died the day before. He was buried in St Jean de Luz in a ceremony presided over by the English chaplain. Gabrielle Fleury-Gissing (she used both names) grieved as a widow for many years, only dying herself in 1954.

Introduction

It is said to be the second fifty years after a writer's death which counts. During his lifetime, his success may be great or small but it will inevitably be to some extent dependent on his own relationship with those times in which he is living; he must speak for others besides himself. He may have the kind of perception and insight which transcend time, and the equally rare capacity for putting this down on paper, but his success in his own time is also likely to be due as much to the coincidence of his own thoughts with those of others. To be a fashionable writer, you have to see or think what your readership is just preparing itself to see and think. The celebrated 'influence' of the great writer —Dickens is the obvious example—is really the action of a precipitant upon a substance (the public viewpoint) which only needs that precipitant in order to crystallize into a new form. Writers do not 'create': they discover and explain.

But, once dead, the writer—to push the chemical metaphor one stage farther—becomes inert. Whether famous or obscure, he can no longer be an innovator. He is overtaken by time, by change: the living, moving on, lose touch with him, and therefore it seems to them that *he* has lost touch with them. If much of his fame during his lifetime was apparently based on his ability to depict and explain their own world to his audience, then that ability becomes revealed as a rapidly depreciating asset. Dated insights have little attraction—and the more keenly particularized they were at the time, the more rapidly they date, especially if, as is often the case, subsequent writers have made use of them in newer ways. This, I believe, is the real reason (rather than any arbitrary 'swing of the pendulum') why a novelist who has known even a modest degree of fame during his lifetime, usually suffers a period of eclipse for several decades afterwards. The world moves on. No one is interested. The books sleep.

Whether they are ever disinterred from their sleep, and the writer himself resurrected to join the exclusive lists of those known to posterity, depends upon something more fundamental than his appeal to his own generation. After fifty years, when all but a handful of the books' original readers will be dead, there is no more question of the books' relevance, topicality, shock value, originality; no one is likely to feel, reading them, 'But this is about *me*!'—that warmly subjective, small-minded response which accounts for so much success which fails to last. The writer who is resurrected must have some fundamental, more durable quality —that mysterious X-factor, a core of inner truth and clarity, which distinguishes real writing from book-making. Of course the X-factor must have been there all the time, even when the books were being acclaimed for purely ephemeral reasons. But few wise critics would confidently predict which, of the writers of their own day, possess this quality. 'May well become a classic' must be one of the most over-optimistic and over-worked terms in the reviewer's lexicon (as well as one of the dullest). Only time tells—time, which shortly after the novelist's death seems to be the enemy, eventually turns out to be on the side of the exceptional writer, separating him at last from his hordes of competitors and emulators, finally establishing him in a niche from which no further swings of fashion can sweep him.

George Gissing provides a classic example of this progress. Acclaimed in his own time (and also reviled) for his novels' 'modern realism', their alarmingly avant garde tendency to deal with 'sordid subjects', after his death he rapidly sank, if not into oblivion, at least into the shadowy limbo of the obsolete. The time-span of his own comparatively short life had much to do with this descent: dying in 1903 at the age of just 46, he thus remained a Victorian for a world which, within a few years, was rapidly consigning the old century and the old reign to the quaintly antique past. Indeed the bulk of his novels were in the traditional, mid-nineteenth century three-volume form; although he tried his hand at the more attenuated, one-volume novel which abruptly took over the market in the 1890s,* he never really adapted to it. In a number of ways, though by no means all, his books seemed to belong more to the world of Dickens than to that of Wells or Bennett, his immediate contemporaries; and,

* See Appendix.

unlike them, he did not live on to become a twentieth-century man. He did not survive to see his 'daring' subjects become commonplace nor his more advanced ideas vindicated—nor, by the same token did he live to compete with such writers as Lawrence and Joyce, or even to envisage a world in which such writing as theirs would be possible. By 1910 his novels must already have seemed to belong to a world that was passing: another decade, and a world war, later, they were completely 'period': everything—style, social assumptions, reticences, plot-formation— all belonged to another era.

And yet the books were not quite dead. At long intervals one or other of them (by no means always the best) would appear in a fresh edition, and a few of them found their way into 'classic' series such as Nelson's Library. A film was made of *Demos* (under another title) in the 1920s. Two biographical studies had appeared in 1912, one by Frank Swinnerton and another, in a curiously hybrid, fictionalized form, by Gissing's old friend Morley Roberts. The amount of dissent and animosity these two works aroused at the time—and continued to arouse spasmodically in literary journals during the twenties and thirties—are an indication of the extent to which Gissing the writer was still alive in the minds of a select body of readers, though many of his novels were only available in what George Orwell called 'soup-stained editions from public libraries' and several were virtually unobtainable. Orwell considered him a very important writer and did a certain amount to publicize his work. The two Georges, in fact, had a number of odd affinities, and at least one of Orwell's own novels, *Keep the Aspidistra Flying*, has a central character who might also have come from a Gissing novel—a bookish, penniless, socially insecure, embittered yet warm-hearted young man alone in London. Virginia Woolf, also, found Gissing interesting enough to devote an essay to him. Both in his lifetime and after it Gissing was a writer's writer, more readily appreciated by his own kind than by the public at large—not surprisingly, since his best and best-known book, *New Grub Street* is the oldest and most classic portrait of the writer's existence. This meant that, although among the general public in the fifty years following his death his literary reputation dwindled to vanishing point, it had not really vanished but had gone underground—into that literary underworld of a diffuse, unorganized, often solitary yet purposefully telepathic and collective movement which is typified by unsigned articles in *The Times Literary Supplement.*

Eventually it began to re-emerge, conforming with absurd coincidental neatness to the fifty-year maxim. A biography of Gissing appeared in 1954, and another a decade later, both by American academics. Articles, and short, specialized studies of particular aspects of Gissing's life and work have also appeared. He has one extremely devoted French biographer, and, since 1965 there has been a quarterly publication called *The Gissing News-letter.* In 1971 a careful and comprehensive Gissing exhibition of letters, photos, and manuscripts was held at the National Book League in London. One can only hope that, if Gissing himself still exists in any other world in any conscious state, he is pleased at all this activity on his behalf—though, if his personality has remained true to itself, that pleasure will be tinged with considerable irony, a histrionic resentment that it could not have happened during his own lifetime, and perhaps also a well-bred alarm at the thought of his private life being scattered now through the libraries of the world like pieces of a dismembered corpse dispersed to different laboratories for the scrutiny of dozens of experts, carefully dated, labelled and pickled. Despite all his rashness, his volubility (both on paper and when in the company of those he liked) and his tendency to change his mind, Gissing remained all his life an oddly private person, prone to keep different aspects of his life, perhaps even of his personality, in separate compartments. This, I think, is one of the sources of what his biographer, Jacob Korg, has called 'the Gissing mystery' —a peculiar appeal in both the man and his work which seems to go beyond the intrinsic merit of many of his novels.

Gissing, simply, appeals to people. He touches them. Despite his nineteenth-century themes, his personal obsessions, his blind spots, we often feel near to him. We feel, perhaps, that pressing desire to reach the reader; that 'craving for sympathy' which his friend Edward Clodd noted in the man is perceptible also in his work, taking craving (as surely Clodd himself intended) not in the vulgar modern sense of 'wanting people to be sorry for him', but rather in the sense of wanting understanding, wanting warmth —wanting, in fact, a reciprocation of those feelings he so often and so readily extended towards others. Gissing has been labelled, usually by people who know little of his work, a 'depressing' writer. While it is evident that he was, in the medical sense, a depressive personality, 'depressing' seems an absurdly inept term to apply to a man whose work contains such bountiful evidence of an unquenchable idealism and a desire to love and help others. Several themes occur and reoccur in Gissing's novels with an obsessional frequency. One, certainly, is the malignity of Fate, but another, almost as omnipresent, is the joy of giving. Daydreams of giving—helping—assisting—educating—appear in book after book. The sympathy that Gissing craved from others, he also longed to offer.

'Gissing the dreary realist' is the oldest and best-established of the false images his name conjures up to many people, but the birth of Gissing-scholarship in the last dozen years has spawned several others. Because his life was at moments colourful, containing many of the traditional ingredients of tragic romance, its outlines have now become quite well known—better known, in fact, than many of his books. We live in what a French critic has called 'l'age des petits papiers'—meaning that a writer's private life now often arouses more interest, and certainly provokes more scholarly efforts, than the works which are, after all, the only reason he is being studied at all. Occasionally one feels that Gissing the writer is in danger of being pushed aside by those not themselves fundamentally interested in the process of writing, and in his place is raised a popular romantic figure to whom are ascribed motivations owing as much to the mental climate of our own times as to that of his own.

The popular legend runs something like this: Gissing was a scholarship boy from a poor family. He was at college, and all set for a brilliant academic career in the classics (his true bent) when disaster struck. He fell in love with a prostitute, and, in order to save her from the streets, stole money from other members of his college. He was caught, dismissed and imprisoned for a month. On his release, friends of his family sent him to America to start afresh, but he returned from there six months later, sought out his girl and married her. They lived in obscure London lodgings, where Gissing gave lessons to support them. The marriage was predictably a failure, the couple eventually separated, but Gissing for years faithfully sent 'Nell' money, though on the point of starvation himself. Disgraced in the eyes of decent society, in order to live he frantically wrote novels, although—

so the myth runs—he would have greatly preferred to be devoting himself to classical authors. Nevertheless—a contradiction is apparent here—he was a champion of the working classes and of the Radical movement. Finally Nell died and Gissing married again but, still prevented by poverty from picking a wife who would be any sort of intellectual or social equal, he chose a working girl. That marriage also ended disastrously after two sons had been born. Only toward the end of his life—approaching forty, worn out with labour—did he achieve a modicum of literary success and felt able to meet his fellow writers socially. Shortly afterwards he met a French woman who appeared to be everything which his previous wives had failed to be. Unable to marry her legally, he lived in a devoted common-law union with her, abroad, until his death from a lung condition four years later.

The basic outlines are true. But much myth has accrued around them—myth which, in the course of this study, I hope to do something towards dispersing. For not only his letters and diary, but also his novels, tell a somewhat different story. Although here a point needs underlining. *No* one—least of all no one who is a novelist—should make the vulgar error of assuming that the novels of Gissing or any other writer are simple *romans-à-clef*, and that it is sufficient to know about the events of the writer's own life to make the key work—to say 'Ah, yes, of course, Carrie is Nell and Mr Hood is Mr Gissing, and, dear me, so that's how it happened, now we know!' Writers—born compulsive writers like Gissing—simply do not write like that. Even when such a writer does set out to put chunks of his own life straight into a book (a wasteful method of working by the way) the writing-mechanism inevitably proceeds of its own volition, subtly altering, transforming, sharpening, making the fictional account different in a number of ways from the reality—but sometimes more fundamentally true, more representative of basic elements in the writer's mentality or the situation described. The axiom that truth is stranger than fiction may be paraphrased to mean that fiction often has a coherence, a probability and a truth of emphasis which the muddled 'true facts' lack. George Gissing himself appreciated this. 'What a farce is Biography!' he wrote towards the end of his life to a woman friend, Clara Collet, with whom he was in regular correspondence. 'The only true biographies are to be found in novels.' One might wish that this letter—not to date published—had been read by some of the critics and commentators who have so vociferously condemned Morley Roberts' *biographie romancée*,[1] a work which, while unreliable on dates and similar material details, gives, in my view, a better and truer overall impression of Gissing the man than many subsequent and more scholarly writers have done.

The point is this: while it should never be assumed that Gissing 'put his life' and the lives of others straight into his books, in an unworked, unprocessed form, it is certainly fair to say that he is one of those novelists whose books are closely associated with his life, and act therefore as a running commentary on it. Sometimes, if taken too literally, they distort and mislead: the widespread misinterpretation of his pseudo-autiobiography *The Private Papers of Henry Ryecroft* provides a classic example of this. But sometimes they appear to embody a more faithful, sensitive and perceptive view of his world than do his personal papers. In diaries and letters we are all of us myopic and over-preoccupied with immediate events and moods to the exclusion of long-term themes. In fiction, the view is longer, the perspective better. The judgement—of personalities and situations—is often keener. Gissing is by no means the only novelist who appears to know with his pen things which, in his daily life, he singularly failed to grasp.

All writers are two people, writer and ordinary person. In that the two share the same environment and experiences, the same eyes and ears, one might be tempted to call them Siamese twins— except that, though inescapably joined together, they are non-identical twins. There are subtle differences—in intelligence, in sophistication, in maturity, even in prevailing mood. There are often irreconcilable differences in needs. It is the inter-relation between these two persons, their points of communication and their failures in communication, which concerns me in the following chapters.

1 The Born Exile

'One may remark in passing,' wrote Gissing in his book on Charles Dickens, 'that English people are distinguished among nationalities by the profound mutual ignorance which separates their social ranks.' We are indeed, as has often been observed, a remarkably class-ridden nation and our literature has been correspondingly class-obsessed. Even today, one of the most significant facts one can know about a man or woman is his or her class of origin: almost always, the fact will be found to explain much, from large-scale assumptions about the nature of life to minor habits of speech, manners or tastes in food. We may no longer be divided into Disraeli's two nations of rich and poor, but we are still divided into two—or more—separate cultures, in a way that other European nations are not and never have been.

Of course—as we are always telling ourselves or assuring other people—the divisions have become far easier to step over than they were in Gissing's day, but the assumption often made that the class structure in the past was a rigid one in which everyone stayed put, knowing his place, born, living and dying within the same culture, is misleading. It would be much more nearly true to say that every age has been one in which a degree of social mobility has been apparent; the 'rise of a new middle class' seems to be one of those perennial phenomena cited for any and every period as if it were a unique one. A fresh middle class was appearing in the fourteenth century, it was appearing in the sixteenth, it was appearing in vast numbers during the Industrial Revolution and it was still coming up, as new and as self-conscious as ever, during the latter half of the nineteenth century, roughly the span of Gissing's own life. To regard Gissing, then, as he tended to regard himself and as many others have accepted him since, as something exceptional, a social misfit with quite peculiar and individual problems owing to his lack of a solid upper-middle-

class background, is to make a fundamental error. 'Born in exile'
he may have been—exile, that is, from the life which he was
temperamentally and intellectually best suited to lead—but in this
he was simply typical of his kind, his own generation, and many
others before him.

He was not (as some readers of his first novel, *Workers in the
Dawn*, assumed) of working-class origin, but lower-middle-class:
that clerking, trading class which has produced by far the greatest
number of English writers. It was from this class that Shakespeare
came, and Dickens (the major literary influence upon Gissing's
childhood); from this class also came Gissing's contemporaries,
Arnold Bennett, Hardy, with whom he had a slightly self-
conscious literary acquaintance, Barrie, H. G. Wells who became
a close friend of his and indeed attended his dying. Even Meredith,
whom he revered as the elder literary statesman who had achieved
security and fame, had had similar modest beginnings a generation
earlier. Such ambitious young men from the provinces were not
only a commonplace of the London of Gissing's own time; they
always have been. His oft-quoted remark, that his literary heroes
belonged to a 'class of young men distinctive of our time—well-
educated, fairly bred but *without money*'[1] was inaccurate simply
in that the class he was citing was by no means new—and in any
case, if they were numerous enough to form a class why did
he himself feel so alone? His own social isolation, which he felt
so strongly and which he lamented intermittently throughout his
life, cannot then be attributed to any great extent to his humble
beginnings and consequent lack of money 'behind him'. The real
sources of his exile lay deeper, were more complex and self-
contradictory.

The Rural Dream

He was born in 1857, in Wakefield, an industrial town which was
even then becoming a part of the extensive Leeds conurbation,
but if this suggests the 'northern writer' on the lines of Bennett
this is another false trail: his family beginnings did not lie there.
Both his parents came from East Anglia, and since there is a small
village in Suffolk called 'Gissing' one may assume that their
roots had been there since the middle ages. It is said that Gissing's
mother was the daughter of a solicitor at Droitwich, Norfolk:
if this is correct, then the Gissing family represented a recogniz-

able pattern in the genesis of remarkable men: a mother who marries slightly beneath her station, socially, but in this obscurity rears at least one child who far outstrips his early environment. (D. H. Lawrence is the classic example.) Typically this son, on whom so much thwarted ambition must be fixed, is the first born: so it was in Gissing's case. Not that Thomas Gissing, George's father, was by any means a stupid man; on the contrary, but he appears to have had only a limited formal education—Gissing, when a precocious schoolboy himself, was shocked to discover that his adored father had never realized Greek and Latin poetry did not have rhymes. He was a pharmacist by trade, and his move, the year before his eldest son's birth, from the pleasant country town of Halesworth to the smoky, fast-expanding mill-town in the alien north, was presumably typical of the immediately post-Industrial Revolution wave of socio-geographical mobility—the move from the impoverished stagnating countryside to the new towns where the money was. The original exile was Mr Gissing senior.

Wakefield was one of those old towns which, in the nineteenth century, were transformed out of all recognition. Situated on the River Calder, in Yorkshire, it had always been a centre for cloth-making and coal-mining, but new methods in both these fields brought devastation to the landscape. In 1871, the year after Thomas Gissing died, when his son was thirteen, a local historian wrote of the river:

It was clear and sweet, and fish lived in it thirty years ago; but I doubt whether at this day fish can exist in any part of its length of forty-five miles . . . Notwithstanding the state of this great stream, which from the above circumstances is also a great sewer, the Wakefield people are constrained to use its waters for drinking purposes. The liquid doubtless undergoes, in the Water Company's reservoirs, filtration through substances which have counteracting properties; but the distasteful fact remains that the indispensable beverage of the town is obtained from diluted sewage.[2]

The message is clear: not merely was the Wakefield to which Thomas Gissing moved a despoiled area, but even during the course of George's childhood it grew progressively uglier, progressively more tainted and blackened by the detritus of mid-nineteenth century commercial prosperity. I have seen a print

of St Mary's Chantry, Chapel-on-the-Bridge[3] (one of the few
medieval buildings Wakefield possesses) dated only a decade
before George Gissing's birth: it was then a sylvan landscape,
the very prototype of that rural England—decorated with the
odd venerable pile—which Gissing was later to enthuse over in
his writings but never gave the impression of knowing deeply.
The small Gissing, trotting at his mother's side, must have seen
the last vestiges of this arcadia disappearing before his eyes. No
wonder, in adult life, though he made so little direct use of his
northern background, the sense of man as a despoiler, and of the
sheer filth of nineteenth-century civilization, crops up so consistently in his books. He was one of the earliest writers to display
that romanticism about the English countryside which comes
from knowing it at second hand—what George Orwell, in the
next century, was to stigmatize (with some justice) as that *rentier*
snobbism and sentimentality so characteristic of the British middle
classes once they have become rootlessly urban. The only book
in which he describes the landscape of his childhood with any sort
of precision is *A Life's Morning* (published 1888, but written
earlier), a novel whose main theme is that of escape, social and
physical, from that very place and all it represents. 'Dunfield' is
Wakefield. 'Banbrigg' is Agbrigg, the suburb of Wakefield to
which the family removed after Thomas Gissing's death:

At no season, and under no advantage of sky, was Banbrigg
a delectable abode. Though within easy reach of country which
was not without rural aspects, it was marked too unmistakably
with the squalor of a manufacturing district. Its existence
impressed one as casual; it was a mere bit of Dunfield got away
from the main mass, and having brought its dirt with it. The
stretch of road between it and the bridge by which the river was
crossed into Dunfield had in its long, hard ugliness something
dispiriting. Though hedges bordered it here and there, they were
stunted and grimed; though fields were seen on this side and on
that, the grass had absorbed too much mill-smoke to exhibit
wholesome verdure; it was fed upon by sheep and cows, seemingly
turned in to be out of the way till needed for slaughter, and by
the sorriest of superannuated horses. The land was blighted by
the curse of what we name—using a word as ugly as the thing it
represents—industrialism.

Emily Hood, the heroine of this novel, has returned for a stay at
home from her post as governess in a wealthy Surrey household—

a locale probably modelled on Meredith's home at Box Hill which Gissing had visited and physically on another house in that area which had once belonged to Fanny Burney. Emily, like her creator, is full of enthusiasm for this new-found-land, and tries to convey its beauty to her father:

'How I wish you could see the views from the hills in Surrey!' Emily exclaimed when they had stood in silence. 'I can imagine nothing more delightful in English scenery. It realizes my idea of perfect rural beauty, as I got it from engravings after the landscape painters. Oh, you shall go there with me some day.'
Her father smiled and shook his head a little.
'Perhaps,' he said; and added a favourite phrase of his, 'while there is life there is hope.'
'Of course there is,' rejoined Emily, with gaiety which was unusual in her. 'No smoke; the hills blue against a lovely sky! trees covered to the very roots with greenness; rich old English homes and cottages—oh, you know the kind; your ideal of a cottage—low-tiled roofs, latticed windows, moss and lichen and climbing flowers. Farmyards sweet with hay, and gleaming dairies. That country is my home!'

One reason Gissing supplies for Emily's enchantment with the scenery of the home counties is that she has fallen in love with Wilfrid Athel, the son of the house in which she is employed, and he with her: this is why Surrey is described as 'her heart's home'—contrast the title of this chapter which is 'the Shadow of Home', the actual, wearisomely familiar home at Dunfield. But to the reader it is readily apparent that Emily Hood, though presented as being without any conscious snobbism or social aspiration as such, is enchanted by the landscape of the Athel establishment for other reasons besides the presence of Wilfrid. Or, rather, her attachment to Wilfrid is all part of a much wider desire in her for the things which Wilfrid, his family and their environment represent: ease, comfort, freedom from anxiety, pleasant surroundings *removed from the contaminated sources of the money which supports such things*, servants to do the dirty work, time and space to pursue cultural activities (Mr Athel senior dabbles in Egyptian antiquities). In short, the bourgeois idyll, leavened with sufficient admixture of culture to avoid the charge of grossness or complacency. To a novelist born into such a home, the tame prettiness of upper-class houses in Surrey (not

then, of course, a suburban commuterland) would hardly have
seemed the apotheosis of the Good Life, but to Gissing, who was
making his way in the world and to whom such places were
relatively new, they represented much for which he had always
longed. For this very reason, he does not describe them well. To
the end of his life, even when he had become accustomed to
visiting comfortable establishments, his descriptions of them
tended to be both flat and fulsome: it is as if he never came to
any understanding of how such households are run—as, never
achieving one himself, he probably did not.

It is highly significant that Emily's enthusiasm for her new
habitat is expressed in terms of an already romanticized ideal of
rural beauty, a consciously cultured, second-hand appreciation[4]
rather than a spontaneous response. Surrey 'realizes her idea of
perfect rural beauty . . . as got from engravings after the landscape painters.' Not even from the landscape painters themselves,
you note, but from copies. Dunfield-Wakefield possessed no art
gallery; we know from a subsequent conversation in the book
that Mr Hood, Emily's father, had never been to London; Emily
herself had presumably never come south till she was adult. Rural
beauty for her in her childhood then was represented by a mere
hieroglyph—a monochrome engraving of an unseen, idealized
picture of a reality that was quite beyond her ken. Even her
first post as a governess, in Liverpool, in the house of a man
who owns many landscape pictures only confirms her early
experience rather than altering it. Her remarks are more
poignantly revealing than Gissing himself was probably aware,
and they are also very typical of his own approach to a number
of things. He had the literary, cerebral, some would say over-
educated person's habit, of progressing from the representation
to the reality rather than the other way round. When he first
saw the more picturesque parts of his native country he saw them
as 'landscape' or as settings for portions of history which had
fired his imagination. When he wrote, in his *Charles Dickens*
(1898): 'Dickens always had a true love of the country, especially
of that which is near to picturesque old towns of historic
interest', one feels that at that moment he was ascribing to his
favourite novelist an outlook in reality more typical of himself.
By the same token, when he first lived in London as a young
man—

what I chiefly thought of was that now at length I could go
hither or thither in London's immensity, seeking for the places
which had been made known to me by Dickens . . . making real
to my vision what hitherto had been but names and insubstantial
shapes . . . Thus, one day in the City, I found myself at the
entrance to Bevis Marks! I had been making an application in
reply to some advertisement—of course, fruitlessly; but what was
that disappointment compared with the discovery of Bevis Marks!
Here dwelt Mr Brass and Sally, and the Marchionness. Up and
down that little street, this side and that, I went gazing and
dreaming. No press of busy folk disturbed me; the place was
quiet; it looked no doubt, much the same as when Dickens knew
it. I am not sure I had any dinner that day, but, if not, I dare
say I did not mind it very much.[5]

At other moments, the eyes through which he looked were those
of Hogarth, a book of whose engravings was another favourite
in the Gissing household. It is interesting to speculate what the
effect on Gissing's work might have been had his imagination been
fired in youth by a specifically northern writer or artist, someone
who would have made him 'see' his own native environment and
understand what actually went on in its mines and mills. Nowhere
in his books do we get farther into a mill than its counting
house. When he was writing *A Life's Morning* he had to write to
ask his brother what was 'the nature' of the big mills in Wakefield.[6] We hardly visit a single northern working-class home. He
remarks that Dickens was no good at showing the 'representative
wage-earner battling for bread' and attributes this to the fact that
Dickens had never lived in a northern town, but he himself, who
was brought up in one, writes as if he were an outsider. The
workers whom he did eventually write about were Londoners,
that is people whom Dickens' novels had already made him see
as suitable literary subjects. Even in *A Life's Morning*, where the
descriptions of the north have an authenticity and a grasp of
detail lacking from the Surrey landscapes, he writes more like
someone visiting from elsewhere, and being disgusted by what
he found, than like someone born to it:

Dunfield offered no prominent features save the chimneys of its
factories and its fine church, the spire of which rose high above
surrounding buildings; over all hung a canopy of foul vapour,
heavy, pestiferous. Take in your fingers a spray from one of the
trees even here on the Heath, and its touch left a soil . . . Emily
tried to believe that this at length was really the country; there

were no houses in view, meadows lay on either hand, the leafage was thick. But it was not mere prejudice which saw in every object a struggle with hard conditions, a degeneration into coarseness, a blight. The quality of the earth was poor to begin with; the herbage seemed of gross fibre; one would not risk dipping a finger in the stream which trickled by the roadside, it suggested an impure source. And behold, what creatures are these coming along the lane, where only earth-stained rustics should be met? Two colliers, besmutted wretches, plodding homeward from the 'pit' which is half a mile away.

The passage is loaded with meaning. Why should Emily (and Gissing) brought up in a region of pits expect earth-stained rustics? Why should the landscape be seen as deceptive, alien to expectations? Because, presumably, Gissing himself and the younger children of the family were reared, as far as was possible, in isolation from the grimy, industrial world on their doorstep, and were led to believe that the norm of life was something quite other and that intimations of this world were to be gleaned from books, pictures, 'education', and the occasional trip to some modestly picturesque and unspoilt resort such as Seascale on the Cumberland coast. The contamination, the leaf whose touch soils, the stream which 'suggests an impure source' seem to represent not merely the actual, physical muck of industrial prosperity but the contamination of that prosperity itself—the spiritual 'filth' of the commerce on which Victorian England's greatness was actually based. Gissing had, by the time he wrote this novel, had his period of youthful Radicalism and political 'awareness': he was familiar with arguments about capitalism and the exploitation of the workers, but his general attitude to money through his books betrays a fundamental naïvety about the sources of wealth. This is the case with a great many novelists, and it is not really their fault. The professional, full-time novelist is, by the nature of his work, cut off as a man from those very sources of information and experience which might, in fact, be of the greatest possible use to him as a writer: this is one of the basic problems of the writer's existence, and one to which I shall be returning. In economic terms, novel-writing is a cottage-industry belonging to a pre-industrial system (which is also why it is a more satisfactory occupation, in many ways, for women than it is for men). Although the theme of money—the need for money, the social significance of money, the psychological harm done by a shortage of money—is one of the paramount themes both in Gissing's life and in his work, he displays the typical novelist's ignorance about how finance actually works, and is made to work by those who possess it.. Unexpected legacies abound in his books, and those of his characters in comfortable circumstances usually obtain their wealth in some quite vague and unspecified way. Later in life he wrote in a letter[7] 'I find it a great effort to understand the daily life of people free from money cares.' He gives the impression of believing that those who do not actually labour directly for money themselves never have to think about it at all. It is as if Gissing himself, despite his consciousness of the sufferings of the exploited classes, in general accepted the prevailing middle-class idea that, sitting on your lovely lawn in Surrey, you are not 'tainted' by commerce or industry even if that is the true source of the wealth you are enjoying.

Rurality then, or *apparent* rurality, of an old-fashioned, traditional, pre-industrial kind, was extremely meaningful to Gissing. In *A Life's Morning*, and also in the two other novels he wrote at the same period within a remarkably short space of time, *Isabel Clarendon* and *Demos*, it represents escape, not merely from the actual and moral filth of industrial civilization into a supposedly purer past, but escape from a lower class into a higher one, and from ignorance and prejudice toward wisdom and enlightenment. Dunfield in particular is stigmatized as the dwelling of the second rate, even within its own terms:

If any Dunfield schoolboy exhibited faculties of a kind uncommon in the town, he was despatched to begin life on a more promising scene; those who remained, who became the new generation of town councillors, of independent electors, were such as could not by any possibility have made a living elsewhere. Those elders who knew Dunfield best could not point to a single youth of fair endowments who looked forward to remaining in his native place.

Gissing himself was just such a promising youth, despatched elsewhere in his teens to school. The escape was an insecure one, however, and the fear of slipping back again very real. Thus, Emily Hood's reaction on her return visit to Dunfield; she sincerely loves her parents with all their limitations, but: 'by no effort could she expel the superstition that she had only escaped from that for a time, that its claws would surely overtake her and fix themselves again in her flesh.'

The image verges on the obsessional. Gissing himself was a great escaper: his life-story, indeed, is chequered with escapes from situations or persons, some more rationally based than others, but because he (like Emily Hood) was also warm-hearted and conscientious, these escapes were rarely complete. Emily's anxieties were evidently well-founded.

In *Isabel Clarendon* (1886) his first proper attempt at depicting a leisured society, Gissing's equation—upper class = rural setting —is particularly distinct. The hero, or rather anti-hero of the story, Bernard Kingcote, is a man of education but modest origins (though this is not made clear at the beginning of the book), whom we meet rambling in the Gloucestershire countryside with haversack on his back, the typical 'unworldly' gentleman's occupation of the late Victorian era. He has come from London but intends to settle for a while in the country, an atavistic step the meaning of which is indicated in his choice of roads in the first few pages; in this book and in several others Gissing made use of the Meredithian device of linking landscape with fate, weather with mood:

He looked for a moment along the new road, then his eyes wandered to the old, and he turned at once to the latter. There was a sign-post at the parting; both its arms said, 'To Winstoke', but one was crumbling, fungus-scored, its inscription barely legible; the other a stout piece of timber, self-assertive, with rounded ends and freshly painted in black and white. Kingcote passed with a mental comment.
'The road was just what it promised, perfectly rural . . .'

It is down this road that Kingcote finds . . . 'a cottage of ideal rusticity. It was very old, built of brick which had become finely toned wherever it was not hidden by ivy, and the tiles of the roof were patched with richest hues of moss and lichen.' (Incidentally, as if in proof of its genuine rurality, its authenticity in Gissing's back-to-front terms, someone is sketching the place. The reality is living up to its image as Art.) It is this cottage which he subsequently rents, for half-a-crown a week. Later in the novel we find him writing to a friend in London:

'. . . I delight in the conditions of rustic life as it exists here about me. At times I talk with a farm-labourer, for my solace; to do so I have to divest myself of the last rag of civilization, to strip my mind to its very kernel . . . The absence of any hint of townish Radicalism is a joy to me; I had not expected to find the old order so undisturbed. Squire and parson are still the objects of unshaken reverence. It is not beautiful, but how wholesome! If only the schoolmaster could be kept away; if only progress would work its evil will on the children of the slums, and leave these worthy clodhoppers in their peace . . . Local charity abounds; in the cottages there is no hunger, no lack of clothing. Oh, leave them alone! Would I had been born one of these, and had never learned the half-knowledge which turns life sour!

'But I have news for you. I have lunched at Knightswell, and in a manner have made acquaintance with Mrs Clarendon. She astonished me by presenting herself at my cottage door, holding in her hand a book which I had left by chance out in a field . . .'

The ironic juxtaposition of these two paragraphs is surely no accident. Kingcote may be playing at living like a peasant (Gissing's own Petit Trianon syndrome) but in practice his retreat into rural simplicity has brought him the social advancement of an acquaintanceship with the local great lady—an acquaintance made (how typically!) over a book—and the subsequent development of his relationship with Isabel Clarendon is the main theme of the novel. Gissing here seems aware of the flaws in Kingcote's rural solitude; for the passage immediately quoted above is preceded by a guileless complaint of Kingcote's about the loneliness and aimlessness of his existence. This is one of those many, many instances, of the author perceiving as a writer something he was apparently unable to perceive effectively in his personal life. Nevertheless the basic situation, that of the upper-class life as lived in a picturesquely rural spot, mirrors faithfully both the English class pattern of the period and Gissing's recent experiences.

Isabel Clarendon, coming after his two early working-class novels, was a new departure for him and indicated a new phase in his life. When his second book *The Unclassed* was completed it was read by Meredith, then a publisher's reader for Chapman and Hall, who praised it in glowing terms (though suggesting various alterations) and had several personal interviews with the author: this was how he and Gissing met. In the same year (1884) the Harrison[8] family, whose two young sons Gissing had been tutoring since 1880, took him with them for a fortnight in the Lake District, thus giving him a taste of family life and country holidays such as he had not known since boyhood, and also his first stay in a moneyed household. Since this was also the first year in which he was entirely free of his first, disastrous marriage (save for the financial burden of continuing to pay Nell fifteen shillings a week) he was no doubt in a receptive mood for new relationships and new experiences. It was through the Harrisons that he met a Mrs Gaussen, whom Morley Roberts thought was the original for Isabel Clarendon (though there is no evidence of any overt sentiment between them). Mrs Gaussen lived in a house on the Oxfordshire-Gloucestershire borders which had once belonged to Ann Boleyn; 'Mrs Clarendon' lived in a similar setting in a house by a well with a romantic, historic legend attached to it. Mrs Clarendon was a widow; Mrs Gaussen was not, but Mr Gaussen was often away, and the atmosphere of the household, though not markedly intellectual, was apparently the most open, hospitable, attractive and casually sophisticated that Gissing had yet encountered. Here, evidently, was the Good Life of which the young man had often dreamed. He was invited to stay there. When he returned to London Mrs Gaussen continued to show kindness and interest. She visited him in his lodgings (and he actually moved to new lodgings in a hurry in order to have somewhere decent in which to receive her). She sent him snowdrops and primroses from the country—flowers which, in the foggy, sooty London which had come to typify for Gissing the limitations of his own existence, must have seemed like signs from another world. (She also sent him hampers of food, a nice detail which indicates the kind of protective, intimate, semi-maternal feeling Gissing must have inspired in her: she was in fact older than she appeared.)

But, though relations continued to be cordial, the Gaussens had their life and Gissing his. Though he acted as tutor to a Gaussen boy for a while, nothing much 'came' of his relationship with the mother—and, translated onto a more dramatic plane in the novel, where a nebulous daydream was made explicit, nothing came of that either. In the end the love-affair between Kingcote and Isabel Clarendon flounders, and not for any of the material reasons provided in the tortuous plot (a typically Victorian affair of Wills and legacies) but fundamentally because their assumptions about life are too different. The worldly elements in his beloved's exis-

tence begin to grate on Kingcote: when she comes to see him in
London in a fashionable dress, she carries 'the atmosphere of
the Season' about her. He for his part is unwilling, or unable,
to play the usual social game of formal invitations to lunch or
dinner. And here an interesting divergence between the original—
Mrs Gaussen—and her fictional shadow becomes apparent. One
may presume that Mrs Gaussen's assumptions about life and
Gissing's were essentially alien to each other because they did,
indeed, come from very different backgrounds. Certainly the
relationship between Mrs Clarendon and Kingcote bespeaks just
such an inbuilt incompatibility. Yet these two fictional shades
should have understood one another at a deeper level since, in the
book, the author provided Mrs Clarendon with a socially and
financially insecure past of her own. She eventually reveals the
fact: 'We were wretchedly poor, my brother, and myself. I
have been hungry often and often. We had to keep up a respectable appearance . . .'

But although an important part of the plot hinges on this
revelation, somehow it fails to convince. It comes too late in the
book, the image of Isabel Clarendon as the *grande dame* is too
firmly established. It is fairly obvious what happened: for
fictional purposes, Gissing grafted onto his original an extra
dimension of experience which was not present in the reality, but
failed to make the logical adjustment either to her fictionalized
personality or to Kingcote's relationship with her. A circumstance which, in life, would have formed an implicit bond between them, only serves, in the book, to drive them farther apart.
Isabel Clarendon simply does not display the deep-seated social
insecurities and awareness which would in reality have been part
of the make-up of a woman with her history. In the end—and this
is entirely convincing—she marries an old friend, a moneyed
cosmopolitan of her own kind, one of Gissing's interesting and
curious gallery of Fairly Decent Chaps who were not his own
sort. Kingcote retreats to Norwich with a widowed sister and
enters the book-selling trade. Books inevitably—but also
stationery, and bottles of gum. He has returned to the social cadre
of his upbringing. Defeated in love, socially demoted once more,
looking 'prematurely aged', he is 'content' but 'joyless'. (The
reader may also note that he has become sexless, too, a life with
a widowed sister being the nearest possible approximation to the

intimacy of marriage without its usual physical component.) The escape route has failed him or he has failed to live up to it: the chance came, but he lost it.

A footnote to this most Turgenev-like novel is that it met with small success. Gissing was particularly chagrined when Meredith, who had provided at least some of the impetus for his literary excursion into upper-class settings, told him firmly that he was making a mistake and that if only he would stick to low-life scenes success would certainly be his.

The theme of retreat to a rural idyll in some way superior to other alternatives of life, crops up again and again in the novels. Godwin Peak, the central character in *Born in Exile* (1892) takes to a similar solitary, rural life as Kingcote's, in a quiet cottage near Exeter. While Peak should never be taken as if he *was*, simply, Gissing (a mistake several critics have made) this novel is so central to an understanding of Gissing's writing that I do not propose to deal with it at length here. It is sufficient to point out that Peak, like Kingcote, finds in his rural retreat a family of higher social status who take him up, and that he, like Kingcote, is, and finally remains, the outsider whose tortuous attempts to become identified with the desirable life eventually fail.

The same equation, country setting = upper-class family, occurs most blatantly right at the beginning of the first published novel, *Workers in the Dawn* (1880), where the child Arthur Golding is rescued from the slums of London by his dead father's old friend, clergyman Edward Norman—and Arthur rejects his foster family and returns to his old haunts. Perhaps Arthur is right. Just such another sexless, refined, cultured rural widower in poor health as the Rev. Norman, appears in *Thyrza*, written some seven years later, but by this time Gissing seems to have begun to suspect that there was something subtly wrong with the rural idyll, at least in its upper class form, though it continued to tempt him. In later books the country retreats become humbler, and the image of the Good Life in them becomes blended with that of love in a cot away from worldly temptations.

The ultimate, full and finally overt treatment of the rural retreat theme is to be found in *The Private Papers of Henry Ryecroft*, written towards the end of Gissing's life when he was not living in England at all and entertained little real prospect of doing so ever again. He remarked when he was working on it that the idea of such a book had been in his mind for years: it is as if he had come gradually to recognize a persistent tendency in his own thought-patterns and aspirations and had decided at last to capitalize on it. I do not personally admire *Ryecroft*. It contains some fine and memorable passages, but in that it is *not* a novel but a piece of bogus autobiography and blatant wish-fulfilment, it seems to me to display far less real perception, common sense and sophistication of thought than are apparent even in his less good novels. In *Ryecroft*, it is not really the writer speaking but the man—and, at that, the man on his off-days: physically ailing, mentally morbid and self-limiting. In fact it is a neat illustration of that dichotomy that exists between man and writer that Gissing could have penned *Ryecroft* five years *after* he had already, in *The Whirlpool* (1897), lightly satirized the same sentimental, unrealistic *rentier* sentiment of which *Ryecroft* is redolent. This is the *Whirlpool*'s Alma Frothingham speaking, an affected, socially ambitious, unstable and ultimately tragic character. She remarks how nice it would be to have 'ancestors'; she goes on:

'But one ought to have an interesting house to live in. Nobody's ancestors ever lived in a semi-detached villa. What I should like would be one of those picturesque old places down in Surrey—quite in the country, yet within easy reach of town; a house with a real garden, and perhaps an orchard. I believe you can get them very cheap sometimes. Not rent the house, but buy it . . .'

Ancestors. A house with a real garden. Not rented but bought. What was to become for the next generation the Metroland dream. Such are the aspirations that haunt the lives of those born into the insecure classes. Gissing, though he might in that instance be mocking such desires, knew all about them. At Wakefield, his family rented their houses. And though they did have a garden when he was a child, that was rented too; it was some way from their house and shop in Westgate, in the centre of Wakefield. It was a kind of allotment, and if you wanted to pay it a visit you took the key with you; such an arrangement was not uncommon in the north of England. (The place is described precisely in *A Life's Morning*: it is 'laid out with an eye less to beauty than to usefulness'. It is there, 'on two Windsor chairs', that Emily gives holiday lessons to a local girl Jessie Cartwright whose family rent the plot.)

But the book in which the theme of a confrontation between aristocratic rurality and plebeian industralization is made explicit, is *Demos*. Vaguely planned before both *Isabel Clarendon* and *A Life's Morning*, though actually written after them,[9] it gets to grips with a number of the themes aired—often incompatibly —in all the earlier books, and attempts to turn to good account a fundamental conflict in Gissing's own view of life. It is a complex and important book which I do not propose to deal with at length in this chapter,* but it is relevant here to draw attention to a central and curiously fairy-tale theme in it: that is, the transformation of a valley, in the course of the novel, from a green retreat to an industrially blighted spot and then back again to what it was before.

'Stanbury Hill, remote but two hours walk from a region blasted with mine and factory and furnace, shelters within its western slope a fair green valley, a land of meadows and orchard, untouched by poisonous breath. At its foot lies the village of Wanley.' So the novel begins. The traditional appurtenances of a picturesque retreat are sketched in: one street, stone-built cottages, associations with a medieval order of monks, a manor house, a church and vicarage, 'these also unmolested in their quiet age'. The description continues, with that tone of irony which is Gissing's usual version of humour:

Wanley, it is to be feared, lags far behind the times—painfully so, when one knows for a certainty that the valley upon which it looks contains treasures of coal, of ironstone—blackband, to be technical—and of fireclay. Some ten years ago it seemed as if better things were in store; there was a chance that the vale might for ever cast off its foolish greenery, and begin vomiting smoke and flames in humble imitation of its metropolis beyond the hills.

In the course of the book, the transformation is set in motion. Mutimer, a working man and distant relative of the family at the manor, has unexpectedly inherited a large fortune; having Radical-progressive ideas he sets out to establish at Wanley a Robert-Owen-style industrial collective. Mills are built, rows of back-to-back houses begin to rise. But, for various reasons,

* See Chapters 2 and 5.

the project eventually fails, and the money finds its way back
to the son of the manor, Hubert Eldon. He and his mother
had previously been ousted by Mutimer, but he now returns.
Under his patrician ownership, the place is restored to what it
had been before Mutimer—the name suggests 'the changer'—
ever came:

A deep breath of country air. It is springtime, and the valley
of Wanley is bursting into green and flowery life, peacefully
glad as if the foot of Demos had never come that way. Incred-
ible that the fume of furnaces ever desecrated that fleece-sown
sky of tenderest blue, that hammers clanged and engines roared
where now the thrush utters his song so joyously. Hubert Eldon
has been as good as his word. In all the valley no trace is left
of what was called New Wanley. Once more we can climb to
the top of Stanbury Hill and enjoy the sense of remoteness and
security when we see that dark patch on the horizon, the cloud
that hangs over Belwick.

It may be objected that this is a staggeringly unlikely ending to
an otherwise realistic book. Never, in real life, is the clock turned
magically backwards in that way, and in any case areas that
have once been disturbed by industry cannot be turned back
into rural England again just like that in a matter of a year or
two. This is true. But fantasies can have their own rightness,
dreams their own internal logic, and I believe that what is
depicted at the close of *Demos* is a long-standing Gissing dream.
(Mutimer's own creation was the realization of a dream too, a
social one.) It seems as if the young Gissing, brought up among
the mills and courts of Wakefield, seeing the River Calder
grow dirtier, the medieval chapel on the bridge dingier and
more hemmed in by buildings, the open country between
Wakefield and Leeds more and more encroached on and
despoiled, nursed from his earliest days a fabulous dream of
time turned backwards and of a beauty-loving classically educated elite taking over—a dream which was nourished by several
elements in his upbringing and education. In his life, he could
do nothing about Wakefield; he could merely escape from it
when he was old enough and seek his 'spiritual home' elsewhere[10]
—a location which, as is the way of supposed spiritual homes,
proved more elusive and disappointing than he foresaw. But in
novels one can achieve things that are impossible in life: in

his novels Gissing could triumph over his place of birth, he could even destroy it. In *Demos*, I suggest Gissing was killing off, among several other things, that physical environment of childhood which had pleased and inspired him so little.

The Real Home

But why, in practice, should George Gissing have grown up like a stranger in his own town and class? The question is an obvious one, but it is not one which is anywhere explicitly answered by Gissing himself, though there are a number of hints. Several times, notably in Godwin Peak of *Born in Exile*, and in the persons of various of his *female* characters in other books, he presents the 'natural aristocrat', the person whose in-intellectual and (more important) spiritual endowment is mysteriously alien to the class and family from which they have sprung. But this concept of personality is less convincing today than it was then, and anyway Gissing himself seems elsewhere to have his own doubts about it—he also several times referred, both in letters and in a novel (*The Whirlpool*) to the 'genetic trap', more commonly known as the 'Blood Will Out' view.

I believe that the essential reason for the Gissing children's alienation from ordinary Wakefield life is to be found in the fact, already mentioned, that their parents were 'furriners', East Anglians put down in a northern mill-town. What's more, both parents seem to have considered themselves, with some reason, 'a cut above their neighbours'. Years after, Gissing noted in his Commonplace Book:[11] '. . . we *never* came in contact with the families of other shopkeepers; so that we hung between two grades of society—as I have done ever since in practical life.' It is arguable, of course, that a chemist *is* a higher form of life than a publican or a pork butcher, but since young George attended, as a small boy, an ordinary local school in Back Lane, five minutes from his home, you would think that he made friends with plenty of shopkeepers' sons there. Apparently not; apparently he, and his two younger brothers, Will and Algernon, all born within three years, were considered company enough for each other. (There were subsequently two girls; the whole family of five children was born in the space of ten years.) That they were in fact a united and happy

family is clearly demonstrated even by the few childhood draw-
ings, stories and papers from pretend games that have survived.[12] All the evidence points to the Gissings' childhood, at
any rate till the death of their father when George himself was
barely thirteen, having been a fortunate, indeed almost idyllic
one, at least within its own rather limited terms. Gissing's subsequent remark, also in his Commonplace Book, that his childhood
was 'of no practical use' to him, being passed 'in mere comfort'
must be placed in the context of his habitual forms of expression,
as exemplified in his letters and diaries, and his constitutional
tendency to make a tremendous fuss about things (to put
the matter in unkind, everyday terms). 'Mere comfort'
is a fairly high term of approbation from one whose
almost constant complaint, in adult life, was a lack of comfort,
physical and emotional. Certainly had there been anything
seriously wrong with his early years it would have figured, in
the books of such a hyper-sensitive man, with as much or even
greater importance as the blacking-factory held for the adult
Dickens. Whatever was wrong with Wakefield as a town it was
allowed to impinge as little as possible on the socially-segregated
little family in Westgate; it is indeed, in all probability, this
same unreal insulation from local life that Gissing is vaguely
feeling after when he says that his childhood was no 'use' to
him. (The dichotomy between the needs of the writer and
those of the person is, incidentally, perfectly illustrated in this
remark. The traumatic blacking-factory that sears the soul of
the person as a person, provides the best possible grist to the
writer's mill: Gissing himself knew that he couldn't have it
both ways, but, as usual, he wanted to.)

One enormous emotional benefit George Gissing had in childhood and sorely missed later was that as the eldest son of a
united family he was never solitary, but at the same time occupied a rather special position. While the Gissing family do not
seem to have been overtly demonstrative—Gissing once said
that he never recalled his mother caressing him—there is little
doubt that, throughout childhood, he was surrounded by the
admiration and encouragement not only of his small brothers
and sisters, but also that of both his parents, since he early
showed himself to be 'a gifted scholar'. Our needs are partly
inborn but they are also partly conditioned by childhood ex-

pectations: throughout his life Gissing craved, and really needed, that constant admiration and support that was more readily come by in childhood than in later years. In my view it has been insufficiently recognized that he was also a natural teacher and helper. Frederic Harrison, who employed him to tutor his sons, used the phrase 'born teacher'; his own youngest sister Ellen wrote, years afterwards '. . . his desire to instruct others was free from all thought of self; let it be but necessary to instruct some fumbler in learning, though it were but one step on the way, and all else was forgotten in the wish to be of use'.[13] This was one of his great, positive characteristics counterbalancing much that was negative and even destructive. He had a richly generous side to his nature; he loved to encourage and advise others.* In this respect, he must have played the eldest-boy role to perfection. His childhood certainly laid the basis for a love and loyalty to his family which he maintained throughout his life, despite occasional assertions from him to the contrary which have misled some biographers. Ellen Gissing spoke of his 'consistency of affection and faithfulness'; nor indeed was there any real reason why he should have become totally alienated from his origins in the ruthless tradition of the socially mobile which has sometimes been ascribed to him. Although they did not fully share his adult world—or series of worlds—neither Ellen herself, nor the other sister Madge, nor Algernon the surviving brother (Will, the third boy, died in early manhood) was a fool; all were to some extent educated. Although Gissing wrote in his Commonplace Book: 'I never in my life exchanged a serious confidence with any relative— I mean, concerning the inner things of one's heart and mind', this seems belied by a lifelong and at least fairly intimate correspondence he maintained with Algernon. Presumably by 'inner things of one's heart and mind' he meant those most intimate of all and (in the Victorian era) literally unspeakable confidences. Indeed he goes on to say: 'This may in part be a personal characteristic of our family; in part, I feel it is due to the innate puritanism which also forbids us to hint at anything like sexual relations—even to the extent quite permissible in other English households.'

In other words, a characteristic peculiar to the lower-middle

* See Chapter 2.

class of his time who regarded themselves as being above the
frank crudeness of working people but who never attained that
other frankness and freedom from the fear of 'what people
will think' which is born of effortless social security. It was
as if the Gissing family were always having to demonstrate,
even to each other, how refined they were. And the children's
recreations—reading, notably Scott, Dickens and Tennyson,
looking at engravings by Hogarth and Dürer, going for long
walks out in the country beyond Wakefield's taint, 'botanizing',
sketching and painting—are precisely what one would expect
of a family brought up to reverence 'culture' rather consciously,
and to seek to escape from their physical surroundings. It was
an attitude to life at once broad and narrow—broad, in that
there was certainly more culture in the cramped household
than one would normally expect of a Wakefield chemist's family,
but narrow in that it betrays an exclusive, carefully elitist attitude to life and its pleasures which is essentially petit bourgeois
in tone. The phrase of the time 'plain living and high thinking'
might have been coined for the Gissing family.

To say that the father provided the high thinking and the
mother the plain living would be neat but not entirely true.
Although it is probably fair to say, as H. G. Wells said and
many others since, that George Gissing's father was 'the chief
formative influence' on his son's character, I suspect it is also a
fact that George Gissing himself wanted this to be true, and
tended to discount, throughout his life, the presence of his
mother in his life. Certainly he himself seems to have resembled
his father in personality rather than his mother, but that is not
saying quite the same thing. As significant to him as his father's
life was probably his father's death, when he himself was on
the edge of adolescence.

The Lost Father

To lose a parent before you are adult yourself means that you
never have the experience of a relationship with that person
from an adult standpoint. Instead of the joint alterations and
adjustments that time otherwise brings, the adjustment is all
one-sided and can only be both retrospective and speculative.
The dead parent remains fixed in time; there can never be any

further 'getting to know' and new, maturer assessments of the parent cannot be checked against the reality; rather the image grows less familiar and accessible as the years pass. One is left with a problem: an adult's view of another adult but only a child's memories to fit into it, and for this reason the dead parent becomes faintly mysterious, an object of curiosity, hard to pigeon-hole. For the rest of his life Gissing behaved intermittently toward his father's memory as if he were turning it over in his hands, trying to fathom its significance but never quite succeeding. He jotted down notes about his father—first in 1884, the year in which he began to surface from the traumatic experience of his first marriage and his early years in London; then again, continuing on the same sheet of paper, in 1896. (That was the year his second marriage began to break up. It is tempting to see a pattern here.) That same year, he looked through the Index of British Botanists in the British Museum, and was very pleased to find his father's name in it—Thomas Waller Gissing had been a keen amateur botanist, and though Gissing himself did not really share his father's interest in this he liked the idea of it: [14] 'How well I can see him, on a Sunday morning, busy over his herbarium! The smell of camphor always brings it back to me.'[15] George Gissing was very pleased when, toward the end of his life, his own eldest son (by then lodged with his sisters back at the family home in Wakefield) was showing an interest in plants. As late as 1902, the year before his death, he interpolated a sketch of his father into an article on Dickens which he wrote for *The Critic*, as if the author who had been *the* novelist for him in childhood was forever associated for him with the father who had been the model for manhood.

What, in fact, was this lost father like? We know from his son's notes that his formal education was not great, and that —rather surprisingly for a pharmacist—he was 'strangely deficient in knowledge of practical science', though apparently ever ready to learn. In fact, like a number of characters in George Gissing's novels, he was a self-taught man with a genuine liking for books and a taste for disinterested learning. As Arthur Golding in *Workers in the Dawn*, Julian Casti in *The Unclassed*—who actually was a chemist's assistant—Gilbert Grail in *Thyrza*, Sidney Kirkwood in *The Nether World*, this is one of Gissing's basic types, presented in different variations but always sympathetically, even idealistically. The type must be carefully differentiated from the self-made man in *Demos*, Richard Mutimer, whose book-reading is all directed toward political ends and who is entirely ignorant of literature. Thomas Waller Gissing had evidently imbibed somewhere in his life— or evolved within himself—the gentleman's ethic of reading for the sake of reading. He subscribed to a Book Club, which, his son noted:

> once circulated a life of Albert [*sic*] Dürer, with good illustrations. This book rejoiced me, and gave me the love of Dürer I have had ever since. When the time came for sending it away, I must have looked regretful, for Father said—'I can't afford to buy it; I wish I could.' At once my instinct of delicacy was moved; I felt ashamed at having appeared to *ask* him to go to such expense; and I replied hurriedly, 'No, no—of course not— I didn't mean that.'

This entry, incidentally, seems to encapsulate the financial atmosphere of the Gissing household, composed of genteel poverty and an equally genteel desire not to refer to the matter, even within the family circle. Several times in his novels Gissing was to remark that well-bred families, in contrast with working-class ones, simply do not discuss the cost of things. But, for all this culture, Thomas Gissing had (like Richard Mutimer) Radical sympathies, and was active in local party politics. He was an atheist: he had 'strong prejudices', to the extent of making enemies. However much he reared his sons to look towards another world than Wakefield, he himself was involved in an entirely practical way in the affairs of the town. He was one of the founders of the Mechanics Institute and some of the friends he made there were extremely helpful to his widow and children when his early death left them badly off. Years later when his own eldest son was a small boy, George Gissing wrote in a letter to a friend: [16] 'One of my misfortunes in boyhood was that my father had exceedingly little time to give me. His leisure was devoted, mostly, to municipal business.' By a nice twist of fate George Gissing himself received, towards the end of his life when he was no longer living in England anyway, an invitation to stand for election on the London County Council. He treated the proposal as an absurdity—yet one can't help thinking that, had circumstances been otherwise, some such gregarious and partisan activity might have corresponded admirably to certain traits in his temperament, and would at the very least have brought him in contact with people who might have been congenial to him as a man and useful to him as a writer.

George Gissing's image of his father seems to have been of a man at peace with himself, a gentle personality, a personification of restraint and good sense. Yet even the brief 'Reminiscences' provide evidence of a man in the grip of conflicting tastes and attitudes—as his eldest son was also to be. For this provincial Radical and local chemist (almost the prototype, one might say, of a responsible spokesman for the people) had apparently an inbuilt aversion to those very people to whom he devoted his time. Not only did he not allow his children to associate with those of other tradesmen, even the other chemists in the town were objects of scorn to him. Essentially he had a low opinion of the citizens of Wakefield. Once, when the shop caught fire, and there seemed a risk that it might be burnt out, he told his son afterwards that, if this had actually happened 'the mob would have stood in the streets and cheered as each floor fell through'. Note that the shop did not in fact burn out, the crowd did not cheer—indeed it is hard to see why they should have done, since a chemist, unless unusually unpleasant (and Thomas Gissing was apparently a kindly and courteous man) is normally perceived as a friend, the 'poor man's doctor'. In short the remark seems to represent less of a real possibility than a degree of paranoia about the working classes on the part of Gissing senior. Even his son seems to have realized this, for he added to the note 'I don't know the cause of [this] feeling'. Yet the remark obviously made sufficient impression on the boy for it to form one of the relatively small sum of significant Memories of his parent. And indeed it would be hard to find another impression from childhood which crystallizes so well George Gissing's own fear and almost abhorrence of the working classes *en masse*—an attitude which crops up in novel after novel with his equally fundamental philanthropy and social concern. The conflict reaches its peak in *Demos*, indeed it is there brought out into the open and thus to some extent externalized, for it is in *Demos*, which is about a Radical dream put into practice, that the mob (*demos*) is also revealed as the killing horde, senselessly brutal, the ones who 'cheer as each floor falls through'. Yet, in spite of having written *Demos* in 1885–6, Gissing never quite disposed of the problem posed by his ambivalent viewpoint, and it continued to haunt his novels.

Thomas Gissing seems to have had, like his son, an obsessional, perfectionist streak in him; several of the 'Reminiscences' are concerned with his pedantic concern for the use of language. In an England where speech was (and still is) an instant indication of class, this concern must also have had purely social overtones—the concern of the tradesman to appear gentlemanly. 'He was very refined in his choice of words, never anything from his lips approaching coarseness or vulgarism. He liked to nicely discriminate certain words, e.g. Tart and Pie. Was always eager for derivations . . .' His method of blotting out the coarseness and vulgarity of the world all around him is neatly indicated in another note: 'I was once coming with him in the train from some place to Wakefield. A man got in and began to talk in a blackguardly way. When the offender had got out, father said to me, "I always go to sleep when conversation of that kind begins".'

Not, you might imagine, a man well-fitted to be a popular leader. Yet it is possible that in the assumption of the leader-role Thomas Gissing was in fact suiting his own sensitive fastidious personality the best way he could. Fated to live in a world of small commerce and ignoble human suffering, he could only cope temperamentally with this world by adopting towards it the role of helper, guider, good influence—in fact, the role of a superior. Very much the same dilemma is apparent in the personality and life of George Gissing, but, as a writer, he attempted to solve the problem rather differently. Thomas Gissing, having only his life through which to express himself, turned himself into the practical leader, Magna Carta-man. George, having that extra dimension of expression that novel writing represents, transposed the problem of his ambivalent attitude to the common people into that dimension. At first this involved a piece of role-playing for himself: when *Workers in the Dawn* came out, he wrote to Algernon that he wished to make his name as 'the mouthpiece of the advanced Radical party'. But this phase of enthusiasm in his actual life fairly quickly passed. The fastidious and conservative elements in his

nature revolted against the society into which his Radical
sympathies had carried him; and he presumably realized, as a
writer, the limitation which being a 'mouthpiece' for any polemic
viewpoint imposes. So he transferred the role-problem to his
heroes; in subsequent novels and short stories it is they who
act out for him the role of people's-friend-and-yet-superior. So
we have Osbert Waymark, in *The Unclassed*, befriending and
educating a girl of the streets (a theme which of course had other
close personal associations for Gissing at that period); we have
Walter Egremont in *Thyrza* lecturing to the working men of
Lambeth and opening a public library, we have Sidney Kirkwood in *The Nether World*, an ordinary working man with
cultural aspirations who manages, at any rate for a while, to
play the role of councillor and fairy-godfather to his less fortunate friends. Most clearly, in *Demos*, we have an actual 'mouthpiece of the advanced Radical party' attempting to do things
for people—and, ultimately, being defeated by his own
egotism.

It is as if the essentially split nature of his father's interests
and sympathies (like his own) was something which Gissing
never fully comprehended in his ordinary life, but his semi-
awareness of it surfaced in his novels. This theme of helping
others, the moral ambiguity of it and the moral dilemmas it can
bring in its train, is a major one in his works.

Though George Gissing himself often betrayed, in his life
and his novels, the desire to play a father's (and eldest brother's)
helping role, one also finds here and there in his books obvious
wish-fulfilling Father Figures, replacements for the parent he
himself had lost, the man whose last thinking act was to dictate
to his thirteen year old son a list of magazines which the
Mechanics Institute should subscribe to . . . There is, most
obviously,* Mr Tollady in *Worker in the Dawn*, who befriends
young Arthur Golding and teaches him how to print, and who,
like Gissing senior, dies. (He also comes from East Anglia.)
There is an odd councillor-clergyman figure in *Demos*, just
such a sophisticated and contemplative influence as the young

---

*The identification is made explicit: 'If ever Arthur endeavoured to
recall to his mind the aspect of that father whom he had so bitterly
mourned years ago, he was quite unable to dissociate the dim memory
of his features from the look of those grave, kind eyes which so often
rested upon him during the day with affectionate interest.'

man Gissing had lacked. There is old Mr Snowden in *The Nether World*, who also dies (and whose ideals are ultimately found self-centred and wanting in common sense). There are various wise, middle-aged men, tending to give counsel or practical help to the tormented central characters of novels and to live in circumstances of rural seclusion, like Mr Warricombe in *Born in Exile* or Annabel's father in *Thyrza* or Basil Morton in *The Whirlpool*. There is—but the point has been made. Gissing lost his adored father when he himself was on the point of growing to manhood, and for the rest of his life he both identified with him and felt the lack of him.

One probably should not leave the subject of Thomas Gissing without a look at James Hood, Emily's father in *A Life's Morning*, whom several commentators have readily accepted as something of a 'portrait' of Mr Gissing, senior. The book's description of him as 'a man marked for ill-fortune' significantly pre-echoes Henry James' well-known remark about Gissing himself. (See p. 238.) However too much should not be placed on this coincidence. The preceding pages will have shown why I regard the view that James Hood 'was' Thomas Gissing—or indeed George Gissing—as much too simple. In any case, contrary to an extremely prevalent myth, novelists do not usually 'put' people, whole, into their novels, certainly not compulsive novel-writers like Gissing. They put in bits of them only—the bits that happen to fit the particular story they are writing. Clearly James Hood shares some of Thomas Gissing's characteristics: his 'refinement', his love of books, his eagerness for random knowledge, his Sunday afternoon hobbies, his close relationship with his child,* but not his Radicalism, not his energy, not even his degree of modest commercial success. Thomas Gissing was not a failure, but James Hood was. True, Thomas Gissing failed his son (in a slightly different sense of the word) by dying on him, and in *A Life's Morning* James Hood also dies, but the real-life father died respectably, if tragically, of a lung condition, after being let down by a friend for

* 'To Emily, who strove to interest herself in his subjects out of mere love and compassion, he appeared to have gained not a little knowledge of facts and theories. She liked to encourage herself in the faith that his attainments were solid as far as they went, and that they might have been the foundation of good independent work; *it helped her to respect her father*.' (Italics mine)

whom he had stood surety, while the fictional one dies horribly by his own hand after a shattering dismissal for theft from his place of business.

Theft? Clearly it is here the author's *own* life, not his father's, that is being recapitulated and examined. I leave the analysis of the chain of events that lead up to James Hood's misfortune till Chapter 3. It is hard to imagine the sober Wakefield chemist, father of five and prominent citizen, being nearly as impulsive, as unwise, as readily swayed by the needs of the moment, as plain *silly* as poor James Hood appears. But silliness, or at any rate a crippling lack of practical common sense, was indisputably a part of George Gissing's make-up: it was the reverse side to much that was also best in him: his warmth of heart, his idealism, his capacity for living in the moment.

Also present in James Hood (though not, as far as is known, in Mr Gissing senior) is a vein of depression, of a gentle, melancholic, contemplative variety. The remark quoted as typical of him, 'While there's life there's hope' is not really an optimistic one but, rather, defeatist. It is the remark of one who has collapsed under the pressures of living and who has renounced control of his own destiny after a whole series of disasters, and indeed it is in this light that this gentlest and kindest of characters is presented. Now, while Gissing himself rarely if ever attained James Hood's resignation in the face of circumstances, a melancholic, despairing flavour permeates his letters and diaries. Though he did not actually commit suicide himself (nor, in my view was he really a suicidal type) he certainly played with the idea, and more than one of his more obvious fictional alter-egos resort to it.*

It is as if Gissing the writer had, in *A Life's Morning*, grafted on to the Father image salient features of his own personality. Perhaps he was trying to synthesize his father and himself, by taking elements from each, into one quintessential figure of an essentially fine man pursued by malignant fate. The lost father was both himself and not himself. He was an idealized figure whom the adult Gissing aspired to emulate, but he was also a projection of himself, containing some of his own weaknesses, beset by some of the same troubles. A similar synthesis appears, in a less carefully worked out form, in the person of Arthur

* See Chapter 6.

Golding's father in *Workers in the Dawn*, who though presented as a good father, is given a criminal lapse in his history and a prison sentence. He also dies early in the book. After his death, the child Arthur, though taken in by kindly and well-to-do people in the country, leaves them and makes his own way back to London with some shadowy idea of 'looking' for his father, even though he is quite old enough to be aware that his father is dead and what that means. The psychological rightness of this, in a novel which in other respects embodies some fairly unrealistic ideas of human motivation and response, is striking.

Yet another father who dies when his son is young (ten in this case) appears in a late book *The Whirlpool*, and, with it, an interesting new point about the ambiguity of a son's feelings towards a loved parent, which perhaps Gissing himself had been unable to admit till then, even in fictionalized form:

When it was too late, too late by many a year, he mourned the loss which had only startled him, which had seemed hardly a loss at all, rather an emancipation. As a man of thirty, he knew his father much better than when living with him day after day. Faults he could perceive, some of them inherited in his own character; but there remained the memory of a man whom he could admire and love—whom he did admire and love more sincerely and profoundly the older he grew. And he held it the supreme misfortune of his life that, in those early years which count so much toward the future, he had been so rarely under his father's influence.

There is a clear echo there of Gissing's expressed regret to Clara Collet about his own father's preoccupation with municipal business. It comes as no surprise that the early manhood of Harvey Rolfe (the character in *The Whirlpool*) has been somewhat chequered. Rolfe senior is a railway engineer—not badly off but presumably, at that date, the occupation would indicate the self-made man. Just as the novelist must always be one jump ahead of his own characters in perception, sophistication or simple success, so Gissing seems to have needed, both as a man and a writer, to be one jump ahead of the toiling, self-educated man who had given him birth, and to take trouble to portray his fictional fathers as mere men, with men's failings. ('Faults he could perceive . . .') Our parents are not just our earliest models; they are also our first competitors in the race of life—and Gissing was, for all his self-defeatism, an ambitious racer.

Perhaps one could leave the last word on fathers to *Thyrza*, Gissing's own favourite among his books and one in which many of the themes apparent both in his life and in his other books are worked out in an artistically satisfactory manner, if not always a realistic one. Speaking of a minor character, Bunce, who is bringing up motherless children, he writes:

What more pathetic, rightly considered, than the story of those fathers whose lives are but a preparation for the richer lives of their sons? . . . Perhaps there is compensation to the parent if he live to see the lad conquering; but what of those who fall into silence when all is still uncertain, when they recognize in their offspring an hereditary weakness and danger as often as a rare gleam of new promise? One would bow reverently and sadly by the graves of such men.

To those who know Gissing's own background, this passage, incidental and even irrelevant in context, is eloquent. Add the unrelated facts that Bunce is an atheist, that Bunce's marriage was apparently an unmitigated waste, and that Bunce's son is showing an aptitude for chemistry: and the whole Bunce-situation (culminating in a happy marriage with a woman who asks nothing better than to help and give) is revealed as a melting pot of items drawn from the depths of Gissing's own experience.

The Unknown Mrs Gissing

When Mrs Gaussen was visiting Gissing at his London lodgings in 1884, she looked at a photograph of his mother he had there and 'said it was a strikingly handsome face, and extraordinarily full of character. I amazed her by explaining that I was really quite unable to say whether the character was in reality there or not; so utterly a stranger, on reflection, do I find my own mother to be to me. A curious state of things; one which I fancy would have been pretty much the same under any circumstances.'[17]

Much has been made of this passage by at least one commen-

tator, Mabel Collins Donnelly,[18] who makes it the basis for an
interpretation of Gissing's relationship to his mother which
possibly owes more to mid-twentieth-century Freudianism than
to nineteenth-century realities. The portrait she draws of a
limited, sternly moralistic woman with much influence but little
in common either with her husband or her eldest son, is tempting in its simple dramatic emphasis: ('For years Mrs Gissing
was the source of her son's ambivalent feelings towards women,
and only towards the end of his life did he break the tie he hated
yet preserved.') There is, however, little evidence for such a
view. For one thing, so many men feel vaguely ambivalent towards women, at once the sex-objects and the nannies of life,
that such an attitude may almost be taken as a normal part of
the male psyche and therefore goes little way towards explaining Gissing's eccentrically disastrous choice of wives. And for
another thing Gissing appears to have remained both attached
to and detached from his mother to the same extent throughout
his life. Far from 'breaking' a 'hated tie', during the last years
of his life he sent his own son to live at Wakefield in the family
home with his mother and sisters—a step which, even though
forced by circumstances, was a pretty fair indication of basic
confidence and love. Throughout his life Wakefield remained a
place of refuge for him when life in London seemed particularly depressing; indeed in the years immediately preceding his
second marriage (1889, 1890) he spent long spells in Wakefield
and did a great deal of concentrated work there—doubtless
waited on hand and foot by his female relatives. His sister Ellen
played the piano for him in the evenings, something he much
enjoyed. In the latter year, he went to the family home intending to stay there 'three weeks' but in fact stayed for most of
the summer: this hardly suggests an environment totally alien
to his tastes however his conscious mind might view it. Though
the happy families in his novels tend to be of slightly higher
social level than his own, and his books show a wide and grue-
some array of lower-middle-class ménages which are *un*happy,
essentially happy parent-and-child relationships, and brother-
and-sister relationships (like the Milvains in *New Grub Street*)
were something Gissing knew about. A passage in his Diary[19]
for 1890, when he was returning from a spell abroad and was
shortly to leave London again for his home in the north, seems

to sum up much of his own essentially warm family feeling; he had travelled from Tilbury to London in the same carriage as an actress returning from Australia, who was met by her brothers: 'They were a trifle vulgar, but the family affection between them all very good. Spoke of their mother as sure to make a great "scene" on daughter's reaching home; also said she had fallen into the habit of perpetual "fretting and worrying". Evidently a good, bourgeois family.' Gissing, who had been alone much of the time abroad, sounds homesick.

To return to Dr Donnelly's portrait of Mrs Gissing as an exceptionally repressive Victorian mother, distorting her son's sex life for him, here too, I think, caution is needed. That he kept his marriage with the utterly unsuitable Nell secret from his mother and sisters for a long time was hardly an unusual step for a dutiful son of the period, particularly for one who must have been trying hard at that moment to re-create an image of his own worthiness in his parent's eyes after the appalling débâcle of the Manchester episode. No doubt hard things had been said, in the small house in Wakefield, about this terrible girl who had 'led George astray' and perhaps he himself knew the marriage would not last. Nor was it particularly remarkable that, years later, he kept silent to his then elderly mother on the subject of his relationship with Gabrielle Fleury. This circumstance, incidentally, was much resented by that French lady herself, who was clamorously insistent on being recognized as Gissing's 'wife' in all but law, but it did not—as she once claimed—betoken any morbid regard on Gissing's part for his mother's peace of mind. Men in late nineteenth-century England, particularly men of Gissing's chequered and 'bohemian' way of life, simply did not attempt to share their private affairs with their female relatives[20]—the fact was noted several times by Gissing himself, and mildly lamented, but he himself made no break with conformity in this respect. As already quoted, the Gissing family suffered from the then-prevalent petit bourgeois inability to call a sexual spade a spade, or even to refer to it at all. (Neither of the girls had married.) Gissing, despite his expressed wish that speech between educated men and women might be freer, was not without a fastidious dislike of things expressed very frankly. His was in any case a secretive temperament, and to construe this secrecy as a sign of fundamental estrangement from his mother and fear of her opinion is to view the period at which these events were taking place too much through modern eyes. Ellen Gissing, who was in a position to know, gave a rather different explanation: '. . . he never appealed to his own home for money, nor allowed his mother to know of the extreme privations through which he was passing. In no circumstances would he draw upon her small resources, some of which he knew would be at his disposal if all the truth were revealed.'[21]

That hardly gives the impression of a stern and unforgiving parent. If a more independent witness is preferred, a life-long friend[22] of the family regarded her as 'most kindly and charming' and 'severe' only 'after the manner of the time'. In fact, Mrs Gissing did send her son money regularly in those early years, but a note added to his Diaries, dated 1902, makes it clear that this was his own money, which was kept for him in a Wakefield bank in his mother's name. Presumably this arrangement suited both of them, Mrs Gissing in that it gave her credit in the town, and Gissing himself—? Well, perhaps his prison record made the young Gissing wary of opening an account in his own name, when routine banker's enquiries might conceivably turn up the hateful secret. The extent to which his secret weighed on his mind and probably influenced in a permanent way both his life and his writing, is discussed in Chapter 3.

The part of the remark, quoted above, about Mrs Gissing being 'a stranger' to her son is easy to misconstrue. Evidently there was a sympathy between them, and an understanding between them, albeit of a clearly-defined kind. To suggest that he 'hardly knew his mother' is, given the homely circumstances of his upbringing, absurd. What Gissing himself failed to note is that, in a sense, it is always the very-familiar figure in our life that is harder for us to place than the slightly known one— though perhaps he was feeling after this general truth when he added: 'A curious state of things; one which I fancy would have been pretty much the same under any circumstances.' It is a commonplace of psychology that children have difficulty in perceiving the mother, the person they are more intimately associated with than anyone else in the world, as a *person* at all. She is just—Mother; an element, a personification of home, a basic fact of life. Although this primitive reaction usually gets modified as the child grows to adulthood, shreds of it must remain. Gissing's inability to tell Mrs Gaussen whether his mother was really a woman of great character or not, could indicate, not that he failed to 'know' her, but that he knew her too well and at too intimate and non-verbal a level to express any idea about her to the articulate, upper-class lady who was paying a call on him.

Much interpretation, too, has been laid upon the one reference to Mrs Gissing senior in the 'Reminiscences': 'Occurs to me now as very strange,' Gissing wrote, 'that he [Father] did not exercise more intellectual influence over mother. In my memory, he clearly had accepted the difference between their points of view, and was content to enter a protest now and then.'

This presumably means that Mrs Gissing did not share her husband's Radical sympathies to any great extent, and that she was religious. (She was a Unitarian, and brought her daughters up to be religious; they remained devout throughout their lives, particularly Madge, the elder.) Thomas Gissing, as we have seen, was an atheist, and once or twice made this clear to his eldest son. But this was not at all an uncommon pattern in late nineteenth- and early twentieth-century households and is reflected in plenty of Gissing's fictional marriages. Atheism, or at any rate agnosticism, had become respectable enough to be almost the rule, rather than the exception, in intelligent men of progressive sympathies, but a degree of religious conviction was still regarded as part of the equipment of the 'nice' woman, and becoming to a lady, particularly a mother. In spite of his anti-clericalism, and his often-voiced disgust with dogma, Gissing himself seems to have subscribed to this 'double standard' where religion and women or children were concerned. In *Thyrza* he makes the essentially honest and thoughtful Gilbert Quail reject militant atheism, and say: 'I'd a good deal rather hear children say the ordinary prayer.' In his Commonplace Book he wrote: 'Religious sentiment, as such, by no means irritates. It is the bad, poor, intolerant utterances of it that I cannot endure.' He had too many atavistic yearnings himself to reject entirely the validity of religious fervour. Though he acquired a reputation as an unbeliever he was probably, like Mallard, the central character in *The Emancipated,* 'one who had no faith but felt the need of it'.

I do not think that one should construe the entry in the 'Reminiscences' quoted above as meaning that Mrs Gissing was stupid or quite uneducated. None of her children was stupid, and certainly she considered education to be of great importance—otherwise, once she was widowed and in poor financial circumstances, her children would never have been encouraged to continue their schooling in the way they were, both boys and girls. She took an interest: the papers from Gissing's childhood contain poems written by him for her, and sent to her from boarding school. A letter[23] Gissing wrote to his sister Ellen in 1888, when he was staying at Algernon's Worcestershire home in September just after spending some time on holiday with his mother and sisters, makes two interesting points about Mrs Gissing's attitude to life:

Never do I hear a word in Worcestershire about household concerns; never is a meal discussed; never is the servant referred to in our conversation. Everything of that nature *comes to pass* merely; it is not wearisomely laboured over . . . Now *is* it worth sacrificing this human progress and peace for the sake of making sure that there is nothing in the kitchen that might not be better? . . . No, but then, of course, the inhabitants of a house must unite in recognizing that the mind is of more account than the body. Mother would grant you that hypothetically, but we know sadly enough that her paradise is in precisely the opposite direction. It is a sad, sad thing that anyone should be rendered incapable of spiritual activity by ceaseless regard for kitchen-ware and the back-door steps.[24]

In short, Gissing regarded his mother as a woman potentially capable of 'higher things', whose life had been arbitrarily circumscribed by the burden of mundane duties to which she brought a neurotic perfectionism. There's something very familiar about that in the Gissing ethos: in fact it is precisely the problem which is so often apparent in Gissing himself. While he had an image of himself as a contemplative scholar who asked nothing better than to be left to read in peace, at almost every stage of his life he seems to have devoted to the trivial, practical arrangements of living an excessive amount of emotional fervour. He hated to be required to bother about domestic matters and claimed, as he wrote to Algernon, to dislike seeing other people wasting their energies in such plebeian concerns, but at the same time he was exigent in his own requirements and sometimes downright fussy about food or surroundings to the point of obsession. He quite often sabotaged his own 'progress and peace' in this way. Such traits are partly inherited, partly learnt in childhood. It begins to become apparent that there was perhaps more of his mother in Gissing than he himself was willing to recognize.

In *Born in Exile* (1892) the poor-but-proud family that have produced Godwin Peak and in particular the mother of it, are of especial interest, for the light they may throw on Gissing's own family relationships. While, as I have already said, one should beware of reading Peak's history as if it were simply Gissing's in a thin fictional guise—apart from anything else, Godwin Peak lacks most of his creator's nicer qualities[25]—his antecedents replicate Gissing's own so very nearly that it is hard to believe that Gissing did not make use of other attributes of his own family also. In fact there are a number of things in this book (more fully discussed in Chapter 3) which seem to have been imported, unchanged in essence, from Gissing's own personal experience, and which do not really suit the fictional setting in which they are placed. It is as if, rather than making creative *use* of his own mother (who, in any case, he had difficulty in 'seeing') Gissing was content to let her sit, barely disguised, in the background of an otherwise much more complex and figurative re-working of personal experience.

Peak's father, like Gissing's, is a dispenser by profession, and a Radical by conviction. His wife is (like Mrs Gissing) 'of better birth than his own' though of impoverished family, and he dies when his eldest son is just thirteen. So far the autobiography is identical in outline, and therefore one is much tempted to read the comment on Mrs Peak that follows as a sketch of Mrs Gissing herself:

For some years she had nourished a secret antagonism to her husband's spirit of political, social, and religious rebellion, and in her widowhood she speedily became the pattern of the conservative female . . . Long ago she had repented the marriage which connected her with such a family as that of the Peaks, and she ardently desired that the children, now exclusively her own, might enter life on a plane superior to their father's.

At the same time '. . . she often stood in awe of her son, who, though not yet fourteen, had much of his father's commanding severity'.

The adolescent Peak's reaction to his mother is delineated in one of Gissing's mordant and suddenly perceptive phrases: 'As women . . . he despised these relatives.' [His mother and aunt.] 'It is almost impossible for a bright-witted lad born in the lower middle class to escape this stage of development.'

Note that Gissing does not say the mother-figure deserved despising; merely that her snobbish and restless teenage son had this reaction to her. *Born in Exile* was written long after Gissing himself could be assumed to be in any state of youthful revolt. Moreover, though the lower-middle-class mother is presented through the novel as being only a background figure in her ambitious son's life, the project which is the main theme of the novel, and the ultimate cause of Peak's downfall—his plan to get himself ordained for reasons of social advancement—is partly her idea in the beginning: 'It would have gratified her to discern any possibility of Godwin's assuming the priestly garb.'

Gissing was evidently aware in his books, if not always in his life, that the influence of the original home is a long, long one. I believe that the title *Born in Exile*, too often taken as a slogan for Gissing's own life, is intended to be at least partly ironic. The phrase occurs too early and glibly in the book for it to represent Gissing's own final word on the subject, and is moreover put into the mouth of the adolescent Peak in a particularly self-dramatizing mood:

. . . He had not ventured to say plainly, that he was leaving Twybridge for good, and henceforth would not think of it as home. In these moments of parting, he resented the natural feeling which brought moisture to his eyes. He hardened himself against the ties of blood, and kept repeating to himself a phrase in which of late he had summoned up his miseries: 'I was born in exile—born in exile.' Now at length had he set forth on a voyage of discovery, to end perchance in some unknown land among his spiritual kith and kin.

What romantic rot, the voice of the maturer Gissing seems to be insinuating. In fact it is possible to read the whole book, not as the description of Gissing's own sense of having been born for better things, which it is usually taken to be, but as a warning *against* any such delusion. It is as if, by the 1890s, Gissing was learning that you can't escape from your family entirely,[26] still less pretend that they are totally irrelevant to your personality, and that, if you try too strenuously to exile yourself from your origins, you will end up in exile from everything, dying (like Peak) alone in an inn in a foreign country, and it will be *your own fault*.

I think that Gissing was, in this novel, using his central character—a version of his own self when younger—to explore the concept of having been 'born in exile' which was still attractive to him, emotionally, but which his maturer knowledge was beginning to perceive as something of an adolescent fantasy. The ending of the novel, in which a friend of Peak's declares, on receiving the news, 'Dead, too, in exile!' reads like one of those fine, symbolic endings which the novelist has in sight from the novel's early stages, but which, by the time the last page comes to be written, has been to some extent outpaced by perceptions and theme-developments which have taken place in the course of the writing. Since novel-writing is not simply a method of putting down what one has already thought, but also is itself a means of thinking matters out and reaching new conclusions, this problem of maintaining a consistent attitude through the book is one which troubles novelists quite often.

Although Godwin Peak's conscious sense of alienation from his home background is many times expressed, Gissing allows him to be warmed, in spite of himself, by the kindly welcome he receives on his rare return visits there, and there is no suggestion that its modest domesticity, as such, is anything but agreeable to him. Mrs Peak appears to belong to the same category of women as the mother in *Mary Somerville's Memoirs*, a passage of which Gissing copied into his Commonplace Book: 'My mother was quite of the old school with regard to the duties of women, & very particular about her table, &, although we were obliged to live with rigid economy, our food was of the best quality, well-dressed & neatly served . . .'

Ellen Gissing stated[27] that '. . . one of Gissing's most strongly marked characteristics [was] his desire for a home of his own, and for the kind of domestic life which he had seen about him when a boy, and which, to him, was an ideal'. One should, perhaps allow for a degree of overstatement here, since, when his sister wrote that, she was trying to excuse to the reader, in somewhat veiled terms, her brother's hasty and ill-considered marriages. All the same, Ellen Gissing would hardly have made the remark if the Gissing family home had been, even remotely, a forerunner of the disorderly and squalid homes run for Gissing by Nell or Edith, his second wife, and hence of the wretched ménages which frequently crop up in his works. In fact one may reasonably surmise that the reverse is true—that at least part of Gissing's obsession about being unable to find domestic comfort in any household of his own stemmed from the extremely high standards (albeit of 'mere comfort') set by his mother and sisters. Significantly, he remarked in a letter to Algernon late in life: 'The oftener I think of *our* mother, and the kind of holidays she made for us in days gone by, the more do I respect the sterling elements of her character.'[28] With our altered, present-day attitude to the male role versus the female one, we would now say that Gissing's womenfolk had spoilt him, and made him so fussy that even the relative comfort of the Fleury household was to fall below his own exacting standards. Typically, for all his self-examination, this simple explanation of his perpetual domestic dissatisfaction never seems to have occurred to Gissing himself.

On occasions, when poverty made him resort to preparing his own food entirely, the circumstance was sufficiently remarkable to be noted in his Diary. Not that he was uninterested in food; far from it, and from time to time he developed an obsession about one or another food being particularly good for the health, and badgered his brother to try it, enclosing recipes and, once, a sample of the right sort of lentil to buy! But Nell was living with him then, and was presumably persuaded to do the actual preparation. When quite alone, in 1889, after his return from his first long trip to France and Italy, and consequently low in funds, he noted sadly in his Diary: 'For Sunday I buy ½ lb. of "brisket" which costs 8d., and this lasts for Monday dinner as well; with it I eat vegetables, which I have to pare and cook.' The picture of Gissing standing at the sink resentfully peeling potatoes, no doubt with unnecessary perfectionism, is one which lingers in the mind. But though the writer's self-pity

c

in this instance strikes the modern reader as funny rather than
touching, he was merely reasonable in feeling sorry for himself
within the context of his own time. In nineteenth-century
England, men of any class simply did not, as a rule, do 'women's
work'; still less did gentlemen do it, even poor gentlemen. Gissing, although he was extremely perceptive in suggesting certain
social changes which have, indeed, come about between his day
and our own, does not seem to have foreseen the time when
many husbands would peel the potatoes as readily as their working wives, or indeed make up the baby's feeds—another chore
which once fell to the lot of the horrified writer.

Another version of the mother-of-a-higher-social-origin-living-
in-straitened-circumstances, which we have already seen in Mrs
Peak, is Mrs Hood, the wife of the ill-fated James Hood of
A Life's Morning. She is an ex-schoolmistress: 'Mrs Hood possessed still her somewhat genteel furniture. One article was a
piano, and upon this she taught Emily her notes. It had been
a fairly good piano once, but the keys had become very loose.
They were looser than ever, now that Emily tried to play on
them, on her return from Surrey.'

But although Mrs Hood appears to inhabit, with her husband
and her daughter, the very house at Agbrigg ('Banbrigg') to
which the widowed Mrs Gissing and *her* daughters had by that
time moved, such appearances can be misleading: to live in a
known house is no proof of fictional identity. There is no
reason to suppose that Mrs Hood 'is' Mrs Gissing, or that
Thomas Gissing ever let himself be walked over by his wife
as the downtrodden James Hood does. All the same, there are
scenes in the Hood household which one tends to think must
have been taken from the Gissings' own:

Saturday was from old a day of ills. The charwoman was in
the house, and Mrs Hood went about in a fatigued way, coming
now and then to the sitting-room, sinking into a chair, letting
her head fall back with closed eyes. Emily had, of course, begged
to be allowed to give assistance, but her mother declared that
there was nothing whatever she could do.

'Shut the door,' she said, 'and then you won't hear the scrubbing so plainly. I can understand that it annoys you; I used to
have the same feeling, but I've accustomed myself. You might
play something; it would keep away your thoughts.'

'But I don't want to keep away my thoughts,' exclaimed

Emily with a laugh. 'I want to help you so that you will have
done the sooner.'

'No, no, my dear; you are not used to it. You'll tell me when
you'd like something to eat if you get faint.'

'I am not likely to grow faint, mother, if I do nothing.'

'Well, well; I have a sinking feeling now and then, I thought
you might be the same.'

The Gissing family ethos is there—the children ministered to
with a genuine kindness, mingled with a snobbish desire that
they themselves will achieve a higher social station for which
they must therefore be prepared. In similar passages there is also
the well-meant but unfortunate tendency, noted by Gissing
in his letter to Ellen regarding the merits of the Worcestershire
household, to make a great to-do about practical trifles, out of
a concern for others' well-being (real or assumed) when they
would be more comfortable to have no cake and less fuss:

'Didn't I ask you to bring a cake? I suppose my memory is
going; I meant to, and thought I mentioned it at breakfast. I
shall have nothing for Emily's tea.'

Emily protested that it was needless to get unusual things on
her account.

'We must do what we can to make you comfortable, my dear.
I can't keep a table like that you are accustomed to, but that I
know you don't expect. Which way are you going to walk this
afternoon? If you pass a shop you might get a cake, or buns,
whichever you like.'

'Well, I thought we might take a turn over the Heath,' said
Mr Hood. 'However, we'll see what we can do.'

Mrs Hood is also prey to headaches—a sign, no doubt—of her
socially superior origins. We have no evidence that Mrs Gissing
was subject to such inconveniences, but one feels that someone
in the household must have been (Madge, perhaps, the more
rigid of the two sisters?) since headaches are such a frequent
feature of Gissing's women characters. You could write a
scholarly monograph on the Headache in the Gissing Heroine.
It is notable that, in his books, headaches are usually only
suffered by ladies, or near-ladies. His lower-class women have
fits or savage tempers instead, or else are splendidly robust. In
such details are a writer's most deeply-rooted class prejudices
betrayed.

To conclude, however much Gissing may have *thought* he disliked to hear about the humdrum details of housekeeping, he was, like everyone born into modest circumstances, entirely used to living in such an atmosphere. One might even say that he was addicted to some degree of ignoble domestic fuss and went out of his way to find it, or at any rate to form relationships with women who would provide it. It provided, in turn, some of his liveliest and most keenly observed writing. However much he enjoyed, at certain periods, visiting households wealthy enough to keep domestic concerns out of sight, he never describes such surroundings as if he felt at home in them, and indeed, once the novelty of this or that affluent household had worn off, was rather quick to criticize it as 'conventional', 'plutocratic' or over-occupied with frivolous Society pastimes. The fact that well-to-do women did not, at that period, concern themselves with mundane household duties, may have been one reason—only one of several—why he apparently had great difficulty in ever seeing a lady as a potential wife for himself. It was as if, at a sub-conscious level, 'ladies' and 'wives' were to him a different species, not so much because of any sexual aspect of the problem, but simply because of the way the two groups spent their time, as he saw the matter. He was thus in the problematical situation of having an essentially lower-class concept of 'wife' while actively disliking many lower-class traits. When he expressed, a number of times both in fiction and *in propria persona*, the view that ladies ought not to think themselves above domestic concerns, he was perhaps not just stating a rational view but also betraying a subjective wish.

It is also worth noting that the women in his books who seem most closely modelled on his mother and sisters and their kind —Mrs Hood and Mrs Peak, Miriam Baske in *The Emancipated*, Kingcote's sister in *Isabel Clarendon*, the sisters in *The Odd Women* and in *New Grub Street*—are not the destructive ones. They have their limitations, but essenially they are seen as benign, friends not enemies. The female-as-destroyer is other, for Gissing, and comes in two versions. One is the lower class one, impossible to the point of being unbalanced (Harriet Smales in *The Unclassed*, Carrie Mitchell in *Workers in the Dawn*, to some extent Clem Peckover in *The Nether World*), a type who so strikingly pre-figured Edith Underwood, whom Gissing did not marry till 1891. The other is the middle-class woman who is 'merely silly', but whose silliness leads to a situation inherently vicious and who thus *is* an agent for evil: Amy Reardon's foolish, snobbish mother in *New Grub Street* is a classic example of this type, and so, in many respects, is Alma Frothingham in *The Whirlpool*. Whatever will o' the wisps Gissing pursued over the course of his life—or wills o' the wisp,[29] as he would pedantically have it—he was never led astray by the seductive simplicities of straightforward snobbery, or by the showily unworthy. His marked lapses of judgement were due not to shaky ideals as such, but to a lethal tendency to idealize a situation or person without sufficient regard for the reality. His personal failures—perhaps even the first, ignominious one—were not an indication of a lack of integrity, sense of moral priorities, or even discrimination, but simply of a crippling lack of common sense. And he knew this himself, at moments. In *The Whirlpool*, where the central characer, Harvey Rolfe, is yet another of those shadowy alter-egos—the writer himself minus the vital moving part that makes him what he is—Gissing reflects: 'Surely something must have arrested the natural development of his common sense [at twenty-one]. Even in another ten years he was scarcely on a level, as regards practical intelligence, with the ordinary lad who was leaving school.'

The un-ordinary lad, who left school precipitately at nineteen in dark disgrace, had many qualities, but a sense of base self-preservation was not one of them.

2   The Escape Downwards

In the very concept of escape from one's origins is the recognition that the origins from which you are escaping continue to
have an ominous significance for you: why else should you still
be needing to get away? As Gissing said of Dickens: 'The
landed proprietor of Gadshill could not forget (the great writer
could never desire to forget) a miserable childhood imprisoned
in the limbo of squalid London; to the end his personal triumph
gratified him, however unconsciously, as the vindication of a
social claim.'[1]

Gissing himself never achieved his scarce-admitted dream of
becoming a 'landed proprietor', but in essence that paragraph
might be about himself, and was obviously drawn from his own
perception of what writing means to the writer. There is even
the nice discrimination between the needs of the writer and
the needs of the man—the former would not wish to forget
the shaming past, even if the latter did.

In the preceding section, I touched on one of the means by
which Gissing sought to demonstrate an emancipation from his
origins: his introduction into his novels of scenes from an
affluent and essentially rural society with which he was only
sketchily acquainted. In this section, I shall be considering what
might be called 'the escape downwards'—Gissing's descent, at
certain periods of his life into surroundings considerably *lower*
in class than any he had frequented in childhood, and his use,
for this purpose, of that traditional bohemian escape-hatch:
sex.

It may be objected that these sections are in the wrong order
—that Gissing tried the low life before he had any choice to
sample the high. But this is an accident of time rather than an
indication of where his original hopes lay. Brought up to expect
that his brains and his hard work at school and at college in

Manchester would, by a gradual but well-defined path, lead to London University or even Oxford or Cambridge, and thence to an academic career—presumably as a fellow of a University— he was turned from early youth towards an intellectual and therefore upper-class world. (One might add in passing that the life of a celibate classics don—Oxford and Cambridge dons were all celibate till 1877—even in the best University in the world, would have left almost as many of Gissing's needs unfulfilled as the life of a struggling novelist, but this was never put to the test.) The conservative and elitist streak as personified by Hubert Eldon in *Demos*, was very strong in him. It is interesting, if fruitless, to speculate on whether, without the Manchester disaster, the democratic Radicalism which he had learnt from his father and which was grafted on to an essentially conservative nature, would ever have been activated at all.

The Nell Theme

In fact, it is probably unrealistic to speak, as Gissing himself tended to and as some commentators have since, as if his relationship with Nell and the results of it were pure, malignant chance, an adolescent aberration which just happened to have unfortunate and far-reaching consequences. The basis for a curiosity about how the 'other nation' lived was already there, even intellectually; besides his father's Radicalism there was the example of Dickens' famous exploitation of 'low life' scenes. Also, as soon as one mentions his affair with Nell, one is driven to ask why he was so seriously attracted to such a girl in the first place? Many young men at college have consorted with prostitutes—at least one of Gissing's own friends[2] 'went with' Nell. How did Gissing become so hopelessly involved that he flouted a taboo far stronger than the sex one—honesty about money?

The sexual aspect of the matter is far more readily explained. (And indeed if the whole affair had stayed on that level there would be nothing much worth commenting on anyway.) Because of the prudery with which their own women were surrounded and the general de-sexing, in myth, of the 'nice' female ('ladies don't move'), many Victorians undoubtedly found it difficult to regard women of their own class as sex-objects at all. Indeed this observation has become a truism of social and literary history, and no review of Gissing's sexual proclivities is complete without it. It has even been suggested that Gissing (like A. J. Munby[3] and doubtless many other men of the period) was only capable of being sexually attracted to lower-class women. While certain elements in Gissing's life might suggest this (such as his making the mistake of marrying beneath him not once but twice), I do not believe that, as an overall explanation of his love-life, it will do. The emotional threads were more complex than that, and there were purely practical considerations too which, while Gissing himself undoubtedly exaggerated them, still need to be taken into account.

Long after Nell was dead, Gissing expressed in a letter to Clara Collet the idea that the loneliness which had dogged his life, and to which he had become habituated, had direct bearing on his early catastrophe also: 'I feel it a strange thing when I frequently see and talk with people. The bad beginning of it was when, at 16 or so, I was foolishly sent to live in Manchester in miserable lodgings. Hence all subsequent ills and follies.'

As usual when speaking of this long-past event—though Gissing never, as far as we know, actually told Miss Collet *what* event had taken place—he was not being entirely accurate. He was more like eighteen than sixteen when he met Nell: though he had been attending classes at Owens for some time, at first he continued to lodge just outside Manchester at Alderley Edge, his Quaker boarding school. He apparently expressed much the same thing to Morley Roberts (who knew the whole truth because he had been at Owens himself) with the same exaggeration of his own youth and unprotected state: 'It was a cruel and most undesirable thing that I, at the age of sixteen, should have been turned loose in a big city, compelled to live alone in lodgings, with nobody interested in me but those at the college. I see now that one of my sisters should certainly have been sent with me to Moorhampton.'[4]

'Moorhampton' is Manchester. The fact that he felt that, with a sister with him, he would not have needed a Nell, is revealing as regards the strength of his relationship with his sisters, but the suggestion that one of them could have lived with him when he was a student was unrealistic since at that time both the girls were children. It is interesting, however, to compare what might well be regarded as a parallel passage in *Born in Exile*, when the young Peak is a charity student at 'Whitelaw College, Kingsmill':

> Accustomed hitherto to a domestic circle, at Kingsmill he found himself isolated, and it was not easy for him to surrender all at once the comforts of a home . . . His lodgings were in a very ugly street in the ugliest outskirts of the town; he had to take a long walk through desolate districts (brick-yard, sordid pasture, degenerate village) before he could refresh his eyes with the rural scenery which was so great a joy to him as almost to be a necessity. The immediate vicinage offered nothing but a monotony of grimy, lower-middle-class dwellings, occasionally relieved by a public house. He occupied two rooms, not unreasonably clean, and was seldom disturbed by the attentions of his landlady.
>
> An impartial observer might have wondered at the negligence which left him to arrange his life as best he could, notwithstanding youth and utter inexperience. It looked indeed as if there were no one in the world who cared what became of him. Yet this was merely the result of his mother's circumstances, and of his own character. Mrs Peak could do no more than make her small remittances, and therewith send an occasional admonition regarding his health. She did not, in fact, conceive the state of things, imagining that the authority and supervisal of the College extended over her son's daily existence, whereas it was possible for Godwin to frequent lectures or not, to study or to waste his time pretty much as he chose, subject only to official enquiry if his attendance became frequently irregular. His independent temper, and the seeming maturity of his mind, supplied another excuse for the imprudent confidence which left him to his own resources. Yet the perils of the situation were great indeed. A youth of less concentrated purpose, more at the mercy of casual allurement, would probably have gone to wreck amid trials as exceptional.

In this passage, which incidentally has little relevance to Peak's subsequent history, but seems to have strayed there whole from Gissing's own experience, there is a clear element of personal wish-fulfilment—of creating a different past, as if on another loop of time, in which the catastrophe did *not* take place, the dangers were present but were circumnavigated. The day-dreaming, wouldn't-it-be-nice-if element in novel-writing can work retrospectively as well as in prospect. As we know, in life Gissing's purpose was insufficiently 'concentrated', he *did* fall victim to a 'casual allurement' and met with a formidable wreck.

It is partly, no doubt, due to the picture of a hyper-sensitive, solitary intellectual in this situation in *Born in Exile*, that subsequent writers, from Roberts onwards, have tended to gloss over the means by which this supposed pure, high-minded child of sixteen ever became involved with Nell at all. A slightly different picture, however, is given by documents in Manchester University archives which came to light in the 1950s.[5] These consist of letters written to Gissing in the first part of 1876, when Gissing was therefore eighteen, by a friend of his at Owens, John George Black; and also the minutes of the Senate meetings at which Gissing's case was discussed and his expulsion decided upon.

Judging by his letters, Black was a young man of ebullient, not to say flamboyant personality, who had formed a warm friendship with Gissing. (The image of the totally friendless, lonely young man already begins to melt at the edges . . .) The letters make it clear (*a*) that Nell was known to both of them, (*b*) that Black himself had slept with Nell, knowing that Gissing had also done so but without realizing that Gissing was 'serious' about her, and (*c*) that Black somewhere caught a venereal infection, about which he asked Gissing's advice, referring to the fact that Gissing himself had had a similar or comparable 'inflammation'.* One should add that Black seems to have been a good-hearted lad and, when Gissing was taking Nell for a discreet holiday in Southport, he readily supplied the addresses of landladies etc. and added, rather charmingly 'Delicacy forbids me to commend myself to anyone but yourself, I suppose'. By that time he knew Gissing was serious about a preposterous project—which he—Black—had at first dismissed as mere talk: that of marrying Nell. ('I believed everything, except that you had really fallen in love with her.')

Now, young men acquainted—however recently—with girls of the town, and capable of swapping the symptoms of venereal disease, the address of a helpful doctor and so forth, are not the absolute innocents that Gissing later presented himself as having been. Frequenting girls of easy virtue was probably, among the students, the dashing thing to do. The impression is less of solitary adolescence than of young men sowing faintly

* See Chapter 3.

squalid wild oats in the time-honoured Victorian tradition. What went wrong? Why did Gissing fall in love with a girl whom even an equally young and green friend clearly regarded as little more than a convenient outcast?

The term 'prostitute' is deceptive, in that it conjures up a different image in different eras. In our own time, when irregular sexual relationships between equals have become so widely accepted as normal, one can't help feeling that there must be far less call for the services of the prostitute than in the past, and that the true 'prostitute' now can only be the hardened professional catering mainly for those too old, unattractive or exotic in their tastes to find accommodation elsewhere. Hence the image of the prostitute as a brassy figure with a totally business-like approach to her work—hardly the person likely to appeal to an eighteen-year-old student, on any level. Gissing was, at that time, a tall, strong, good-looking young man—indeed Morley Roberts was of the opinion that he was always attractive to women. A student Gissing of today would undoubtedly have a girl-friend with whom he was sleeping—a difficult, unstable girl-friend, perhaps, since instability calls to instability, but someone on whom he could lavish his strong, if immature, affections.

This, I suggest, is what Nell Harrison in essence was; today we should not call her a 'prostitute' at all. The term of the period was 'dollymop'. She was very young—younger even than him—and seems from the start to have had even less idea of running her sex-life efficiently than Gissing himself. Her promiscuity would now be quite unremarkable, in a teenage girl of deprived background. A modern Nell Harrison, without the same dire financial need, and with a weakness for university students above her own social and educational level, would probably have no difficulty in finding a person or persons to whom she could attach herself.

Even the descriptions of her that survive (no photo does) suggest the tatty bohemian rather than the tough professional. Morley Roberts wrote: 'One day he showed me a photograph. It was that of a young girl, aged perhaps seventeen . . . with her hair down her back. She was not beautiful but had a certain prettiness, the mere prettiness of youth, and she was undoubtedly not a lady.' The descriptions of Carrie Mitchell, Arthur Golding's prostitute wife in *Workers in the Dawn*, give the same sort of picture. When Arthur first meets Carrie, in a lodging house, she is dark-haired and very young—'perhaps seventeen or eighteen'. She is a mantle-hand in the garment trade (that was Nell Harrison's trade also) and, like Nell, attracts by her air of need: 'He thought she must be ill, and felt his interest in her grow yet stronger . . .' Much later, after Arthur has married her and she has run away from him, she makes her reappearance in a restaurant; respectable women did not then go into restaurants alone: 'Her hair was of the colour of dark gold, a hue too rich to be natural, and hung in a long single plait down to her waist. As she entered she threw back a heavy paletôt, which the coldness of the night rendered necessary, and displayed a robe of dark blue silk, the front of which gave to view the curves of a magnificent throat and bosom.' The impression is pre-Raphaelite, bohemian rather than flashy. What Nell represented for Gissing, in fact, was probably not the street-girl at all, but the French *grisette* (also by tradition a seamstress) of de Musset and of Murger's *Vie de Bohème*. We know that both writers were favourites with Gissing from his teens, and he re-read Murger at intervals throughout his life, as if, even when he had become older and sadder and wiser, it remained his favourite fantasy. The de Musset–Murger idyll is expressly referred to in conversation between men in *Born in Exile*. The most probable explanation for the depth of his attraction to Nell, at the beginning, is that it stemmed from a desire to create this cloud-cuckoo-land of love-in-a-garret in his own life. He was at his usual practice of matching his experience to what he had read.

The main explanation for his continuing involvement with her, even after he had realized her way of life, was the one he apparently gave haltingly to the college authorities: he wished to save her. This theme makes its appearance in *Workers in the Dawn*; it is worked out, more romantically and less realistically, in *The Unclassed*. But first a little background: when the college became anxious about continuing thefts of money from the Common Room, they called the police and a trap was set. Gissing walked straight into it—he was seen to take a marked piece of money from another student's coat left hanging up. Hauled before the magistrates he was sentenced summarily to one month's penal servitude, and at the next meeting of the college Senate all his scholarships were annulled and he was formally dismissed. Subsequently, in an apparent attempt to win a little sympathy for him, friends of his family in Manchester revealed to the college authorities that this brilliant student, of whom so much had been hoped, had stolen in order to support a girl who otherwise, he knew, would return to her old way of life. In particular, he had stolen money in order to buy her a sewing machine, and thus help her to be self-supporting. Unfortunately the hearts of the authorities were not softened by this pathetic circumstance, which they evidently just regarded as further evidence of young Gissing's general moral depravity. Black's letters came to light and he was also dismissed—though later reinstated. It was obviously a large and unpleasant row.

One may reflect in passing that, just as the Gissing of today would be able to sleep with a girl without making romantic distinctions between those 'inside' society and those 'outside' it, so too, if he were led to steal, his case would probably be more sympathetically dealt with. Indeed several modern explanations have already been advanced for his uncharacteristic lapse in honesty, none of which are probably particularly relevant to his own time. It has been suggested that he was striking 'a blow at society', or again 'a blow at his family's narrow morality'. Personally I don't think either of these ruthlessly cerebral motivations would have been at all typical of Gissing, either then or later: in practice, old-fashioned philanthropy was much more his line than revolutionary gestures. In fact I suspect the real reason behind his idiotic behaviour was a trivial adolescent neurosis, inexplicable on strictly rational grounds. Whether or not you believe that people steal money as a substitute for the love they really want (and neatly, in Gissing's case, he might have been said to be stealing 'love' in order to *buy* love—i.e. the attentions of Nell), it is an observable fact that children and adolescents quite commonly steal, particularly when they feel socially or emotionally insecure, and the great majority of them become reformed characters once they are fully adult.

What is, however, equally relevant, and probably a lot more relevant as regards his subsequent fictional use of the affair, is that Gissing seems to have *believed* he was stealing 'to save Nell' and that he allowed this to blot out all other considerations.

It was the first major manifestation of an obsession with the theme of helping, raising and improving others which is such a dominant one in his books.[6] It was, ironically, this potentially admirable trait in him which brought about his disaster and compounded it with marriage. It was not his loneliness, nor yet his sexual appetite as such that did the damage, but the other emotions he brought to bear on the situation.

His image of Nell seems from the first to have corresponded more to a romantic ideal of his own mind than to the reality. John George Black's description of his own relations with her shows that she was in a disturbed, emotional state, and was possibly drinking heavily, even then. Yet one must suppose that Gissing attributed special qualities to her. (Like many impulsive people he does not seem to have been a good judge of character. Years later he made the same mistake with Edith Underwood, thinking her 'docile' when she was apparently anything but, and he also at times changed his mind drastically about his male friends or publishers.) Certainly when Arthur Golding in *Workers in the Dawn* first meets Carrie, he feels an attraction to her which is not, even in retrospect, put down to purely physical reasons: 'Though her beauty was of a somewhat sensual type, and her features betrayed no special intelligence or good humour, Arthur felt strangely attracted to her for all that.' As already noted, his interest in her is already increased because he thinks she looks ill. It is as if, for him (and Gissing) the very things that were wrong with Nell helped to contribute to the romantic image. Carrie is lodging in the same house as Arthur; their relations are blameless, but Arthur comes across a letter, dropped on the stairs, which Carrie has received from a man. It disclaims all responsibility for the child she 'says' she is carrying, and adds, as a threat 'it's the easiest thing in the world for me to prove that you're nothing but a common girl of the town'. Note that in the fiction reality is here a little softened: Carrie is not yet a prostitute, she merely risks being labelled as one: Arthur has, as yet, no good reason to regard her as anything but an unlucky victim: 'It did not occur to him for a moment that the girl herself might possibly be to blame. He could feel nothing but tender pity for her, passionate indignation against the heartless brute who had cast her off . . .' When Carrie's landlady discovers she is penniless and threatens

to throw her out, Arthur secretly takes over the payment of
her board and lodging—the fairy godfather theme which appears
in many of Gissing's books.

One can have little doubt that Gissing tried to make something like this happen in real life—or would have liked to do so.
In life, the whole project, including the buying of the sewing
machine which he mentioned to Morley Roberts, may have
remained at fantasy level: clearly Gissing had to some extent
lost touch with reality at that point in failing to realize the
risks of his stealing being discovered. What is, however, true, is
that Gissing took Nell away to stay in lodgings with him (at
Southport) just as Arthur Golding takes a room for Carrie—
with again a further idealization in that, in the novel,
Arthur is not actually living with Carrie at this point, but
maintains the chastest relations from a room of his own down
the street. He is, however, quite as dictatorial towards her
as any lover or husband: 'He would have liked to be able to
lock her up from the world, so intense was his passion, and,
consequently, so acute his jealousy.' Carrie wants to go to the
theatre, Arthur refuses: 'In his attempt to exalt her nature
above the level on which it had hitherto moved, he, the democratic agitator, the ardent sympathizer with the most miserable
of poverty's victims, waxed quite aristocratic in his conversation.' What Carrie symbolizes to him has taken over almost
entirely from the reality of her nature: in the words from
Lecky's *Morals* which her creator was to copy years later into
his Commonplace book: 'She remains,'—the prostitute—'while
creeds and civilizations rise and fall, the eternal priestess of
humanity, blasted for the sins of the people.'

Being an eternal priestess of humanity is a difficult role for
any ordinary girl to fulfil, and presumably Nell in life found
it as difficult as Carrie does in the novel. The third volume of
the novel traces the course and deterioration of her relationship
with Arthur. At his insistence they marry, though his anxieties
have already been alerted by an occasion when Carrie has been
out at night without telling him where. The immediate effect
of their ill-conceived marriage is to lock them in a dialogue in
which neither is really speaking the other's language at all, and
indeed the claustrophobic nature of this situation is indicated
in the volume's first sentence: 'Arthur's life was now pent

within a narrower course than ever hitherto.' Carrie has had only two years' formal education; her speech is ungrammatical, her letters are illiterate. Arthur sets to work to teach her, setting her daily lessons of coyping, spelling and learning poetry; he also corrects her when they are in conversation. Carrie resents this (with some reason, as Gissing himself seems to perceive); she gets her own back on him, for this and for his wish that she should sit docilely at home all day, by making jealous scenes on her own account about a picture of a woman she finds among his papers (Arthur is an artist). He reads aloud to her, but she fails to appreciate it.

Gissing destroyed his diary for the early years with Nell, but it is reasonable to assume that he tried reading aloud to Nell since that is just what he did later with the almost equally un-receptive Edith Underwood, and later again, more appropriately, with Gabrielle Fleury. Reading aloud seems to have been part of his fundamental concept of what two people do together in an intimate situation; one can see a good deal of justification for Walter Allen's remark that, from Gissing's books, you would think that 'the sole end of life was that men and women should read'!

All this part of the book, and the worse troubles with Carrie that follow (drinking, lying, running away, taking to a life of prostitution) is written in a mood of hindsight. From the start of their marriage the reader is left in little doubt that this is going to end badly; indeed Gissing himself, addressing the reader, remarks that he hasn't the heart to detail the couple's happier moments, since 'perhaps the shadow of coming events falls already upon me and makes me gloomy'. Now there would be nothing very remarkable in this if the book had been written after he and Nell had finally split up and the whole relationship was thus viewed with a retrospective shadow. But in point of fact *Workers* was finished just about the time Gissing himself married Nell in 1879. Not maintaining the impeccable respect-ability he ascribed to his hero, he and Nell had already been living together for nearly two years; it is reasonable to suppose that Gissing was by then to some extent disillusioned about Nell's nature and had discovered, like Arthur Golding, that a girl's looks are not a reliable indication of her intelligence. But he did marry her—that is, he took exactly the rash, foolishly idealistic step which, in his novel, he had already made his hero take and had shown to be disastrous.

We have a very interesting example here of two things, both of which, separately, are typical of the relationship between Gissing's life and his novels. On the one hand, he appears to have been using his novel to test out in fictional form a possible source of action for himself, and did indeed succeed in proving, within the book, that marrying Nell-Carrie would not do. And yet, in his life, he went ahead and did it, thus making his novel into the most curious pre-recognition of what was actually to come to pass—the reverse process to the far more commonplace one of 'putting one's life straight into a book'. It is not surprising that most people assume, on reading *Workers*, that it is the latter, commonplace process Gissing is employing. It is as if, in spite of apparently using his book to probe and reject the idea of the marriage, he was still unable to bridge the gap between his perception as a writer and his feelings as a man. The writer knew more than the man, and the man was thus unable to make proper use of what the writer clearly told him.

One should, I suppose, make allowances for the fact that what is presented in the book, as in any book, is a *selection* of the real life events, both actual and likely, rather than a comprehensive review of them. While there were clearly times, the times when he was writing, when Gissing perceived with dismal clarity what Nell's eventual fate was likely to be, life is more complex and varied than even a three-volume novel, and there must have been many days, even after Nell had repeatedly disappointed him, when their life together seemed temporarily fresh and hopeful once more. The marriage itself—after nearly two years of living together—may indeed have been the result of a superstitious belief that it would provide a chance for Nell to turn over a new leaf and for everything to be magically 'different'. Gissing in any case seems to have had in his mind at this early period in his life the concept that the emotion of loving has in itself a value and a beauty, irrespective of any more objective assessment of the situation. When in America, lonely and presumably much disorientated, his once bright future now only an ominous question-mark, he kept a notebook (small and brown and bought at Chapin's Cheap Book House in Chicago[7]) into which he copied passages from books, as a young man will when seeking for a viewpoint in life. Here we find copied 'Wherever affection can spring, it is like a green leaf of the blossom—pure, and breathing purity, whatever soil it may grow in (Romola)'; and 'Là ou il y a beaucoup à plaindre il y a beaucoup à pardonner, et là ou l'on trouve à pardonner, sois certain qu'il y a quelque chose à aimer (Carmelo)'; and 'Aimer est le grand point; qu'importe la maîtresse? (Alfred de Musset)'. (The notebook also contains a number of sketch-plots for stories and novels, many on themes concerning fallen women, unconventional or ill-favoured marriages, etc.) Having taken the decision to come home and resume his relationship with Nell, with whom he was maintaining a correspondence, he had presumably got fixed in his head the idea of putting these romantic dicta into practice.

His letters to Algernon, the only one of his family to know, for a long time, that he had taken up with Nell again, show how hard he tried to maintain and demonstrate a harmonious union. In the early letters from London there are domestic references to 'we', to happy excursions made to Richmond or Kew, and mentions of Nell herself, e.g. 'Many thanks for the marrow receipe. I think Nell means to make some.' Nell's 'good wishes' are regularly sent, and one letter ends 'Nell wishes to be kindly remembered. How I wish I could say to mother, as well as to you.' Only gradually, indeed after *Workers* had been completed, do the references to Nell, her 'state of health' and the impossibility of finding her any suitable company, take on a more ominous note. She had an abscess on her arm, 'erysipelis' on her face, 'a form of scrofula' allegedly left over from her childhood, eventually 'fits' which sound like alcoholic seizures. In one letter, written shortly after *Workers* was published, Gissing suddenly admitted to his brother 'If you knew much of my daily life you would wonder that I write at all, to say nothing of writing cheerfully.' Yet in another letter[8] at precisely the same period there is a glimpse of one of the happier moments, those which, in the novel, he had not felt able to detail: he and Nell had a canary and he described how it woke them with its singing at four in the morning. In such hours the old idyll of the Murger vie de bohème, complete with symbolic songbird in its garret cage, must temporarily have re-asserted itself. One must assume that, even at that date, there were many moments of physical tenderness between them, since this was perhaps the one area of life they could truly share.

The hold which the unrealistic, idealized image of Nell had over Gissing's imagination, even when bitter experience must have shown it to be ill-founded, is shown by the way it surfaces covertly in *Workers* despite the overall gloom. In life, it seems fairly clear, Nell was already taking money from men when Gissing met her; why else his determination to 'save' her? But in the novel Carrie, who enters the book pregnant and deserted (providentially the baby dies) is presented as being merely flighty at first. Not till their relationship has deteriorated quite far does Arthur discover that she has new pieces of jewellery in her possession. Soon after this she leaves him for the first time and he catches a glimpse of someone looking like her in a hansom cab with a man near the Strand. But it is still not till some time later again—when Arthur has had a breakdown and been rescued himself, literally from the gutter, by a remarkably generous friend (another fairy godfather)—that we are shown Carrie actually being persuaded by an older woman into the final step towards real prostitution: the taking of money from men. In unromantic reality, would this step really have been so long-delayed? On the other hand the description of the room Carrie rents in her procuress-friend's house, has an awful ring of truth. It has a cracked, gilt-framed mirror, a spittoon and a man's old hat hanging behind the door. You feel that Gissing had been in that room.

In the book as in life, an abortive reunion takes place (in life there were a number of these), and here the sense of the conflict between the reality and the image in Arthur's heart is made explicit:

Arthur, though he could not persuade himself into a belief of reviving passion, yet experienced so intensely the emotion of pity, felt so keenly the full pathos of her broken words, was so profoundly touched by the sense of her helplessness, that the thought of once more being a providence to the poor, suffering outcast melted his heart, and for the moment made him forget to compare her with Helen.

In the book, Helen is the female antithesis to Carrie, a pure, not to say smug and cold heroine, admired by Arthur—and presumably by Gissing himself—but distinctly unattractive to most twentieth-century readers. One hardly need underline the significance of the fact that, in life, Helen in fact was Nell's full name. By such linguistic codes does the author attempt to redress the balance of reality.

Alas for the restored image of the 'poor, suffering outcast'. Once again it does not survive the pressures of daily living. Arthur notes candidly: 'Comfort had a demoralizing influence upon Carrie. In the midst of physical suffering she seemed to become somewhat finer-natured, manifesting sensibilities worthy of respect . . . But as the recollection of pain began to lose its edge, she became perceptibly coarser . . .' The operative word here is 'seemed'. Whether or not Gissing realized it himself, Arthur's view strikes the reader as a subjective impression. Carrie was really always Carrie, stupid, delinquent and addicted to drink: it was just that, when possessed by emotion and by the heady thought of being 'a providence to the poor suffering outcast' Arthur did not see her clearly.

Rather interestingly, one of the most idealistic features of Gissing-Golding's dream, the plan to teach his outcast to read good books, though its failure in Carrie's case is demonstrated, is allowed to survive in the parts of the book which deal with Helen Norman. Helen runs a class in the East End teaching working girls to read and write, of which bounty they are all most gratifyingly appreciative: 'All their fingers bore the impression of the eternal needle, and not a few, on sitting down, had, by force of habit, taken a thimble from their pockets and slipped it on before beginning to spell.' In other words they were all seamstresses and thus Carrie-Nells, nice, decent, docile ones who gave no trouble. The detail of their taking out thimbles automatically is acutely observed, no doubt from Nell herself. The general impression of the passage, however, is one of wish-fulfilling fantasy.

Nor did the fantasy die, even after *Workers* was published. Gissing wrote to his brother 'in that book I have, so to speak, *written off* a whole period of my existence. My next book will be very different.[9] (As *Workers* sold only twenty-nine copies and Gissing himself paid for its publication, all he could reasonably do was plan to make the next one different.) In fact the next completed book, tantalizingly entitled 'Mrs Grundy's Enemies', was never published. One publisher (Bentley) got as far as setting it up in type, but then took fright at the audacity of the subject matter and never went any further with it. So a sizeable gap occurred between the finishing of *Workers* and the time when Gissing, having at last freed himself from Nell, was living on his own in Chelsea (1883) and writing *The Unclassed*, a period of relative tranquillity. He wrote[10] to Algernon at this time: 'I return to the correspondence of past days. One smiles in a grievous way over such things. However, the best part of life is sentiment, and, for my own part, the pain of many sentiments is redeemed by their emotional values.' Evidently the idea of the beauty of a subjective emotion *per se* still haunted him. Haunting him also was the theme of saving a fallen woman, just as bright and complete in his mind as if the experience with Nell had never been. If *Workers* is a fairly realistic—indeed at moments painfully realistic—treatment of the theme, *The Unclassed* is a mere compensatory fantasy. Clearly Gissing had not 'written off' the whole thing at all.

In *The Unclassed* the personality of the prostitute heroine, Ida Starr, is so romanticized that it is hard for a modern reader to see why the book was widely considered shocking. Even Algernon apparently considered it 'offensive', with 'exposition of obscene details', whereas to the reader of today Ida's life is so lacking in realistic detail, obscene or otherwise, as to be more than a little unconvincing. There are good things in it; in particular the conversations between Waymark, the hero, and Ida strike one as timeless and natural, like the realistic chat of brothers and sisters in Gissing's books—which is, in point of fact, exactly what they are, since, although Waymark has set Ida up in a flat, he makes a point of not sleeping with her himself. This central unreality mars the tale for the modern reader but was presumably necessary at the time if the book was to be bought by the circulating libraries, which then had a stranglehold on the British novel-market. One wonders also if Gissing had read De Quincy's romantic little tale of a platonic relationship with a prostitute, *Ann of Oxford Street*.

Gissing insisted to Algernon that Waymark was not himself, but there is clearly much of him in his hero: Waymark even publishes a book. You could say that Waymark is Gissing without most of Gissing's problems (if that were not a contradiction in terms!) while Julian Casti, the other important male figure, is Gissing with the problems but minus the talent and the resilience. It has been said that Casti was modelled on Bertz, Gissing's lifelong German friend, but only certain specific features, such as their meeting one another through an advertisement, seem to fit; in other respects Casti (to whom Waymark is prone to give good advice) is one of those partial alter egos, the depressed unfortunates, like Hood, who carry Gissing's burdens but collapse totally under their weight. Casti falls secretly in love with Ida, thus adding the final touch in the imaginative transformation prostitute-into-untouchable goddess.

Just as the less fortunate aspects of Gissing himself are siphoned off into Casti (who, incidentally, dies in the end) so the bad aspects of womankind are siphoned off into the person of Harriet Smales, who is portrayed as a 'respectable' girl with an inherently louche and sluttish personality—she also has a scrofulous condition and becomes subject to fits and to alcoholism. The mechanics of how Casti, a sensitive, intellectual, chemist's assistant, comes to marry Harriet, are entertaining but are intrinsically rather hard to believe: by taking him up to her bedroom to show him something, she manœuvres him into what she assures him is a compromising position for her. He thus becomes engaged to her out of a combination of pity, guilt and good manners. While certainly such behaviour was not untypical of Gissing himself (his sister wrote '. . . he always had an enormous sense of duty, and no personal discomfort was considered if this could be discharged') to see these traits exemplified to the exclusion of all others does make Casti seem an unusually feeble young man. Perhaps, in a real life story, the truth would have been that Casti married Harriet Smales against his better judgement but mainly out of unsatisfied desire, and Gissing knew this but felt that he couldn't portray the fact.

It occurs to one that a number of Gissing's complaints about loneliness, which are to be found in his personal writings throughout his life, are at least partly a means to referring in code to specifically sexual needs and unfulfilled desires which, at the period, could not be made explicit. The very use of such a code of expression would have helped to obscure for Gissing the distinction which most men make quite readily—that between sexual needs and other affective needs. Certainly many of the problems of Gissing's life seem to have stemmed from a lack of the peculiarly masculine ability readily to separate sexual emotions from the idea of love. I do not mean to imply that Gissing was in any way effeminate; clearly he wasn't, but he does seem to have had in his emotional make-up a rather larger-than-average share of what a Jungian would call 'the feminine principle'—the intuitive, responsive, affection-demanding range of traits. He himself claimed in the persona of a character in a story *A Lodger in Maze Pond* that he was 'not a sensual man', which today seems an odd belief for a man whose life was characterized by rash alliances, but presumably what this meant, in the veiled terms of the period, was that he did not enjoy consorting with prostitutes or any other sexual outlet which takes place without emotional involvement: these things did not fulfil his personal needs. While it was probably true, as H. G. Wells wrote to Edmund Gosse, in a confidential letter after Gissing's death, that Gissing 'was fearfully oppressed by the sex necessity' (between his two marriages) and was 'too poor for prostitutes', the latter fact is irrelevant. Unlike, no doubt, Wells himself, whose sexual freedom was somewhat notorious, Gissing didn't *want* a prostitute, at least not as such.

This might suggest that he was a man who fell violently in love, but, rather, it would probably be truer to say that throughout his life Gissing succumbed to the *idea* of love (and marriage) rather than the reality. Morley Roberts actually considered this passionate man to be semi-incapable of love in an adult sense. 'To my mind,' he wrote, 'all his books betray an extreme lack of this. His characters in all their love affairs are essentially too reasonable. A man wishes to marry a girl, not because he desires her simply and overwhelmingly, but because she is a fitting person, or the kind of woman about whom he has been able to build up certain ideas in his mind'—such as, one might add, romantic ideas which have little bearing on true facts. Roberts' view may seem incompatible with the above remarks on Gissing's inability to enjoy sex for its own sake, but really it is saying the same thing the other way round: if Gissing was unable, as I believe, to differentiate between sex and love, then he would not only mistake sexual passion for love but would also treat what he took to be love as if it had the same transitory and wilful qualities as sex.[11] In a late, slight novel, *Eve's Ransom* (1895), he comments significantly on his central character: '. . . he never regarded his love as of very high or pure quality; it was something that possessed him and constrained him—by no means a source of elevating emotion.' The only major novel of his which is almost devoid of the spark of reality is *The Crown of Life* (1899), his sole attempt to portray a deep, lasting and adult version of passionate love. (This is discussed in Chapter 4.) In his diary, even when he was a man in his thirties, he was capable of declaring himself 'in love' and then relinquishing the idea again within a week or two. The characters in his books often behave in the same manner, as if falling in love—like having a sexual experience—was at least partly a matter of decision, and one could think oneself in and out of it virtually at will. Jasper Milvain's behaviour in *New Grub Street* is a good example of this. He really does 'love' Marian Yule, but switches the emotion off when he has decided that it is not a good idea to marry her after all. True, Jasper is supposed to be a somewhat cold-blooded character—but the same behaviour is found in Everard Barfoot in *The Odd Women*, Walter Egremont in *Thyrza*, and even Mallard in *The Emancipated*, whose feeling first for Cecily Doran and then for Miriam Baske is the thread on which this diffuse book is strung. In practice, Gissing's confusion between sex and love devalues love; his heroes (except for Barfoot on one occasion) seem, typically, unable to admit that sexual passion may be no more than that, but feel impelled to find true love whenever their senses are aroused. ('Though her beauty was of a somewhat sensual type, and her features betrayed no special intelligence or good humour, Arthur felt strangely attracted to her for all that.' 'Though'—or 'because'? Arthur seems to have mistaken the nature of his own feeling.)

An extremely graphic and indeed conscious illustration of the confusion of emotions in his mind is provided by the short story *A Lodger in Maze Pond*, written in the 1890s. In a letter, Gissing directed Clara Collet's attention to the story, adding ruefully that the lodger was himself. He meant by this to explain to Miss Collet how he came to marry Edith Underwood in 1891, but it casts an equally revealing light upon his attitude to his first wife. This story is written in the first person:

I am a fool about women. I don't know what it is—certainly not a sensual or passionate nature; mine is nothing of the sort.

It's sheer sentimentality, I suppose. I can't be friendly with a woman without drifting into mawkish tenderness—there's the simple truth . . . There's that need in me—the incessant hunger for a woman's sympathy and affection.

The Lodger has had a previous abortive marriage with a wife who was subject to—yes—fits. Now, living alone in a lodging house, he receives attention from the landlady's daughter—roughly the social class from which Edith came. He unexpectedly inherits eighty thousand pounds and on the spur of the moment proposes marriage:

And she looked at me—and then—why, mere brute instinct did the rest—no, not mere instinct, for it was complicated with that idiot desire to see how the girl would look, hear what she would say, when she knew that I had given her eighty thousand pounds . . . And the frantic proceeding made me happy. For an hour I behaved as if I loved the girl with all my soul. And afterwards I was still happy. I walked up and down my bedroom, making plans for the future—for her education and so on. I saw all sorts of admirable womanly qualities in her. I *was* in love with her . . .

Evidently it was in essence the Nell situation all over again. In their persons Nell and Edith should not be confused, since one was working class and the other lower middle class, a distinction quite clear to Gissing though often obscured by his critics. Edith's superficial air of gentility puts her in another category and in another chapter (Chapter 4). But as regards Gissing's own emotions the situation was almost identical: here once again was a girl who could be *given money* and *educated*. The public-spirited shadow of Thomas Waller Gissing was very much to the fore.

Even after *The Unclassed* the dream of an idealized Nell figure had not exhausted its literary possibilities for Gissing. In 1886 he returned to it with *Thyrza*, the most romantic and gentle of his low-life novels and the book which, for most of his life, remained his favourite. Exceptionally, in *Thyrza*, the streets and courts and lodging houses of working-class London are shown in a homely, even a cheerful light. Whereas, in *Workers*, people shopping in a street market are shown as harridans and drunkards, emerging from doorways reeking of poverty, in *Thyrza* we are allowed to watch normal and reasonably contented housewives picking out the 'biggest and hardest cabbage, the most appetizing rasher'. Afterwards, when they turn into the pubs, these are full not of Hogarthian monsters, but of 'companies of girls, neatly dressed and as far from depravity as possible [who] called for their glasses of small beer.' By the same token, though Thyrza and her sister are orphaned, unprotected young girls, they manage to support themselves even with some degree of modest comfort. The necessity of their earning a living is mentioned a number of times but it never seems to oppress them; they are never threatened by starvation (as their real life counterparts typically were) and have leisure and energy to worry about love, respectability, religion and similar luxuries. It is as if Gissing, when he wrote this book was looking back on scenes which memory had, for him, softened and idealized just a little. *Thyrza* is not precisely unrealistic—or not in its general social picture: indeed the impression it conveys of a cohesive and humane working-class neighbourhood might well be considered more realistic, because more balanced, than the extremely jaundiced view of working-class existence in Gissing's earlier books. But certainly it is true that some subjects, notably poverty, which had loomed so large for Gissing earlier and were to loom again in *The Nether World*, were, when he wrote *Thyrza*, no longer occupying the forefront of his imagination.

As a novel in its own right, *Thyrza* is a shapely and at times moving work, undistorted by obsessionalism and only occasionally lapsing into sentimentality. In its perception of the flourishing and distinctive nature of what we now call 'working-class culture' and what in Gissing's day was simply considered a lack of culture, it strikingly prefigures a much more famous book: Somerset Maugham's *Liza of Lambeth* (1897). Even the location is the same. But I do not think that for the modern reader, unless he is interested in Gissing's work overall, it is a particularly meaningful book; and one may guess that Gissing himself was attached to it because it was his final attempt to work out the Nell theme: the most artistically satisfying and the farthest removed from reality.

So much do we see of Lydia and Thyrza Trent talking, drinking cups of tea and doing each other's hair, and so little do we see of them going to work or worrying about next rent

day, that it is possible to overlook the fact that they are both—
once again—seamstresses. When Walter Egremont, the central
character, reflects that Thyrza is 'a simple girl who lived by
her needle, who spoke faultily. And he loved her with the love
that comes to a man but once'—we are back again on extremely
familiar and central Gissing ground. Till that point in the book,
the personal theme has been decently disguised. Egremont,
whose nickname is 'the Idealist', is only in general outlines a
Gissing-figure. The son of a self-made man (now dead) he
enjoys a private income, has travelled, and published poetry.
He comes to Lambeth with the idea of benefiting the working-
people of his father's old neighbourhood by instituting a series
of evening lectures. He plans a free library. Gissing remarks:
'With women, he was a favourite, and their society was his
greatest pleasure; yet, in spite of his fervid temperament—in
appearance fervid, at all events—he never seemed to fall in
love.' In short, as with Waymark, in *The Unclassed*, Egremont
is rather like Gissing himself but with money and without
Gissing's fatal sexual susceptibilities. This being so, *Thyrza*,
whose early chapters are concerned with the themes of charity,
education and self-education (Gilbert Grail), turns out in its
second half to be a rewriting of life, a vision of how the Nell-
experience in Gissing's own life might have turned out had
everyone concerned been a rather different person—including,
of course, the girl herself.

Like Nell-Carrie, Thyrza is very young (and provided with
a protector in the shape of her kindly, stable elder sister Lydia).
Like Nell-Carrie she even wears her yellow hair in a long,
childish plait down her back. Unlike Nell-Carrie, however, she
has the refined instincts of a higher class than her own and—
rather improbably—Lydia is doing all she can to foster ladylike ways, to stop her little sister singing in a public house, to
shield her from rough housework, etcetera. Quite early in the
book, too, Thyrza starts having headaches, a sure sign of gentility with Gissing's heroines. Totty Nancarrow, a more original
and far more genuinely emancipated character in the same book,
would never have a headache in her life. At the same time
Thyrza's lack of education is emphasized. When the self-taught
working man Gilbert Grail becomes interested in her, inevitably
—this being a Gissing novel—his first action is to offer to lend

her books from his own patiently acquired library. She accepts, but he has to choose for her. Their respective roles are those which emotionally, so appealed to Gissing—the roles of little sister and big brother, child and teacher: 'The reverence which she had always felt for him grew warmer under his gaze, till it was almost the affection of a child for a father.' What about sex and desire, one might well ask?—indeed Thyrza herself seems aware that some vital component is missing in their relationship and, though accepting his offer of marriage, wonders if she will be the right wife for him since she 'knows so little'. Ironically, she *would* be a good wife for a Gilbert Grail, but Gissing's treatment of their relationship from the start leaves one in little doubt but that this too-careful, too-repressed idyll is not going to flourish. It is not thus that the Nell-problem will be worked out.

Living in idleness in the days immediately before her marriage to Gilbert is due to take place, Thyrza finds ladylike time on her hands and is drawn to the unladylike indiscretion of calling several times at the new free library where Walter Egremont is working alone, arranging the volumes. (Gilbert Grail is to be the librarian—the chance of a lifetime for him.) Gissing works very hard at the plot to make Thyrza's visits seem both blamelessly innocent and socially compromising, and almost succeeds. It is a nice touch of irony that books, which brought Thyrza together with Grail, also bring her together with Egremont but that time to her undoing. Nothing 'happens' between them— except that he falls secretly in love with her, she falls secretly in love with him, and neighbours begin to gossip. With one of those touches of realism with which Gissing highlights female portraits otherwise too romantically pure in concept, the author shows us Thyrza's own humble belief in her essential difference from 'ladies':

'Did ladies think and feel in that way? or only foolish little work-girls, who all their lives had dreamed dreams of a world that was not theirs? Did ladies ever press down a heart beating almost to anguish and say, half-aloud, to themselves: "I love you!"

'No; a stately life theirs, no weakness, no sense of a measureless need, self-respect ever, and ever respect from all about them——'

As for Egremont, his own inner speculations, to those who have already read *Workers in the Dawn*, have a ring of absolute familiarity, save that the situation is more clearly seen by the subject:

Very possibly he saw her in the light of illusion; should his opportunities grant him a complete knowledge of her, he might not improbably discover that after all she was but a pretty girl of the people, attractive in a great measure owing to her very deficiencies.

We have been here before—or have we? Perhaps not, after all. For this is the irony of *Thyrza*, a poignancy only perceptible if one knows of the author's life and other work: Thyrza is not, it is ultimately demonstrated, a commonplace working girl at all. The book is reality not just improved upon but turned inside out. Whereas, in life, Gissing ascribed numinous qualities to a plebeian and unreliable girl, in *Thyrza* Egremont is tempted to do just that but, having more sense than his creator and less susceptibility, resists the temptation; only to find out in the end that he was mistaken in his caution. Moreover, although superficially Egremont with his library has got himself into just the sort of philanthropy-confused-by-sex muddle that Gissing got himself into with Nell, appearances are deceptive. Egremont has not 'ruined' Thyrza (in the phrase of the period) and as soon as he realizes he is compromising her he escapes alone with all possible speed. Unfortunately it is too late; tongues are wagging, and everyone in Lambeth—including Gilbert Grail and Thyrza's sister Lydia—take the same view: 'A gentleman did not fall in love with a work-girl, not in the honest sense.' An identical view is taken by Egremont's middle-class acquaintances, to whom the news of his defection is spread by a zealous local MP, the 'professional philanthropist' Dalmaine. As so often, in Gissing's books, a person is accused of doing something he has not in fact done, though appearances are against him . . . (Another, still deeper layer of personal preoccupation becomes apparent.)

Extremely interesting, in the light of Gissing's own love-life, is the interview between Egremont and Grail who, in a passion of jealousy and justifiable suspicion, tracks him to his rooms near the British Museum. Egremont hotly denies that anything 'improper' has taken place between him and Thyrza, but at the same time cannot avoid feeling guilty because he knows in his heart that he has succumbed to another, subtly different temptation—he has fallen in love with Thyrza. (Or what both he and Gissing take to be love anyway.) Eventually he admits this by implication to Grail, who accepts the confession but replies:

'Then you acted wrongly! . . . You were wrong in allowing her to stay and help you in the library. You were wrong in speaking to her as you did, in asking her to address you as an equal, and to let you be her friend. You must have known then what your real meaning was. It is only half a truth that you said and did nothing to disturb her mind. You were not honest with yourself, and you had no just regard for me. You *did* yield to temptation——'

Gissing the writer had developed a long way in sophistication from the adolescent who believed that love redeemed everything, and that social differences could all be overcome with goodwill, lack of prejudice and reading books together. The subsequent history of Egremont and Thyrza—or rather, non-history, since they never actually meet again—takes the form of deliberation on the theme of social inequality and what demands may reasonably be made of whom, problems of which Gissing had become gradually more aware. In other respects, the events that follow form an artistic pattern, made out of certain factual elements in the history of Gissing and Nell arranged in a new way. Thyrza flees from Gilbert Grail whom she doesn't love and from local notoriety, and takes refuge in a slum the other side of London, where she falls ill. From here she is rescued—not by Egremont himself, but by an older woman friend of his, Mrs Ormonde, who runs a children's convalescent home at Eastbourne, a kind but worldly mother-figure such as Gissing himself would no doubt have liked but never found. Thyrza recuperates in seaside lodgings—one is reminded of Gissing taking Nell to Southport, and indeed the sea figures as a general image of health and purity in this novel. Thyrza, like her predecessors in Gissing's eyes is educated, taught to read and sing—but not by her lover. Mrs Ormonde convinces Egremont how wrong, and indeed selfish and unfair he would be to marry Thyrza—the type of advice Gissing himself presumably felt he had lacked himself ten years before, when he had been hopelessly set on 'doing the right thing' by Nell. She extracts a promise from him that at least he will decide nothing for two years, and will meanwhile leave Thyrza in her care. Unknown to both of them, Thyrza overhears this conversation.

Egremont sets off to spend the two years in America (shades of Gissing again) and, unlike Gissing, manages to extract much good from the trip and returns in a robust and mature frame of mind. The vision of Thyrza has paled a little for him. He still has his same 'fixity of purpose. His plain duty was to go to Thyrza and ask her to marry him.' He has even been writing to Mrs Ormonde describing the sort of domestic idyll—rural of course—he envisages, with Thyrza singing for him in the evenings. But he no longer feels that he is in love with her, indeed—'It was with apprehension that he thought of marrying her. He knew what miseries had again and again resulted from marriages such as this, and he feared for her quite as much as for himself. For there was no more passion.' The Gissing of ten years earlier was co-existing, pen in hand, with the Gissing of the late '8os, attempting with literary hindsight to redress the lived past. Mrs Ormonde has no great difficulty in persuading him to abandon the whole idea—of course she does not realize that Thyrza herself has known of the two-year covenant and that all her apparent cheerfulness and self-reliance in her lonely lodgings has been based on hope.

With a certain inappropriateness in context, Egremont-Gissing muses

The one passion of his life had been for Thyrza. He called it dead; does not one mourn over such a death? He would not have recourse to the only dishonesty, and say that his love had been folly. Was it not rather the one golden memory he had? Was it not of infinite significance?

One loves a woman madly, and she gives proof of such unworthiness that love is killed. Why, even then the dead thing was inestimably precious; one would not forget it——

That thought has in fact little to do with Thyrza, who has given no such proof of 'unworthiness'. But as a final epitaph on Gissing's own first love it is poignant. *'Aimer est le grand point; qu'importe la maîtresse?'*

But—and this is the irony—Thyrza is not Nell, she has spent the last two years passionately educating herself in order to be worthy of Egremont, and then he turns from her. For a wish-fulfilment Might-have-been, this novel is curiously rueful. Thyrza is such a model of Patient Griselda fidelity that even Mrs Ormonde feels shamed by her example, but it is all to no avail. There can be no comfort, either to Gissing or to the reader, in her little speech to her 'benefactor':

'You haven't done me harm intentionally; I know that now. But if you had let him come to me, I don't think he would have been sorry—afterwards—when he knew I loved him. I don't think anyone will love him more. I was very different two years ago, and he thinks of me as I was then. Perhaps, if he had seen me now and spoken to me—I know I am still without education, and I am not a lady, but I could have worked very hard, so that he shouldn't be ashamed of me.'

After this Thyrza becomes ill again, then returns to Lambeth and, as if passion were now for her a thing of the past, a mere immature folly, renews her promise to marry Grail. To the modern reader, such a solution has an inconclusive death-in-life quality, that is both convincing and tragic—indeed Gissing was later to end *The Nether World* on just such a note. But the high romanticism of *Thyrza*, evidently seemed to Gissing to demand a more dramatic end and so Thyrza dies of a heart attack brought on by joy at hearing of her sister's engagement. In the long literary tradition of tragic virgins, it is death, not marriage, which claims her, her hair still plaited like a child's.

Egremont, appraised of her death, has a drawing made of her as she lies in the little room in Lambeth. Later he shows the picture to Annabel Newthorpe, the socially suitable and high-minded girl with whom he is now inevitably going to make his life. Her comment is: 'The crisis of your life was there. There was your one great opportunity, and you let it pass. She could not have lived; but that is no matter. You were tried, Mr Egremont, and found wanting.'

As a comment on an actual girl 'she could not have lived' is nonsense, but in terms of the book's artistic conception and Egremont's own experience, it makes sense. As Annabel also says to him 'You missed the great opportunity of your life when you abandoned Thyrza', and this is the book's central theme:

opportunity lost which almost *had* to be lost because, had it not been, it would have transformed itself into something else anyway. Only by relegating his original Nell-passion to such a level of Might-have-been could Gissing salvage any of the vision intact—the beauty of the love itself—from the erosions of time, fact and bitter experience. The doubtless admirable union that will now take place between Egremont and Annabel is presented as a second best, but not in any spirit of resentment or regret: rather, as if, in life, only the second best were ever possible— or as if Gissing were only ever able to perceive perfection in a situation not immediately present. As he says elsewhere in *Thyrza*, in a sentence which might stand for the spirit informing the whole book: 'Is this not the best of life, that involuntary flash of memory upon instants of the eager past? better than present joy, in which there is ever a core of disappointment; better, far better, than hope, which cannot warm without burning——'

By way of an epilogue to *Thyrza*, one might perhaps note that the year after it was published Nell herself died—in Lambeth. Gissing had not seen her for years and had been unaware that she was living in Lambeth when he wrote *Thyrza*. Her death bed was very different from that of the pure, fictional wraith of whom she was the original inspiration. She appears to have died of drink and syphilis, in a house where her 'profession' was no secret to any of the inmates. No artist was summoned to sketch a moving portrait of her. But Gissing, called to London to pay for the funeral, described the poverty-stricken room very fully in his diary (January 1888): the lack of food or coals, the single blanket on the bed, the scant clothing, the pawn tickets, the fruitless biblical pledge cards, the bundles of old letters from himself, the one or two pictures dating from happier days, and 'a little workbox, the only thing that contained traces of womanly occupation'. He added: 'She lay on the bed covered with a sheet. I looked long, long at her face, but could not recognize it. It is more than three years, I think, since I saw her, and she has changed horribly. Her teeth all remained, white and perfect as formerly.

In spite of those white teeth, the separation of the real girl from the romantic, Murger-inspired myth, seems at last complete. Gissing, in a phrase which probably contains more signifi-

D

cance than the practical one the writer intended, 'could not recognize' his loved object any more. The Nell-experience was at last over.

The experience might be over, but one permanent result remained, to affect his work with a minor but distinctive literary obsession: his books abound, to an unrealistic extent, in male characters, both major and minor, who have 'married beneath them', sometimes for good, sometimes for ill. We shall pick this theme up again in a later chapter, as Gissing himself picked it up in his life in his choice of a second wife, although the emphasis changes (as it did in life) from the abandoned girl-of-the-people to the merely commonplace and uneducated. But one very late example—Lady Ogram in *Our Friend the Charlatan* (1901)—provides an interesting example of the influence of the Nell–Carrie era reappearing twenty years afterwards—interesting, because Gissing's tone is by now ironic. The passage is about Gissing's own original romantic dream, but it is making fun of it.

Lady Ogram (she is old at the time the book takes place) was in youth an artist's model—a person in the Victorian moral hierarchy only slightly better than the out-and-out prostitute—then, as a matter of course, his mistress, and finally his wife and sharer in his family fortunes and titles.

By some freak of fate she had for parents a plumber and a washerwoman—'poor but very honest people', was Quentin's periphrase; their poverty of late considerably relieved by the thoughtful son-in-law, and their honesty perhaps fortified at the same time. Arabella (the beauty's baptismal name) unfortunately had two brothers; sisters, most happily, none. The brothers, however, were of a roaming disposition, and probably would tend to a colonial life. Quentin had counselled it, with persuasions which touched their sense of the fitting . . .

Sir Spencer affected to believe that Arabella, when his son came to know her, was leading the life of a harmless, necessary sempstress, and that only by long entreaty, and under every condition of decorum, had she been induced to sit for her bust to the enthusiastic sculptor. Very touching was the story of how, when the artist became adorer and offered marriage, dear Arabella would not hear of such a thing; how, when her heart began to soften, she one day burst into tears and implored Mr Ogram to prove his love, not by wildly impossible sacrifice, but simply by sending her to school, so that she might make herself less unworthy to think of him with pathetic devotion, and from a great distance, to the end of her days.

Alas for the less realistic aspects of *Thyrza*! Gissing himself is now rather hard on such fragile dreams—but perhaps he has more right to be than anyone else.

It is true that the theme of rescue by marriage lingered for some time in his work, though in more diffused forms. In *The Nether World* (1889) Clara Hewett becomes an actress (an escape from the prison of working-class life) and, as if in punishment for the sin of pride and ambition, has vitriol thrown in her face: she is rescued back into respectability by Sidney Kirkwood. In Gissing's next novel *The Emancipated* (1890) the rescue is *from* extreme, claustrophobic respectability into a freer life (Miriam Baske, when she is married by Mallard). And once, later, Gissing returned more directly to the story of a man trying, consciously flouting convention, to give chances to a woman that she would not otherwise have, in the one-volume *Eve's Ransom* (1895). As a novel, it is without conviction, credibility or, indeed, much interest: one of those works Gissing hammered out to put money in his purse at a time when he had temporarily exhausted his capacities and his ideas on far better ones (in this case *The Odd Women* and *In the Year of Jubilee*). But for the student of his writings it has some interest, for the 'mysterious' Eve (actually she is merely slight) is a late descendant of the Nell–Carrie–Thyrza woman, further transformed by time and the pressures of imaginative romanticism. She is 'refined', yet not a lady. Hilliard, one of those Gissing young men of strong passions, intense honourableness, too much leisure and a modest private income, falls half in love with her and sublimates his passion into a desire to bestow on her leisure and the experience of travel. She accepts his no-strings-attached offer—a circumstance which hardly endears her to the modern reader, but no doubt Gissing's contemporaries saw the matter rather differently. Hilliard reflects: 'The moment was worth living for. Whatever the future might keep in store for him of dreary, toilsome, colourless existence, the retrospect would always show him this patch of purple—a memory precious beyond all the possible results of privilege and narrow self-regard.'

Once again the concept of the golden moment, transcending all subsequent rational analysis. Gissing could hardly have been aware of such moments by theory alone: he must have known them. Perhaps, despite everything that had come to pass with Nell, despite her death-bed in Lambeth, when he came to look back on their early time together from the prison of his 'dreary, toilsome, colourless existence' with Edith, it appeared as a tiny, far-off patch of purple, that 'involuntary flash of memory', a heroic hour which after everything had kept its own value for him, and which he could not quite abandon.

The theme of helping and also improving those of a lower social class, is so prominent in Gissing's books that it needs to be considered apart from its effect on his love life, which is only one way in which it manifested itself. It is not that Gissing was introduced to 'low life' by his sexual proclivities, as a good many writers have been, but rather that it was his earnest desire to improve the conditions of a particular low life that determined his first marriage. From the first, he was not so much slumming as doing missionary work. He did not seek to lose his identity in the obscurity of a déclassé relationship, but rather to impose his upper-class identity, standards and aspirations on people like Nell. Waymark's claim to be one of the 'unclassed' is false; Waymark, like his creator, is transparently a decent English gentleman. The distinction is an important one. There is no *nostalgie de la boue* here but, rather, such a dislike of the *boue* that he felt impelled to raise other people out of it. In his lifetime he was occasionally compared with Zola, a categorization he himself rejected, but though there are elements of a reforming ethic in both writers the differences are very wide. In Zola's *L'Assommoir*, for instance, the writer is a passive recorder; the evils of the drink-shop are allowed to speak for themselves, there is no overt moralizing. Gissing, however, in *Workers*, in *The Unclassed*, in *Demos* and *Thyrza* and *The Nether World* (his five 'low life' books) not only moralized—thus keeping his own distance from his characters —but indulged in extensive fantasies of helping and reforming. Moreover, clearly recognizing that this was for him a central preoccupation, he several times, notably in *Demos* and in *The Nether World*, set to work to examine the whole ethic of charity.

The Theme of Help—Book or Baked Potato?

In Gissing's emotional make-up, if not always in his conscious intellect, the idea of offering practical help was very much bound up with that of education. His brightest day-dream was not to see every denizen of the Mile End Road with its hands suddenly full of its favourite food, but, rather, to see those same people washed and brushed and learning to appreciate Dickens—or at the very least to read Radical pamphlets. It may be argued that this is, in fact, a more enlightened form of philanthropy (it is certainly the theory on which the evolution of the welfare state since Gissing's day has been based!) but one result of it is that Gissing's moral judgements sometimes appear to have a naïvely snobbish, almost superficial basis. As P. J. Keating has ably expressed it:

For Gissing, the man who possessed a highly developed aesthetic sensibility, immaculate table manners and a standard English accent, was inevitably 'better' than other men. This belief was not merely a private quirk, but was frequently expressed in his novels, and rendered impossible that social impartiality theoretically essential to naturalness.[12]

The rough, grubby, illiterate, unambitious but essential *good* working person is almost unknown in Gissing's books except in extremely minor roles. For him, the good working-class man or woman is the one who has aspirations toward better things, and indeed has already made some progress towards them by attending Helen Norman's reading classes, learning to speak with a better accent, buying books off stalls in the Waterloo road or in some other way evincing an earnest desire to be transported out of his or her natal class into higher regions. His low-life novels abound in self-taught people, starting with Arthur Golding himself who, in the Oliver Twist tradition, has all the instincts and apparently much of the speech of a gentleman, though practically his entire childhood is passed in squalid surroundings. There is Julian Casti with his vaguely-indicated London–Italian background and his wistful interest in the classics; there is Gilbert Grail with his room full of literature to which he returns each night from his work in the candle factory; there is Ackroyd, in the same book, whose bent is rather for practical

studies, but who is already by this several cuts above his work-
mates; there is even poor Bunce whose intellectual aspirations
manifest themselves solely in the reading of atheistic pamphlets.
Then, in *The Nether World*, there is Sidney Kirkwood with
his sketching and, in the same book, Jane Snowden, whose ladylike bearing seems a somewhat unlikely result of several formative years spent in being a skivvy for the Peckovers. All these
are shown with great sympathy, though there is little suggestion that, despite all their efforts, any of them actually could
leap over the wall and become real ladies and gentlemen, indistinguishable from the born variety. (It leads one to wonder
whether Gissing believed in his heart that no one was likely to
accept *him* as a real gentleman, despite all that education:
this could be one of the many factors going to explain his
peculiar diffidence in picking a mate from the educated classes.[13])
Lucy Venning, in *Workers in the Dawn*, though she is taken
up by Helen Norman, with whom she goes to live in a determinedly modest home in Hackney, nevertheless still calls Helen
'Miss Norman' while Helen calls her 'Lucy', a sign of their respective positions which hardly impresses one as to the truly
progressive nature of Helen Norman's fervour, though I am sure
Gissing himself did not see it that way.

Meanwhile those persons in the novels who have been shown
the way to better themselves but still obstinately refuse to avail
themselves of the opportunity, are depicted in a consistently
poor light which may strike the reader as a little unfair: When
the young Godwin Peak in *Born in Exile* says: 'I hate low,
uneducated people! I hate them worse than the filthiest vermin!
—don't you?' . . . ; and his brother Oliver can only reply
admiringly, 'You're an aristocrat, Godwin', one tends to feel that
Oliver has a right to his own feelings and if he does not wish
to become a gentleman himself Godwin should not think any
the worse of him. But Oliver, though admitted to have no particular vices such as dishonesty, disagreeableness or even a dis-
inclination to work, is unflatteringly portrayed:

His brother Oliver, now seventeen, was developing into a
type of young man as objectionable as it is easily recognized.
The slow, compliant boy had grown more flesh and muscle
than once seemed likely, and his wits had begun to display that
kind of vivaciousness which is only compatible with a nature

moulded of common clay. He saw much company, and all of a low intellectual order; he had purchased a bicycle, and regarded it as a source of distinction, a means of displaying himself before shop-keepers' daughters; he believed himself a modest tenor and sang verses of sentimental imbecility; he took in several weekly papers of unpromising title, for the chief purpose of deciphering cryptograms, in which pursuit he had singular success. Add to these characteristics a penchant for cheap jewelry, and Oliver Peak stands confessed.

In other words, Gissing did not even wish to examine Oliver as an individual; he was repelled by the type. In this novel, ideas held only to some extent by Gissing himself seem to have become isolated and exaggerated in an unpleasant manner; one is glad to remember H. G. Wells' testimony on the kindlier Gissing he knew as a friend: '. . . That readiness to call common people "base", "sordid", "mean", "the vulgar sort", and so forth was less evident in the man's nature than in his writings.'[14]

Only in a few stories, or in the short, humorous novel, *The Town Traveller*, is the shop-keeping, commercial-travelling type presented sympathetically. (Will Warburton, in the novel of that title, belongs in another category, since it is only by accident that he takes to shop-keeping.) More often, even when a shop-keeping type does evince signs of the kind of emotional yearnings to be found in Gissing's better-bred characters, this is treated unsympathetically—witness poor Mr Bullivant in *The Odd Women*, whose passion for the ladylike Monica is shown in a contemptuous light. It is as if Gissing saw such people as caricatures of gentlemen, and resented them accordingly. In *Demos* the plebeian young man, complete with cheaply smart clothes, is personified by Harry—or, rather, 'Arry, since it is spelt like that throughout the book: the very name suggesting the vulgar music-hall character. 'Arry is presented as being of lazy and self-indulgent habits from the start, and these, when an unexpected fortune transforms the family's status, degenerate into a vicious idleness and finally dishonesty. He serves a term in prison for stealing from his employer, and comes out none the better for this experience. (Gissing's view on the matter obviously came from the heart, though the reference, like all the references to prison in his books, is brief to the point of obscurity.) The implication seems to be that because 'Arry did not make proper use of the chances which money brought, it did positive harm. Indeed a dominant theme in this novel is the inability of the Mutimer family, even Richard Mutimer himself who is, superficially, so socially mobile, to adapt themselves worthily to the privileges of a leisured existence. Obstinately refusing to become either educated or cultured, they therefore collapse under the pressure of their newfound wealth into alarming travesties of their former selves. 'Serve them right!' Gissing seems to be thinking, but the moral, though interesting and instructive, seems to go a little beyond a strict regard for realism. One wonders if old Mrs Mutimer, so perfectly well-adapted to the humble sphere in which she had spent her life, would really have disintegrated into such a state of mumbling depression just because she was required to live in a somewhat more ladylike manner. Does it really matter if she still collects the teaspoons in the slop basin and pours hot water on them at table? Her family don't seem to mind. One wonders also if Alice, who, ironically, has always been called 'Princess' in the family because of her little airs of false refinement, would really have become quite so feeble and indolent under the influence of novel-reading and leisure, though her marriage to a man who turns out to be only an imitation-gentleman himself and in fact a crook, is a neat commentary on the falseness of her view of what matters in life. As for Richard Mutimer himself, the fundamental flaw in his attitude to education is indicated by Gissing from the start in the description of his bookshelf, which contains only political tracts, no literature, nothing that might be read for its own sake—'. . . the chosen directors of his pre-judice taught him to regard every fact, every discovery, as *for* or *against* something'. Mutimer is a subtle character; Gissing obviously put a lot of thought into him, and manages to con-vince one of his original good intentions in setting up his factory-commune, while at the same time slipping in many indications of a fundamental lack of integrity or sensitivity—in particular his treatment of Emma Vine, the humble fiancée he abandons on the way up. The Vine sisters themselves exemplify Gissing's tendency to equate 'ladylike' qualities with actual moral superiority, for Emma, who has aspirations towards plain living and high thinking, is an angel of kindness, while her sister, Mrs Clay, is of baser clay in every sense, being not only more obviously working class but also much less amiable. Incidentally, the bedtime stories Emma tells her little nephew and niece have, unlike Mutimer's reading matter, no polemic message: '. . . it never occurred to Emma to teach her hearers to hate little Blanche just because hers was the easier lot.'

The rogue-theme of basically harmless people being spoiled, in a deep-seated way, by too much prosperity, crops up elsewhere: it appears in the minor but key character of Mr Bowers the shop-keeper in *Thyrza*. (I call it a 'rogue' theme since it would seem to be directly at variance with Gissing's equal conviction, expressed with vehemence in many other places, that poverty and want are the great corroders of human nature.) Of Bowers, Gissing writes:

The man was a fair instance of the way in which prosperity affects the average proletarian; all his better qualities—honesty, perseverance, sobriety—took on an ignoble colour from the essential vulgarity of his nature, which would never have so offensively declared itself if ill-fortune had kept him anxious about his daily bread.

Gissing seems to be on highly questionable moral ground here; these are the same slippery slopes on which a Carrie, ailing or in trouble, automatically appeared to him more attractive— 'somewhat finer-natured'—than a Carrie who was prospering. For all his interesting varied treatment of the theme of help and self-help, and his terrier attempts to pin down the problems implicit in charity, this was one personal aspect of the dilemma with which he did not get to grips.

The stages through which Gissing himself passed in his attitude to charity, philanthropy, the education of the working classes, democracy, and associated questions of the period, manifest themselves both in his letters and his novels. A number of his novels may be read as a commentary on the progress of his own thoughts in these matters, a personal dialogue with himself. Because his deep-seated attitudes were probably, like his father's, always equivocal and complex, and because he changed his mind as time went on, discarding early enthusiasms, giving rein to previously suppressed feelings, it is impossible to pigeon-hole him accurately as being one thing or anything: 'radical sympathizer', 'natural philanthropist', 'defender of the People', 'natural aristocrat', 'misanthropic conservative', 'sentimental bourgeois', 'depressive realist'—all these terms might fairly be applied to Gissing at different moments in his life and in different moods, but none of them will even begin to do as an overall label. As Ellen Gissing was already complaining by 1927, commentators will seize on just one (true) aspect of this strange man's personality and, by making it out to be the dominant one, create a completely unrecognizable picture. But it is probably fair to say that all writers whose work presents a degree of growth and change over the years tend to suffer from being arbitrarily labelled on the strength of one or more books— works which, from the writer's point of view, are ephemeral projections which may become rapidly obsolete as indications of his beliefs and perceptions. To the reader, particularly a reader with no creative bent of his own, a novel is a solid, permanent object, an expression of a fixed view embodying characters which seem more or less 'real'. Novelists are sometimes irritated, if flattered, at the way their characters are solemnly discussed and criticized as if they were 'real people', for the novelist knows quite well that they are fundamental subjective assessments, vehicles for ideas which happen to interest or convince him at the time of writing. For example, the reason that Mr Tollady, the elderly, book-loving philanthropist in *Workers in the Dawn*, appears a basically different sort of person from old Mr Snowden, the would-be benefactor of the poor in *The Nether World*, in spite of obvious points of comparison, is that in the years between writing his first working-class novel and his last one, Gissing had been debating with himself principles of philanthropy which he did not question in the early days, and had considerably modified his views. Mr Snowden is not essentially 'different' from Mr Tollady; it is the way in which he is seen which is different, and thus the role he is made to play in the story is different also. The real change lies in the writer, not in the subject-matter.

In *Workers*, the book about which Gissing notoriously declared that he wished to be considered as 'a mouthpiece of the advanced Radical party', ideas of charity, democracy and reform are bungled together without much attempt at a coherent view. Moreover, as Gissing was very young at the time, his ideas seem to have evolved and altered in the course of writing it even as a young man's life does. We know that during that period he sought—partly from motives of honest, youthful indignation against the evils and inequalities of the period, but partly also, no doubt, from a desire to give an intellectual colouring to his emotional commitment to Nell—a formal connection with avowedly Radical movements. So, he lectured at a working man's club in Paddington; which also seems to have been a method of trying to get on to terms he himself could value with 'the Paddington people', plebeian relatives of his father's. Gissing's strong family feelings, as noted in the previous chapter, and his awareness of his and Nell's lamentable social isolation, would have made him try hard to find a common ground on which he and these essentially alien cousins could meet, but the attempt seems to have floundered in the end with ill-feeling on both sides: no doubt Gissing's other equally strong feelings of 'natural aristocracy', his squeamish dislike of working-class coarseness and his general tendency to become intolerant after a while of *any* alien mode of life, contributed to the break. This phase in his life is indicated in *Workers*—one should perhaps say 'made use of' in *Workers*—by Arthur Golding's involvement in various working men's self-help groups, each of which eventually founders. There is also the memorable vignette of the old blood-and-thunder revolutionary Pether, a pathetic wreck of a man who leaves one in no doubt as to Gissing's own view of such a histrionic approach to social problems, though at the same time his sympathy with Pether's sufferings from birth onwards is fully apparent: Pether is a man, not a monster, he is one suffering comprehensible human, not a representative of the demon *demos*. Twice in the book Gissing repeats the horrific information (which one feels must have come from an actual case) that Pether's mother was convicted of killing the man by whom she was pregnant, and that her execution was put off for a month till her child should be born, after which she was speedily hanged. Such a story seared Gissing's sensitive, fair-minded heart, but it was the individual case that appealed to him (as to all the philanthropists in his novels): as soon as he began to extrapolate from the particular to the general, he found himself on shifting grounds of abstraction and political theory which did not really suit his pragmatic, essentially emotive responses.[15] The very title *Workers in the Dawn* seems to derive from an early moment of conscious political 'awareness' rather than from any on-going sense of social currents. By the book's end, when the various working men's movements have come to nothing, and Golding himself has committed suicide in the Niagara Falls, the title seems quite inappropriate to what has been clearly an account, not of society, but of one, or at most two, individuals' spiritual odyssey. The puzzled lady[16] who enquired, on finishing it 'But where are the workers in the dawn?' was not far wrong after all. Saying a book is *intended* as an exposition of advanced Radicalism does not make it into any such thing, if the real sympathies and perceptions of the writer lie in other directions.

At the time the novel appeared Gissing was presumably still too involved in playing his politically-conscious role to perceive the contradictions and question-begging the book implies, but by the time *The Unclassed* made its appearance his ideas on the subject had sorted themselves out and he had got to know himself a little better. His own dead political enthusiasm is dismissed almost too summarily by Waymark, speaking of his 'days of violent radicalism':

'That zeal on behalf of the suffering masses was nothing more nor less than disguised zeal on behalf of my own starved passions . . . I identified myself with the poor and ignorant; I did not make their cause my own, but my own cause theirs. I raved for freedom because I was myself in the bondage of unsatisfiable longing.'

Waymark, like all writers' alter egos, is simpler than Gissing, and his remark should thus be taken as a simplification of the real issues at loggerheads in Gissing's psyche, but nevertheless there is undoubtedly *a* truth there. As if recognizing, like Waymark, that it was persons which appealed to him rather than People, from the time he left the Radical scene Gissing seems to have held aloof from giving support to any partisan cause, though he remained objectively interested in 'social questions' and sporadically sympathetic—for example, in 1888 he attended the demonstration in Regent's Park on behalf of the Match-girls' strike. Essentially he seems to have realized that, for a creative writer, any degree of avowedly partisan commitment however 'liberal' and 'freedom-loving' is compromising, and acts as a strait-jacket on the writer's real freedom of thought. He went to considerable pains at one point to explain this by letter to an intellectual acquaintance of his, a Miss Sichel, who had reviewed *The Nether World* as if it were a polemic view. It is, incidentally, a lesson which large numbers of literary bureaucrats and busy political-animals writing both in England and in other countries could well learn today: novelists perennially need warning against 'smelly little orthodoxies'[17] and such cosy in-groupism, the writer's trade being essentially a solitary one. But in Gissing's case this valuable knowledge was complicated by a less-admirable emotion—his conservative elitism as such. In a letter to Algernon[18] in 1895, he wrote:

Do you see the report of the row the Socialists have had with the police in the East End? Think of William Morris being hauled into the box for assaulting a policeman! . . . But, alas, what the devil is such a man doing in that gallery? It is painful to me beyond expression. Why cannot he write poetry in the shade? He will inevitably coarsen himself in the company of Ruffians.

Keep apart, keep apart, and preserve one's soul alive—that is the teaching for the day . . .

As a creative writer, Gissing was undoubtedly quite right. As a man, he was possibly quite wrong. Certainly his general tendency, remarked by Roberts and other people also, to shun the company of people he did not know well and in particular the company of anyone of inferior station, sensibility or education, made his personal life far more lonely and hard than it might have been. For he was the least self-sufficient of men, he suffered greatly from solitude and was not without his gregarious side. People who knew only his books and who eventually managed to meet him commonly remarked that he was a good deal more cheerful and outgoing than they had expected him to be. Without the creative dimension to his personality which kept him alone, imprisoned at a sedentary and introspective occupation, he might have done many things: one can imagine him as a vigorous and passionate—if quixotic—local councillor, as a campaigner, a charitable administrator, a personal assistant to a member of parliament, perhaps best of all as a teacher.

I have already said that both his family and Frederic Harrison considered him a 'born teacher'; he was also apparently a success,

young and disturbed as he was, during his brief period of class
teaching in a High School at Waltham, Massachusetts, USA.
Rather interestingly, he made little use of his teaching experience
in his novels; this may have been because, since his débâcle in
Manchester and with the ending of any real hope of an academic
career, the subject was a painful one to him and he would not
allow himself to see tutoring as anything but an uninteresting
stop-gap; it is this for Waymark at the beginning of *The Unclassed*. But in fact teaching is probably the nearest thing to
writing, minus the creative element: it demands the qualities
of conviction, self-expression and the sheer desire to communi-
cate which writing demands, but it avoids many of the dis-
advantages and isolation of the writer's life. The process of
communication is not, for the teacher, the act of faith it is for
the writer: the teacher has the person he wishes to make contact
with there before him. All writers need a sympathetic response,
a sense of making an impression: George Gissing, as more than
one person noted, needed this acutely. Ellen Gissing, speaking
of his 'wish to be of use', wrote: 'No pains were spared, no
patience was too great, so long as the glance of intelligence in
the eye of the listener showed that his words had been understood.' To such a man, the novelist's life must come particularly
hard. Novelists are often useful, in the long run, but it is difficult
for them to perceive of themselves as such.

Though virtually none of his characters are actual teachers by
profession, many of them are teachers in another sense in that
this is the form which their individually orientated philanthropy
takes. Wavering, and turning aside from the sort of organized
political theory of betterment for the masses which was not
really in his line, Gissing came fairly early in his career to base
his ethical viewpoint on what appealed to him personally—the
one-to-one relationship between teacher and taught, superior
and inferior, philanthropist and needy subject. This is what the
good characters in his books do; the relationship is for him a
fundamental one. Lizzie Clinkscales wants to teach Arthur Golding to read; Tollady teaches him to print and to appreciate
books. Helen Norman teaches East End girls; Arthur tries,
unsuccessfully, to teach Carrie. In *The Unclassed* Waymark
attempts with more success to teach Ida Starr, and Casti fails
to teach Harriet Smales. In *Demos* Richard Mutimer, despite

his considerable imperfections, sees himself as an instructor for the masses—indeed a 'mouthpiece of the advanced Radical party', the teacher turned demagogue, and incidentally a mentor to his family, to Emma Vine, the girl he deserts, and to Adela Waltham whom he marries. In *Thyrza*, Egremont perceives and attempts to avoid the pitfalls of demagogy (though his lectures on English Literature stray into being 'Thoughts for the Present') and would like to teach Thyrza, only that office is performed first by Gilbert Grail and then by Mrs Ormonde. In *The Nether World* old Mr Snowden sets out to teach Jane Snowden—though by this time Gissing has begun to question more fundamentally the whole nature of such relationships and what they involve in the way of imposed ideas and idealisms.

Long before this, in fact when he was engaged on *Workers*, Gissing already seems to have become alert to the dangers of the philanthropist-teacher-helper expecting any return for his labours as of right, or even any gratitude. He has Tollady tell Arthur his life story, which significantly includes an early episode of youthful thoughtlessness as a result of which his mother suffers (a pregnant aspect of the subject to which I shall be returning by and by)—and which culminates in Tollady's resolve to devote the rest of his life to helping others. Notably, Tollady discovers and helps a long-lost nephew, finally setting him up in a business in a coffee shop, after which the young man drops him. The coffee shop evokes shades of the common uncle who, in *Born in Exile*, shames *his* nephew by opening shop opposite the college, and one can't help seeing Tollady-Gissing's formal principle of not expecting thanks as the way in which Gissing attempted to cope, emotionally, with his own fundamental shrinking from real involvement in working-class life and his sensibility to rebuff. There is an interesting satirical treatment of this theme in the soup-kitchen in *The Nether World* (1889), but by the time he wrote that Gissing was in any case scrutinizing the whole ethic of giving rather harder than he was in the days of *Workers*, when he was still inclined to let his favourite fantasies have full play.

If *Workers* can be said to be 'about' one thing, it is about the desire to *do good* on the part of the main characters (and the singular failure of certain other characters, such as Helen Norman's uncle, the odious railway director Waghorn, and assorted

Church of England priests, to do the good they might). On Tollady's death Arthur vows himself to emulate the old man's philanthropy; his desire for a private income arises at least partly from a dream of offering practical help to others. The Carrie-situation is, as we have seen, an attempt to fulfil this dream. Helen Norman (who is perhaps most fairly considered as an incarnation of those parts of Gissing's own nature—for example, his interest in German philosophy—not represented in the person of Arthur Golding) is also chiefly preoccupied with well-doing, and has been since her earliest days: her childhood aspiration is to give poor people money—'a shilling at a time—father says it isn't wise to give too much'. The philanthropist's dilemma is already making itself inescapably apparent!

No wonder the occasions, in this and other novels, in which Gissing seems to realize his perennial daydream of giving most happily, are those minor ones where neither the person of the giver nor the help given are important enough in context to warrant a close examination of motive or result. In fairly quick succession we see Arthur Golding as a child receiving this sort of painless help from Edward Norman and his daughter, from a family met on his lonely track back to town, from Ned Quirk, then the Rumballs, then Mr Tollady. In between, he has also been the recipient of a vividly described handout from a kindly baked potato seller, one of those nugget-passages for which Gissing is remembered when much else in his work is forgotten. It is easier to give a hot potato to a hungry child than to debate the topic of social inequality: it is easier to *be* a hungry child receiving a potato than to be the object of the intense, theoretical desire to Do Good of a Helen Norman, a Michael Snowden— or a Gissing. Although, as I have said, I believe that Gissing fairly soon in his career became aware of the depths and complexities of the subject of doing good which preoccupies so many of his characters, the giving of the baked potato (so to speak) remained for him a favourite and comfortable daydream, a periodic resort from tougher problems and realities. Elsewhere I have called this the 'fairy godmother/father theme', and it accounts for some of his most vivid, sympathetic and enjoyable passages, if not always his most perceptive. Many writers betray a weakness for a particular type of make-believe involving elements of wish-fulfilling—most typically a self-comforting eroticism or romanticism: with Gissing, it was the self-comforting dream of making a wish come true, one that must have appealed both to the lonely, penniless youngster in him *and* to the would-be strong father. In imagination, he is both Tollady and Arthur, both Arthur and the anonymous kind old gentleman on a bench in Islington who (at a much later stage in the book) raises Arthur from the depths to which he has temporarily sunk by giving him money. He is Mrs Ormonde running a charity home for poor little girls in *Thyrza*, like a rather similar lady Miss Ledwood in *The Unclassed*, *and* he is the poor children themselves. He is Eve in *Eve's Ransom* being given a holiday in Paris, *and* he is her determined and rather improbable benefactor. He is Thyrza and Lydia giving old Mr Boddy an overcoat (the prime example of the dream in its simplest, most happily imagined form) *and* he is Mr Boddy himself with leaking boots wondering if he will have to pawn his violin. He is Sidney Kirkwood giving the Hewetts furniture, *and* he is the wondering and grateful Hewetts.

Clearly the dream was a deeply satisfying one to him, for it was one to which he returns incidentally in book after book, long after he had explored the deeper and less pleasing implications in the whole giving-situation in *Demos* and in *The Nether World*. He was undoubtedly, like many basically egoistic people, a person of many generous impulses himself. To do a good turn for a friend—to attempt to find a buyer for Bertz' dog when Bertz' finances ran out, to bail Morley Roberts out of Marylebone police station when the latter was involved in a fracas in the street—came naturally to him; he might protest obsessionally in his diary about the interruption to his own work, but it never occurred to him to refuse—any more than it occurred to him not to go on making efforts to save Nell from herself long after she had shown herself an unsuitable recipient for his solicitude. It seems a pity that the essentially self-centred life of a writer afforded him relatively few opportunities for exercising in reality these generous impulses.

One may, indeed, justifiably regard the persistent wish-fulfilment, fairy-godfather theme in his works as a compensation for a life which was for long periods rather sparse in human contacts and human demands. One may also regard scenes like the giving of the overcoat to Mr Boddy, of the seaside holiday to the London waif, as an escape from reality, in that they portray a situation in which the recipient of the charitable act is unfailingly grateful, and the act itself is a gratuitous one without moral strings attached. In life, Gissing had tried, and hoped, to offer to those near to him something rather more complex and ambitious than baked potatoes, overcoats or even seaside holidays. He had been brought up to regard himself as the future provider, material and spiritual, for a widowed mother and a family of younger brothers and sisters. As Ellen wrote: 'Was it not he who had hoped to be their guide and their helper in all matters? And now [after the Manchester episode] all such hopes were dashed to the ground.' It is understandable that after such a blow to his self-image, Gissing should have taken comfort from easy fantasies of benevolence. Such dreams must have been both a balm to his conscience, and also a form of expiation. As mentioned already, Tollady, that early prototype of selfless benevolence, consciously took to philanthropy after an incident in thoughtless youth when, travelling abroad, he allowed his widowed mother to die of neglect at home. The clumsy parallel between Gissing's own case and this fictional one does not need spelling out. Though Mrs Gissing senior, being a woman of character, did not succumb to the shock of her eldest son's disgrace, a shock it must indeed have been to that needy, hopeful, desperately respectable family. It is small wonder that no family letters or other evidence from the actual period of the Manchester affair have survived. Then again the whole long drawn-out affair of Nell baulked further his instincts of a generous helpmeet and educator. He wanted to offer her a new life, a new world of love, thought, sympathy, respectability, books—particularly books. But money was what she immediately needed, so money it had to be, with devastating results. Then, years later, when all his other offerings had been rejected, he was reduced once again to giving her nothing but money— fifteen shillings (later one pound) a week so long as she kept her distance. It was charity, of a sort, and given of his own choice, for certainly no court of law would have compelled him to go on supporting a wife of such known 'bad character'. But it was hardly even on the baked potato or overcoat level, and there can have been little pleasure, even masochistic, in this particular giving, only a dire sense of expiation for past errors and failure of judgement. As Morley Roberts said apropos of another event in Gissing's life (actually his ill-conceived second marriage): 'I have often thought it was his one great failure in rectitude which occurred at Moorhampton that made him infinitely more tenacious of doing nothing which might seem in any way dishonourable, however remotely.' Or, one might add, anything that could be construed as grasping or mean.

It is thus that Gissing's books betray an ambivalence in his attitude to charity, and charitable urges, of all dimensions. On the one hand the theme of helping and giving was the fantasy with which he comforted himself; on the other hand he knew it to be a dangerous temptation which could lead the giver into deeper waters than he bargained for and result in disastrously inappropriate long-term commitments. When he wrote *Workers* he was not yet fully aware of this, and Helen Norman is not forced to discover the essentially self-enhancing vanity of her schemes for East End girls. But later books—with the exception of a poorish novelette called *Sleeping Fires* (1895) which returns to the early fantasy—deal with schemes such as Helen Norman's more thoughtfully and critically, till outright condemnation is reached in *The Nether World*. And before he came to *The Nether World* he had already published *Demos*, the novel which, more than all the others, attempts to get to grips with the problems implicit in doing good to people.

Demos deals perceptively with the fact that philanthropy, when elevated and systemized into a political viewpoint,[19] can become a source of destructive pride and egotism, a monstrous conceit in which any means justify a theoretically 'moral' end. Richard Mutimer is not a bad fellow, given a certain social context. He is presented as the 'best' type of London artisan, good worker, 'good Radical' without extremism, a reader of polemic tracts, a natural leader with a certain cool acumen, a man without any true culture but an honest and even perceptive fellow within the limitations of his station in life. His views early in the book on the physical tiredness that crippled the working classes of the time, making even Sunday churchgoing a luxury in which they did not feel inclined to indulge, are worthy of Gissing himself. (Indeed it is not hard to guess that Gissing is so unforgiving to Mutimer later in the novel because he has ascribed to him certain discarded parts of his own opinions and experiences from the Paddington men's club days: novelists always tend to remorselessness with characters who represent, however partially, superannuated versions of themselves.) In short, Mutimer in Islington, working for his daily bread and toiling obscurely in the cause of Socialism is a useful and sufficiently moral person. But Mutimer transformed, by means of a legacy, into a hard-headed visionary enabled to make his vision of a Robert Owen community come true, is revealed as unequipped to resist the temptations that power brings in its train. In the consciously egalitarian community he sets out to develop at Wanley he rapidly assumes the role of the big boss, almost indistinguishable in style from a capitalist like Dagworthy in *A Life's Morning*. With legal right, but moral shabbiness, he loses no time in ejecting the Eldons from the Manor House, and speedily sets out to marry one of the few suitable middle-class girls the hamlet offers. By steady and predictable degrees, he becomes, not the workers' 'brother' but their traditional enemy, the hard master using his power over the future of wives and families to browbeat the restless working men.

This portrait of the making—and unmaking—of a man would be distinguished in any case, but what gives it an extra subtlety and power is the way in which Gissing parallels Mutimer's performance as a Radical employer with his performance as a private individual. When the novel opens, Mutimer is engaged, suitably, to Emma Vine—the inevitable seamstress—to whom he is a source of genuine support and help. But, once established in the big house in Wanley, he quickly perceives that his changed status demands someone rather different from Emma. '. . . To have a "lady" for his wife was now an essential in his plans for the future.' So, not sharing his creator's concern to 'do nothing which might seem in any way dishonourable', he deserts Emma, in a particularly cowardly way, leaving her without news, explanation or confession while he quickly becomes engaged to Adela Waltham. The limitation of his imagination, and the ruthless selfishness of this professional do-gooder, are thus made fully explicit for the first time: 'Her love for him he judged by his own feeling, making allowance, of course, for the weakness of women in affairs such as these. He might admit that she would "fret", but the thought of her fretting did not affect him as a reality.'

If he does not perceive other people's needs as being real like his own, still less does he appreciate the way in which one aspect of life affects another:

It never occurred to him . . . that in forfeiting his honour in this instance he began a process of undermining which would sooner or later threaten the stability of the purposes on which he most prided himself. A suggestion that domestic perfidy was in the end incompatible with public zeal would have seemed to him ridiculous . . .

One might add that, in this, he makes the same fundamental mistake as Godwin Peak in *Born in Exile*, who persuades himself that he can pretend to religious conviction as a means to a desirable end. Both men compromise their integrity, and both eventually, because of this, fail ignominiously—even, one is tempted to add, as Gissing failed in compromising his honesty in the attempt to help Nell . . . But this brings me to the theme of the Guilty Secret in Gissing's characters, and thus to another chapter. Essentially, the theme of *Demos* is the 'process of undermining', the moral deterioration which affects not only Mutimer himself but all the members of his family. And, in that this deterioration so speedily sets in as a concomitant to prosperity, it begs the question as to whether Mutimer's original beliefs, principles and ambitions were ever quite what they seemed in the days of supposedly honest men's clubbery: 'In a nature essentially egotistic, there is often no line to be drawn between genuine convictions and the irresponsible changes of resentment.'

In that sentence, I believe, Gissing touches the core of all his justifiable doubts about the true nature of the emotions involved in Doing Good, both his own and other people's. But he does not, in *Demos*, elaborate the point further. When circumstances force Mutimer to abandon Wanley, he organizes a working men's benefit club—a supposedly 'Radical' scheme with an essentially Capitalist basis. But I think that Gissing, with his fundamental lack of interest about the sources of money, sees Mutimer's ultimate defeat—and indeed death—at the hands of the howling, mindless mob, more as the result of stupidity, gullibility and spiritual pride than as an ironic retribution for

political bad faith. The theme of the egotism of the would-be
reformer wavers somewhat towards the end of *Demos*, losing
itself in Gissing's own obsession about the dangerous and repel-
lent nature of People in the mass. It surfaces again in *The
Nether World*, in a smaller-scale study of personal motive better
suited to Gissing's special skills.

The *Nether World* (1889) was Gissing's last 'low life novel'
and, in my view, the best. It is the only one where no distracting
pseudo-moral comparisons are made between one social level
and another—too many of Gissing's novels remind one of a
medieval diagram of the estates of man, with the ladies and
gentlemen inhabiting the top floor in such refined isolation that
one cannot imagine that they even belong to the same species
as the creatures toiling in the pit below despite self-conscious
intercourse between the two levels. While such an elementary
view may be said to be implicit in the very title *The Nether
World*, in practice, since the novel is exclusively concerned with
the inhabitants of this sub-world—in fact with the area round
Clerkenwell Green—the effect is homogeneous and realistic.
All are workers, more or less, all share, or have at any rate
known, the same problems. In this book there are no knights
in shining frock coats riding in to rescue distressed and uneducated maidens—no Osbert Waymarks or Walter Egremonts.
The would-be rescuers, Sidney Kirkwood and Michael Snowden, are basically of the same social level as those in need of
rescue, and when they fail there is no escape for them to the
upper airs.

Gissing wrote this book during the year after Nell's death
(1888), a period of relative peace and ease for him—relative,
since he was in fact lonely and restless when few demands were
made on him. But he had the leisure to plan this book and to
accumulate factual detail for it in a way he did not do for his
previous ones, and the difference shows. *The Nether World* is
carefully constructed, the dominant themes in it are allowed to
surface gradually and subtly without distorting the story too
far in any direction; there is little of the romanticism or glossing
over of the facts of daily living which mars some of the earlier
books. In setting out to write it Gissing can hardly have avoided
a mental comparison with Zola's *L'Assommoir* (published a decade
before) and, though his attitude to Zola tended to be cautious,

tinged with an element of professional jealousy for the foreigner's freedom of expression untrammelled by the dread library public, this time he followed Zola's well-known method in paying deliberate visits to his chosen setting, familiarizing himself with the details of Clerkenwell's small industries. For instance the artificial flower-making in the book is no Murgeresque 'property' occupation, but the genuine, carefully observed trade. Things seen years before were also able to surface in his memory now without the distortions of either sentiment or shuddering repulsion. One believes in almost everything in this book: the room where the Hewett family live, which has cane chairs with bulging seats, and a mantelpiece that slopes forward so that the ornaments have to be kept there by a piece of string; the pawn shop with its box of old-fashioned gritty sand for sprinkling on the ink of the tickets; the way one of the Hewett children takes nips of vinegar in preparation for an adult addiction to spirits; a sick child looking like 'a wax doll that has gone through a great deal of ill-usage', its browbeaten mother's awful diet consisting of coarse mince pies, lumps of pudding from a cook-shop, tea, and the odd two ounces of treacle which she eats obsessively.

The nearest thing to a Gissing-character in this book is Sidney Kirkwood, a self-taught working man something in the style of Gilbert Grail, who has had (yes) rather a wild youth abruptly terminated by the shock of his father's death: 'Saved from self-indulgence he naturally turned into the way of political enthusiasm . . . he reached the stage of confident and aspiring Radicalism, believing in the perfectability of man, in human brotherhood, in—anything you like that is the outcome of a noble heart sheltered by ignorance.' So much for idealism: clearly, in this book, we are to be on our guard: things are not necessarily what they seem. So, when old Michael Snowden appears in Clerkenwell like a cross between the Ancient Mariner and the beggar-king of folk-tale, and we hear that he rates compassion above all other virtues, we must beware—though, because the book is cleverly written, we do not. He rescues his grand-daughter Jane from the clutches of the Peckovers, and educates her to a new self-awareness as Tollady educated Arthur Golding: they live in Hanover Street (now Noel Road, Islington) where Gissing once lived with Nell, and are happy.

Gradually we learn more about the roots of Snowden's personal ethic. As a young man he married a wife of whom he expected much; he was always lecturing and admonishing her and trying to get her to save money, till—'At last she began to deceive me in all sorts of little things; she got into debt with shop people, she showed me false accounts, she pawned things without my knowing. Last of all she began to drink.' Shades of Nell.

You might think that this unfortunate early experience of the difficulty of helping others to help themselves would have turned Snowden away from the whole idea, but in fact it has been a main factor in the development of his 'life controlling purpose', as he goes on to explain it—a plan for helping the poor without losing touch with them. The prototype of the working man made-good, he has earned a fortune in Australia and has now come back to Clerkenwell to lay his plans for a trust fund, to be administered after his death by a chosen kindred spirit. It is inevitable that his choice will fall on Jane, so docile, so gentle, so eager to help others. 'Part of his zeal for the great project had come of a feeling that he might thus in some degree repair his former ill-doing; Jane would be a providence to many hapless women whose burden was as heavy as his own wife's had been.' But, ironically, just as he long ago expected too much from his wife, he is now expecting too much from his grand-daughter also. Jane is not, after all, of the stuff of a Helen Norman, a Lucy Venning or a Mrs Ormonde, nor—now that he has become more sophisticated—does Gissing expect that she should be. She is just a nice, ordinary, rather especially kind girl who loves Sidney Kirkwood and whose chief delight, in hearing about all the money she will inherit, is at the thought of being able to lay it at her future husband's feet. In this, she resembles Totty Nancarrow, the sturdier but similarly good-hearted working girl in *Thyrza*, who eventually offers herself as a wife to Bunce mainly because she can't resist the pleasure of giving him the small legacy she will receive: these women are an interesting extension of the simple *giving* motif which is commoner in Gissing's male characters.

The intellectual do-gooding female now appears as Miss Lant, the spinster with the soup kitchen who is supposed to teach Jane the business of charity. We never actually meet this lady, but Gissing described her and her ideals in essentially slighting terms:

. . . Unfortunately the early years of her life had been joyless, and in the energy which she brought to this self-denying enterprise there was just a touch of excess, common enough in those who have been defrauded of the natural satisfactions and find a resource in altruism. She was no pietist, but there is nowadays coming into existence a class of persons who substitute for the old religious acerbity a narrow and oppressive zeal for good works of purely human sanction . . .

One might fairly accurately say that Miss Lant *is* Helen Norman, ten years on and viewed with clearer eyes.

Sidney Kirkwood, fairy-godfather in his own right in a small way, perceives the mistake Snowden is making regarding Jane, but precisely because the man is old and his cherished idea has become everything to him, Sidney feels unable to say to him what he needs to hear: 'This money will be the cause of endless suffering to those you really love, and will never be of as much benefit to the unknown as if practical people dealt with it. Jane is a simple girl, of infinite goodness; what possesses you that you want to make her an impossible sort of social saint?' The money, because of the responsibilities it brings, is beginning to appear as a curse rather than a blessing—just as it was in *Demos* when it was used for a comparable high-minded but ill-conceived scheme. Sidney's worst fears are confirmed when Michael Snowden's mania pushes him to the decision that he does not, after all, want Jane to marry Sidney or anyone: he wants her to devote herself entirely to the 'life controlling purpose'. Thus he finally reaches 'that horrible intensity of fanaticism which is so like the look of cruelty, of greed, of any passion originating in the baser self'. Altruism itself stands exposed and condemned as the classic resort of the egotist.

Unlike *Thyrza*, *The Nether World* does not end with several of its characters marrying and living happily ever after, nor does the tragic princess die. Unlike Thyrza and Emma Vine, those other prototypes of unrequited love in women, Jane Snowden lives on, without Sidney or many hopes. Sidney himself marries the girl he had originally wanted to, but only after her own life (and her face) have been unredeemably blighted, and he takes

on the burden of supporting her family also. At the end, Jane
and Sidney face one another across Michael Snowden's grave:

In each life little for congratulation. He with the ambitions
of his life frustrated; neither an artist, nor a leader of men in
the battle for justice. She, no saviour of society by the force of a
superb example; no daughter of the people, holding wealth in
trust for the people's needs. Yet to both was their work given.
Unmarked, unencouraged save by their love of uprightness and
mercy, they stood by the side of those more hapless, brought
some comfort to hearts less courageous than their own. Where
they abode it was not all dark. Sorrow certainly awaited them,
perchance defeat even in the humble aims that they had set
themselves; but at least their lives would remain a protest against
those brute forces of society which fill with wreck the abysses
of the nether world.

We are very far here from free baked potatoes or holidays in
Paris painlessly bestowed. Gissing was rather proud of this last
paragraph of *The Nether World*, which he had thought out
before reaching the end,[20] and I think he had reason to be.

I have said that I believe Gissing, like many writers, used
his books as a way of thinking out themes which were not
entirely clear in his own mind when he sat down to write. In
particular in several books he seems to be using the novel to
'try out' ideas about life or relationships which were relevant
to his own existence. Sometimes, having tried the concept out
in fictional form, he went ahead and did that very thing himself
months or years later: it is this that sometimes gives his books
their odd, apparently 'pre-recognitive' quality when placed
alongside the events of his life.* But at other times he appears
to have been using the fictional exploration of an idea as a way
of disposing of it and rejecting it for his own use.

Once his early days of Radical alignment were over, there is
no history of his having gone in extensively for pet schemes,
philanthropic or otherwise: he had, he felt, learnt better. On
the other hand, he was attracted emotionally to schemes, cam-
paigns and other 'life-controlling purposes'; despite the rude
things he occasionally had to say about partisan attitudes to life,
his was essentially a partisan nature, warm-hearted, liable to
sudden enthusiasms. Throughout his life, he tended to urge his

* See Chapters 4 and 5.

varied and varying panaceas on his friends, and particularly on his brother: Positivism, vegetarianism, a meat diet, life in the country, life abroad, life in England, a method of buying provisions in bulk through a scheme started by Lord Winchelsea—all these things, at one time or another, figured for him as 'solutions' to the manifold ills of his own life and those of other people.

It is not hard to see that he was, emotionally, the sort of person who would very much have liked a 'life-controlling purpose' of the kind Michael Snowden evolved, particularly one that corresponded to his generous instincts. But intellect, sensitivity, and perhaps also his pessimistic and negative tendencies, led him to feel that such projects were a snare and a temptation. I believe that he wrote *Demos* and, more especially, *The Nether World* partly as a way of demonstrating the dangers inherent in 'finding a resource in idealism' as much to himself as to others. The rather self-indulgent fantasies of philanthropy which crop up in his slighter books become, in his best books, the very thing which is analysed and found wanting. Like many writers, he did not just make his characters do what he himself had done: he also at times made them do what he had *not* done and thus avoided the act himself.

One should also perhaps add that the whole concept of altruism and of grand philanthropic plans was not just a private obsession of Gissing's own but was a theme of the period, or at any rate of the 1890s. (Like many good writers, Gissing's own sensitivity to certain ideas may be seen to develop rather in advance of the popular awareness.) In one of his best books, *The Odd Women* (1893), he makes use of the idea of the 'life-controlling purpose' in an objective and non-obsessional way. There is Mary Barfoot, a good Fabian type who has a scheme for benefiting educated but fortuneless girls by training them to be secretaries. The conflict between Miss Barfoot's hopes and ideals, and the ignoble needs of her protégée Monica Madden, an attractive but not very intelligent or secure young woman, form a key part of the book, but Gissing's own preoccupation with the subject is kept within bounds; his view of Miss Barfoot is reasonable, not over-enthusiastic nor morbidly derogatory.

For a final, more acid view of the subject, and an indication of the way Gissing's views on it continued to mature and alter

over the years, one should turn to *Our Friend the Charlatan*
(1901), a splendidly ironic novel in which Gissing's considerable
capacities for wry sub-humour are displayed to the full and
his earlier sentimentality or gullibility appear totally in abeyance
—if not extinct. For this reason, one might find this book rather
sad reading as a comment on his own existence, but as a book
it is most successful. Dyce Lashmar, the 'charlatan' of the title
(Gissing was going to call the book 'The Coming Man' but
his contempt for his central character seems to have increased
in the course of writing) is an example of a type of person
whom Gissing evidently considered had by then become fashionable. He is the type who has:

a habit of facile enthusiasm, not perhaps altogether in-
sincere, but totally without moral value . . . convictions
assumed at will as a matter of fashion, or else of singu-
larity . . . the lack of stable purpose. Worst, perhaps, of all
these frequent traits is the affectation of—to use a silly word—
altruism. The most radically selfish of men seem capable of
persuading themselves into the belief that their prime motive is
to 'live for others'.

Essentially a snob and an anti-democrat, Lashmar stands as a
Liberal candidate for reasons of social advancement—one may
compare Denzil Quarrier in the novel of that name—and is
sufficiently naïve to let fall at a late stage in the book that he
would just as soon have stood as a Conservative had he seen
a better opening there. Nor is he the only character in the book
against whom the charge 'affectation of altruism' is levelled.
There is 'The Parliamentary Mr Roach . . . an idealist of a mild
type, whose favourite talk was of "altruism", and who, whilst
affecting close attention to what other people said, was always
absorbed in his own thoughts.' There is also Constance Bride,
an honest, sensible, no-nonsense girl (with a physical resemblance
to the photographs of Clara Collet) whom one thinks for a
while is destined to be the book's shining heroine. But she does
not escape the author's censure either: 'She, too, for all her
occupation with social reform, was at core a thorough indi-
vidualist, desiring far less the general good than her own attain-
ment of celebrity as a public benefactress.' More gross examples
of the essentially self-centred quality of much philanthropy are

provided by May Tomalin, an on-the-make young miss who thinks it would be so good for the working classes to be taught Old English, and her aunt, a terrifying old person of considerable wealth and a boundless desire to control other people's lives. As Constance Bride (who is eventually to put Lady Ogram's schemes into action) says herself: 'To tell the truth, she wanted not only to do substantial good, but to do it in a way which should perpetrate her name—cause her to be more talked about after her death than she had been in her lifetime.' Indeed Lady Ogram, with her manic refusal to take account of anyone else's personal wishes, far transcends Michael Snowden in egotism, and forms the ultimate—and indeed comic—indictment of the ideal of philanthropy which Gissing himself so long cherished. One may perhaps reflect that, as time went by, he felt personally injured at seeing his own personal and private fantasies become vulgarized into a fashionable cult.

It is rather a relief to turn to the one moderately sympathetic and dignified character the novel contains—the weak-willed but sensible and discriminating Lord Dymchurch. This last, one of those literary wraiths constructed out of a small selection of his creator's own traits, is also drawn to vague yearnings toward Doing Good, as exemplified for him, the classicist, by dictates of Marcus Aurelius. But in the end, like Rycroft, he abandons the idea of any 'life-controlling purpose' in favour of a 'wise passiveness', with plans to cultivate his own farm in Kent and not bother about anyone but his immediate circle.

As a method of living decently, this may have much to recommend it—*The Private Papers of Henry Ryecroft*, written soon after, makes Gissing's own yearnings in that direction depressingly clear—but as a final comment on the large and glorious theme of altruism which had played such a distinctive part in his own life and works, it hardly seems adequate. To be sure, the theme of disillusionment itself was something of a perennial one with him. Long before, in 1880 shortly after *Workers* had come out, he had written to Algernon[21] telling him that he was already engaged on a new book to be called *Will o' the Wisps*: 'The subject of the novel is the dissipation of illusions, the destruction of ideals, in short the failure of a number of people to gain ends they have set up for their lives, or, if they *do* gain them, their failure to find the enjoyment they expected.' The book was later abandoned, although one may reasonably surmise that much of the material for it was used in the later books—and used, no doubt, in more sophisticated ways than Gissing would have been able to in 1880. But for most of his life, like all people much subject to violent and painful disillusionment, Gissing had a correspondingly lively capacity for finding new ideals, new enthusiasms. Only when his spirit had been eroded by years of assorted anxieties (most of them of his own making, but that is irrelevant) and by the essentially draining, self-consuming nature of a creative writer's life, did his resilience really begin to crack.

His sour abandonment, in *Our Friend the Charlatan*, of those most profound and general ideals of altruism which had informed so much of his previous life and work, is, I believe, just one of several sad pointers to his physical and spiritual decline. He became obsessed, in his last three or four years of life, with the state of the world and the 'decline of society', without apparently suspecting that the real decline might be in his own stamina, and hence in his own capacity for enthusiasm, generosity and belief in human nature. In Wells' words, he 'spent his big, fine brain' deprecating and pillorying those aspects of life which, in more buoyant days, he was able to place in perspective. Moreover the theme of escape—justified, rightly or wrongly, on grounds of health—became more and more marked, both in life and work. *Our Friend the Charlatan* was written, not while he was in any way involved in the scenes of British life it depicts, but in the social isolation of a semi-secret alliance and a rented Parisian flat—a self-limiting exile, though Gissing could not bring himself to see it as that. *Ryecroft*, with its theme of a self-centred and quiescent identification with the British landscape, was begun in the attractive but different landscape of central France. It was as if those very aspects of human society which so exasperated Gissing, in practice brought out the best in him, not only as a writer but as a man also. Left too much to his own devices, undisturbed by the philanthropists, charlatans, *poseurs*, self-seeking society matrons and fools of the busy world, his spleen became not less but greater. Many of us are not particularly good at knowing what is good for us: Gissing was singularly incapable of this knowledge.

3   The Guilty Secret

Of the various personal themes which run like significant, persistent yet often irrelevant threads through Gissing's novels and
stories, that of the Guilty Secret is perhaps the most ubiquitous
and at the same time the most elusive. You can read a number
of his books before even spotting it as a theme, yet, once noticed,
it makes its presence felt everywhere. It crops up attached to
important characters and to minor ones; it plays a key part in
the development of some plots, and elsewhere it is a mere incidental, a part of the background of particular significance only
to those familiar with Gissing's own experiences. Sometimes the
'secret' is something clear-cut and unequivocally shameful—an
actual prison sentence or similar early misdemeanour. Sometimes
it is something far more generalized, like a humble background
carefully dissembled, a present lack of cash similarly dissembled,
or a family disaster. Twice it is a secret marriage. Sometimes,
again, it is something more in the nature of an overall fault
of character that is being concealed—a devious ambition, a
lack of integrity, an ulterior motive, even just the basic fact of
egotism (traditionally cloaked under the desire to Do Good,
as discussed in the previous chapter). In a few instances it is
something still harder to pin down—in fact Gissing never does
nail this one properly: a vague suggestion of male nastiness and
'impurity' as opposed to the essential niceness of women. Not
that Gissing's books don't contain plenty of nasty women with
vaguely unclean secrets of their own: Harriet Smales in *The
Unclassed*, with her 'scrofula', her drinking habits, her fits, her
way of coercing Casti into marriage and her scheming against
Ida, is a distillation of female nastiness, as Gissing saw it. In
The Odd Women, Virginia Madden, though well-intentioned
and merely feeble, is another secret drinker, and presently
develops 'a shrinking, apologetic shyness only seen in people

who have done something to be ashamed of'. But Gissing's main women, with a few memorable exceptions such as Amy Reardon in *New Grub Street*, can, far more than his men, be divided into 'goodies' and 'baddies'. In his world-picture it is chiefly men who may happen to have, lurking in the background of an otherwise tolerably decent existence, a suggestion of shame and buried guilt on which they prefer not to dwell.

The most obvious source for this in Gissing's own life is, of course, the Manchester disaster. This, for Gissing, combined the potent elements of hopes blighted, personal shame (the betrayal of his own private standards), social shame (the betrayal of socially accepted standards, this hurting his family as well as himself) and overtones of sexual 'impurity' in addition. It also included the experience of the prison sentence which, in itself, was a thing so unthinkable for a gentleman at that period that Gissing notably failed to make proper use of this unique experience in any of his works.

What he saw and felt during that month of hard labour in a common Manchester gaol was evidently a subject so deeply buried in shame and distress that he was unable even to regard it as material for fiction, though other aspects of the Nell-affair were used in his books later, in graphic detail. It is true that a number of his characters do get sent to prison—Arthur Golding's father, in *Workers* has been there, as a result of poverty and 'temptation' in youth; so has Northway in *Denzil Quarrier*; so has Mary Hewett in *The Nether World* (significantly, she is rescued and rehabilitated by marriage with John Hewett); 'Arry Mutimer in *Demos* is also sent there; so is Hugh Carnaby in *The Whirlpool*. But in each case the event is referred to in the briefest factual manner, with painful restraint. There is no revelation of what prison is actually *like*. Even in *The Unclassed* when Ida Starr finds herself in prison through a false accusation, engineered by Harriet, Gissing indicates the shock of this obliquely rather than describing it through Ida's eyes. Instead, he substitutes Casti's speculations about it: 'He leaned against the great gloomy wall, and thought of Ida. At this hour she was most likely asleep, unless sorrow kept her waking. What unimagined horrors did she suffer day after day in that accursed prison house?'

The route by which Ida reaches gaol is tortuous, and Gissing

1 George Gissing in the 1890s during his second marriage.

WORKERS IN THE DAWN.

A Novel.

IN THREE VOLUMES.

BY

GEORGE R. GISSING.

1880
(obiit: 23.)

VOL. I.

London :
REMINGTON AND CO.,
5, Arundel Street, Strand, W.C.

1880.

10   The title page of *Workers in the Dawn.*

was at much pains to make the charge transparently false to the reader and at the same time sufficient to convince the fictional magistrate of her guilt. Algernon, who was then studying to become a solicitor, helped him with legal points. In May 1883 Gissing was writing to him: 'I have secured a conviction, but it has been the hardest piece of work I have done for a long time.'[1] It is not hard to see all this section of *The Unclassed* as a wish-fulfilment re-writing of the writer's own past, with the criminal actually a guiltless victim of mistaken identity, just as the personality and past of Ida herself is a fantasy re-writing of Nell's true nature and history. The Manchester gaol would, one feels, have been much more bearable to Gissing had he been able to see himself there as a heroically persecuted character instead of a shabby and deservedly punished thief.

As I have said in the previous chapter, it is not easy for us today to grasp the peculiar horror which Gissing's petty larceny had at the period, both for himself and for others. Twentieth-century commentators, socially more sophisticated, and aware of the high incidence of money-thefts in literally any institution—are inclined to underrate the significance of Gissing's lapse *in itself*: they stress only the miserable harsh consequences. For a viewpoint which combines a charitable approach with a full appreciation of the social climate of the period, there is one book written by a comparative nonentity: the Reverend W. Robertson Nicolls' *A Bookman's Letters*.[2] Nicolls knew Gissing slightly; he was with him at a literary club dinner in 1895 given by Gissing's friend Clodd. Ten years after Gissing's death, when the Manchester secret was finally (due to Morley Roberts) a secret no more, he wrote:

Men who yield easily to other temptations would never under any circumstances yield to the temptation of theft. Even though they were starving they would not pick pockets for money; they would not steal overcoats; they would not steal books. In fact, temptation could not assail them on that side at all. That Gissing gave way on this point was a most calamitous fact. He practically thrust himself outside the pale by these actions, and outside the pale he remained . . .

In other words, Gissing had not just 'sinned' (i.e. in his association with Nell) or even just 'committed a crime'—there were

E

certain crimes which gentlemen were known to commit, improperly and disgracefully, to be sure, but without necessarily losing their label of 'gentleman'. Embezzlement was the gentleman's pecuniary crime of the period, along with its blander cousin 'rash speculation': indeed several of Gissing's characters, notably Alma Frothingham's father, are guilty of these. No—what Gissing had so calamitously done was to commit a *working-class crime*.[3] He had disgraced his family and himself by doing something not just against the law but utterly out of keeping with the class with which the whole Gissing household fervently wished to be associated. In his temporary abandonment of honesty, he had blundered back through those very social barriers which, by dint of work and scholarships, he had himself so laboriously climbed. No wonder that he was to feel after that he had somehow given the game away about himself —that he had betrayed an essential looseness in his nature, and, at the same time, that if he were to keep this secret trait carefully concealed in future, he would be guilty of a lack of integrity and hence another form of dishonesty. Such, at any rate, is the sense of unease and slightly furtive role-playing that one picks up from many of his characters, from out-and-out charlatans like Dyce Lashmar, through less pernicious versions of the same type—politicians like Denzil Quarrier or Richard Mutimer, men on the make like Jasper Milvain in *New Grub Street*, and Everard Barfoot in *The Odd Women* or the tormented Godwin Peak, to essentially high-minded characters like Reardon in *New Grub Street* or Will Warburton in the late novel of that name. To such a profound and double-edged unease, there is no ready solution.

A number of his half-good characters are ignobly tempted by money, usually in the form of advantageous marriage, but only once, in *A Life's Morning*, did Gissing make direct and full use of the theme of a lower-class temptation to steal. One may be inclined to feel that the temptation that faces the struggling clerk James Hood, when he finds a ten pound note, is still harder to resist than that which, in real life, assailed Gissing; one may also feel that, in the way Hood is led from one error to another against his will and intention, there is once again an element of romanticizing, as of Ida's profession in *The Unclassed*. Nevertheless this part of *A Life's Morning* is the nearest thing we have to Gissing's view of his own crime and of the combination of emotions which contributed to it, and it is therefore worth examining.

The chapter in question is called 'Circumstance'. But the whole of Hood's life, as delineated in the earlier chapters, is a background of circumstances, all tending toward the fatal moment. Like many of Gissing's characters, the Hood family's whole existence, emotions included, is deformed by lack of money:

Time had robbed them of their youth, and the injustice of the world's order had starved love to less than a shadow of itself, to a mere habit of common suffering. Tender memories were buried in the grave of children whom the resources of ever so modest a fortune would have kept alive; the present was a mere struggle to support existence, choking the impulses of affection.

Hood is a clerk in the counting house at Dagworthy's mill and finds a ten pound[4] note between the pages of a ledger. As Dagworthy is at that hour absent, and he himself had to make a business trip to Hebsworth (Leeds), rather than hand the note to anyone else he places it in his pocket book fully intending to give it to his master that evening. In the train, however, a mishap occurs—train journeys frequently play a key part in Gissing's novels:

It was a slow train and there were half a dozen stoppages. Hood began to eat his sandwiches at a point where the train was delayed for a few minutes by an adverse signal; a coal-pit was close by, and the smoke from the chimney blew in at the carriage windows, giving a special flavour to the bread and meat. There was a drunken soldier in the same compartment, who was being baited by a couple of cattle-drovers with racy vernacular not to be rendered by the pen. Hood munched his smoky sandwich, and with his sad eyes watched the great wheel of the colliery revolve, and the trucks rise and descend. The train moved on again. The banter between the other three passengers was taking an angry turn; to escape the foul language as far as possible, Hood kept his head at the window.* Of a sudden the drunken soldier was pushed against him, and before he could raise his hands his hat had flown off in the breeze.

* Shades of Thomas Waller Gissing telling his son after a train journey, 'I always go to sleep when conversation of that kind begins'.

To understand the dilemma Hood thus finds himself in, the reader has to project himself back into the era when, strange as it may seem, it was extremely unusual for anyone but the lowest type of working man to go hatless through the streets of a town. For a clerk, to whom the carefully-nurtured appearance of a gentleman was part of his stock in trade, it was *absolutely unthinkable*. The equivalent in today's terms would be for a bank clerk to appear without his trousers. The present-day reader must bring himself to understand this, since otherwise Hood's subsequent behaviour appears not merely rash (which it is meant to) but lacking in any sense of proportion, which it is not. Ironically, it is the desire to appear respectable which leads to the first step on the downward path. One is meant to sympathize with Hood when he solves the problem by cashing the note—having endorsed it on the back, as was then the custom with such a large sum of money—to buy a new hat at a hatters. At this stage he has no intention of concealing what he has done from Dagworthy, but—being as liable to sudden spurts of optimism as he is to sudden depression—he convinces himself that Dagworthy will wish to pay for the new hat anyway. (One may imagine Gissing momentarily justifying his thefts from the pockets of richer students by convincing himself that, if only they knew and understood about Nell, they would be glad to help out anyway.) However his mood alters; he suddenly becomes afraid that, if he goes to Dagworthy with the change from the note in his hand and the true story on his lips, Dagworthy will not believe it anyway, and will suspect him of abstracting a far larger sum and returning just a part of it in order to get credit for honesty. Such is the sensitivity in the poor-but-respectable. Just as he is puzzling wretchedly over this invented horror, he runs into an old friend, very down at heel. They have a drink together, and, suddenly sanguine again, Hood invites his friend to a meal. During the meal, the friend reminds Hood that he owes Hood money from long ago—ten pounds as it happens—and promises to repay it 'soon'. Hood's response is to lend him a few shillings more.

Afterwards, when his business is transacted and he sits at the station waiting for his train back, he is falsely elated with his own generosity, a frame of mind of which Gissing himself obviously had experience: 'He was in that comfortable mood, following upon unusual indulgence of the appetite, in which the mind handles in a free and easy way the thoughts it is wont to entertain with unquestionable gravity; when it has, as it were, a slippery hold on the facts of life, and constructs a subjective world of genial accommodations.' He gradually convinces himself that, as the money must have been in the ledger for a long time, it will not be missed, that it was very likely never Dagworthy's at all but some other person's—that it is, simply, a 'find', just as much as if it had ben picked up by the roadside, and that it will do more objective good by paying his own family's rent than by being given to a mill-owner who does not need it. He returns to the mill, and the moment when he would have had a chance to mention the matter to his master passes without him doing so. After this, conflict and choice are at an end, and though Hood still does not feel comfortable in his mind, he returns home and tells his wife that the unexpected windfall is the repayment of an old loan by a friend, thus turning the encounter in Hebsworth back to front.

With Hood's usual ill-luck, things go from bad to worse. He is tormented by what he has done, and attempts to put the matter right with his own conscience by giving the rest of the money to the old friend, who turns up again on his doorstep, but this merely serves to raise anxieties in his wife. Meanwhile Dagworthy knows about the theft, and has told Hood's daughter Emily, whom he is pursuing, in the tradition of the rich villain and the poor-but-honest maiden, that unless she falls in with his wishes (marriage, actually, not dishonour) he will take proceedings against her father. Emily will not, of course, do what Dagworthy wants but—typically of a novel heroine—she does not think to have the matter out with all the parties concerned, either, or threaten a public scandal to embarrass the mill-owner himself. The reader may perhaps be forgiven for thinking that Emily is a tiresome tragedy queen who lacks mundane common sense—and indeed Gissing himself seems to have had qualms about her, for this novel was never one of his favourites.

The result is that Dagworthy, refusing any offer of Emily's to repay the money herself, summons Hood and dismisses him on the spot. Hypocritically he speaks as if he were a high-principled man, even a kindly one—he tells Hood he will not actually prosecute him out of concern for his age and his family, but since he will not give the clerk a reference the dismissal is, in effect, a sentence of doom. It is strongly implied, though never stated baldly, that Dagworthy planted the note in the ledger in the first place; in any case Gissing leaves us in no doubt that the mill-owner feels ashamed of the course of action in which he is now brutally persisting. The event has not just been the temptation and downfall of James Hood, it has also been the temptation, and downfall in spiritual terms, of Dagworthy himself. By his cruel behaviour, he has merely ensured that Emily will never look at him, now. He has missed his chance of this, and a great deal more. 'Midway in his life, when slow development waited but occasion to establish the possibilities of a passionate character, Dagworthy underwent the trial destined to determine the future course of his life.' Dagworthy too now has his unpleasant secret.

As a result of his dismissal, Hood goes out onto the Heath and poisons himself, one of a number of the suicides that are committed in Gissing's books by partial alter-egos of himself. We do not see into his mind as he commits the act; we—along with Dagworthy—simply find his body.

It is not known that Gissing himself ever actually made a suicide attempt of any kind. But the emotion associated in his mind with the Manchester disaster was evidently of that desperate, horror-struck order. This quality of emotion occasionally crops up in other books, attached to fictional circumstances which, in point of fact, do not warrant it. Thus Gilbert Grail, the literary working man in *Thyrza*, is vaguely described as having had a 'breakdown' at the age of twenty-five brought on by too much sitting up late and reading. 'Breakdown' was the euphemism used in Gissing's family circle to explain his dismissal from Owens, Manchester: the description of Gilbert's own state of mind about his collapse suggests a setback of a much more specific and calamitous order than the novel actually mentions:

The purpose he knew was frustrated. The 'Might have been', which is 'also called No more, Too late, Farewell', often stared him in the eyes with those unchanging orbs of ghastliness, chilling the flow of his blood and making life the cruellest of mockeries.

A similar sense of generalized shame and remorse is attached to the nebulous 'past' of Sidney Kirkwood in *The Nether World*. No details are given, except that his father's death pulled him up short and made him repent of his ways:

His bereavement possibly saved Sidney from a young manhood of foolishness and worse. In the upper world a youth may 'sow his wild oats' and have done with it; in the nether 'to have your fling' is almost necessarily to fall among criminals.

This observation, though doubtless true, reads like a partial excuse for Gissing's own conduct. Certainly had Gissing been a moneyed young man at Owens, his association with Nell would not have led him to steal—or, more exactly, could not have presented itself to him as a valid excuse for stealing. Later, in a sentence which also seems personal, Gissing remarks that when Sidney Kirkwood woos Jane Snowden: '—the memory of passions from which he had suffered years ago affected him with a sense of unworthiness, almost of impurity.' It is not clear in context whether it is Kirkwood's old love for Clara Hewett which is being referred to, or to undefined passions from still further back, but in any case the remark seems more appropriate to Gissing's *own* experience than to Kirkwood's.

The Nether World abounds in secret pasts: Michael Snowden's own past contains the remorse-inducing episode of his marriage (quoted in Chapter 2); his son, Joseph Snowden, carries guilt about with him like an unclean odour:

. . . his talk was at times very persuasive and much like that of one who has been brought to a passable degree of honesty by the slow development of his better instincts. But his face was against him; the worn, sallow features, the eyes which so obviously made a struggle to look with frankness, the vicious lower lip, awoke suspicion and told tales of base experience such as leaves its stamp upon a man for ever.

The same theme of the stamp of a vicious past, combined with the rather questionable concept of a man being 'brought to a passable degree of honesty' in the process of time, is found in Scawthorne, an oddly shadowy character in this novel. Scawthorne's function early on seems to be that of evil seducer: it is he who tempts Clara Hewett away from respectable barmaiding to the life of an actress (then synonymous with immorality). He surfaces again later as an accomplice of Joseph Snowden's in his money-making schemes, yet he is an enigmatic character for whom Gissing is inclined to make excuses: 'Probably no one who is half-starved and overworked during those critical years [of youth] comes out of the trial with his moral nature uninjured.' Later his early problems are made more explicit:

... notwithstanding his keen social sense, his native tact, in all London not one refined home was open to him, not one domestic circle of educated people could he approach and find a welcome ... Suppose he had wished to marry; where, pray, was he to find his wife? A barmaid? Why, yes, other men of his standing wedded barmaids and girls from the houses of business and so on; but they had neither his tastes nor his brains. Never had it been his lot to exchange a word with an educated woman —save in the office on rare occasions.

Here, we touch on a central theme in Gissing's life and work: the impossibility of a penniless man, whatever his breeding and intelligence, making overtures to a 'lady'. This was the reason Gissing proffered, to family and friends, for his quixotic marriage to Edith Underwood: *New Grub Street*, the novel he rapidly completed, after many false starts, once Edith had entered his life, is to a large extent an exploration of this theme.*
Yet his numerous treatments of the subject in this and other books tend to perpetrate a myth, concealing the real state of affairs rather than exposing it. Is Scawthorne really driven to shabby expedients in order to attain for himself a congenial place in society commensurate with his abilities? Or is *a sense of guilt and shame about expedients already resorted to* the thing that actually inhibits him from seizing what social opportunities are honestly open to him? Gissing's own attitude to social overtures made to him by well-to-do and educated people was equivocal in the extreme. He was wont to lament his own social isolation so that the image of the lonely outcast has been perpetrated, yet even a cursory examination of his diary and letters reveals that he often refused such promising invitations as were offered to him, or broke off fruitful relationships for no very apparent reason. Middleton Murry[5] remarked that: 'What is

* See Chapter 4.

peculiar about his heroes . . . is that they are frustrated by something more (and less visible) than their poverty.' In any case
there is a central contradiction in his purported belief that lack
of money prevents an educated man from seeking a wife of
similar level: on the contrary, it is precisely *because* of their
poverty that characters like Jasper Milvain in *New Grub Street*
and, more farcically, Dyce Lashmar the 'charlatan' are led to
approach moneyed young women. And, in the case of the
latter, it is not his moneyless state *as such* which eats into his
spirit by the end of the book, but the sense of his own duplicity:

At moments, so profound was his feeling of insignificance
that he hid his face even from the darkness and groaned.
Not only had he lost faith in himself; there remained in him
no conviction, no trust, no hope of any kind. Intellectually,
morally, he had no support; shams, insincerities, downright dis-
honesties, had clothed him about, and these were now all stripped
away, leaving the thing he called his soul to shiver in shamed
nakedness.

An almost analogous state of mind has also been reached by
Lord Dymchurch, who, except for being similarly money-less,
is everything that Lashmar is not and fails to be everything that
Lashmar is: 'Poverty and loneliness he had known, and had
learnt to bear them with equanimity; he was tasting for the first
time of humiliation.'

The vicious circle of poverty (or whatever) leading to a sense
of unworthiness, leading to devious attempts at making good,
leading in turn to a further and more profound inner humiliation at the loss of personal integrity, is nowhere so completely
illustrated as in *Born in Exile*. I have already (in Chapter 1)
discussed Godwin Peak's morbid sensitivity about his lower-
class origins and his sense of being born for better things. In the
book's early passages, when Godwin is at Whitelaw College,
the problems of the scholar with very little money are spelt out,
in a fact at rather greater length than the story warrants, for later
we never see Peak as actually destitute: his is the middle-class
dilemma of lack of 'prospects', not the acute and immediate
one of lack of cash on which to live. It is as if, in writing the
early passages, Gissing found that memories of his time at
Owens loomed so large that he was unable to select those

relevant to his novel. I have already remarked on the pregnant passage which ends 'A youth of less concentrated purpose, more at the mercy of casual allurement, would probably have gone to wreck amid trials so exceptional'. Rather clumsily, as if unable to leave the subject of Godwin's trials alone—though in the book no particular 'temptation' follows—Gissing continues:

Trials not only of his moral nature. The sums of money with which he was furnished fell short of a reasonable total for bare necessities. In the calculation made by Mrs Peak and his sister, outlay on books had practically been lost sight of; it was presumed that ten shillings a term would cover this item. But Godwin could not consent to be at a disadvantage in his armoury for academic contest. The first month saw him compelled to contract his diet, that he might purchase books; henceforth he rarely had enough to eat. His landlady supplied him with breakfast, tea and supper—each repast of the very simplest kind; for dinner it was understood that he repaired to some public table, where meat and vegetables, with perchance a supplementary sweet when nature demanded it, might be had for about a shilling. That shilling was not often at his disposal. Dinner as it is understood by the comfortably clad, the 'regular meal' which is part of English respectability, came to be represented by a small pork pie, or even a couple of buns, eaten at a little shop over against the College. After a long morning of mental application this was poor refreshment; the long afternoon which followed, again spent in rigorous study, could not but reduce a growing frame to ravenous hunger. Tea and bread and butter were the means of appeasing it, until another four hours' work called for reward in the shape of bread and cheese.

Food meant a great deal to Gissing: the inherent contradictions in his nature were borne out in his culinary tastes. As Morley Roberts said, his idea of cooking was 'fatness and a certain amount of gross abundance'. He loved also the *idea* of certain particularly English victuals, such as beef and beer; succulent references to thick slices of meat, bread-and-dripping, hot potatoes and steak and kidney pies crop up throughout his books. At the same time he was fastidious and was liable to sudden accesses of moralistic distaste for this or that food, and even spent a period as a vegetarian. At moments 'grossness' revolted him: certain disgusted descriptions, such as a house smelling of bubbling cooking fat, are memorable. It is very noticeable—though I have never seen the fact mentioned, all biographers seeming to take Gissing's protestations on diet at their face value—that whenever Gissing was unhappy he tended to complain about the food, and in particular of being 'half starved'. I think one might be justified in interpreting the memories of inadequate diet in Manchester, as lent to Godwin Peak, as an emotional reaction rather than a strictly literal one. The evidence is that absolute lack of money was not the real problem in Manchester anyway: Gissing held several scholarships, Morley Roberts could never think how he came to be in such apparent difficulties. If the above passage expresses anything meaningful in terms of Peak's later history, that something can only be his generalized sense of social inferiority and frustration.

Peak's hunger-pangs do not, at any rate, lead anywhere in particular. By an irony which I am not at all convinced was intentional on Gissing's part, his downfall, his 'guilty secret' and the reason for his departure from College is simply the fact that a brazenly working-class uncle of his appears in the town with plans to open an eating house opposite the College called 'Peak's Dining and Refreshment Rooms'.

How much Gissing means us to sympathize with Godwin Peak's well-bred distress at this prospect, and how much he intends that we should regard him as a snob with false values, is difficult at this distance in time to determine. One should, undoubtedly, make allowances for the vastly different social climate of the period, for the contempt in which 'trade', particularly ignoble, obvious trade, was held by the upper classes, and for the fact that scholars from humble homes formed only a tiny proportion of College students. A common old uncle from Dalston Junction was just the sort of relative a boy at 'Whitelaw'—or Owens—would reasonably prefer to keep secret, or at any rate at a safe distance. At the same time, however, Peak's subsequent career, with its emphasis on appearances rather than on integrity, allows us to suppose that Gissing himself did think Peak's reaction somewhat extreme. The fact is, there is something obscure about this whole section, no doubt because the awkward fictional device is weighted illogically with all the secret passion of Gissing's own, far more shaming experience. Plot and emotion threaten to part company: in place of Gissing's actual guilt is substituted Godwin Peak's innocence—yet Godwin *behaves* as a guilty man.

Perhaps this discrepancy is the main reason why, throughout the book, Godwin Peak, for all his intelligence and sensitivity, remains a rather unlovable figure. Of all Gissing's heroes he is the one that excites the least ready sympathy and yet the one that most needs it. Again and again he behaves like a man with a shameful secret to hide—yet when, as through all the early part of the book, this secret is presented as being merely his base origins, the reader is bound to feel that far too much is being made of this, even by Victorian standards. Peak is educated, he is not totally without resources, people are kind to him; he seems to be obsessional without sufficient excuse. For instance, when he re-meets the middle-class Warricombes, he is totally preoccupied with the impression he is making: 'Peak, after each of his short remarks, made a comparison of his tone and phraseology with those of the other speakers. Had he still any marks of the ignoble world from which he sprang?'

Essentially Godwin Peak has a very low opinion of himself —irrationally low, in the context of the novel: 'That his male friends held him in any warm esteem always appeared to him improbable, and as regards women his modesty was profound.'

The central theme that develops is an odd one. Peak decides that the best way of social advancement for a young man like him of no background and few means, is to take holy orders, since Church of England clergymen traditionally 'counted' as upper class whatever their origins. He thus sets out to convince those round him (the Warricombes and their friends) and also himself that he is a believer—or at any rate that an adequate degree of belief for a cleric is not incompatible with the new Darwinism, then a burning question. (The novel is set back a little in time.) Since he has in fact, like Gissing himself, no belief at all, and has written the occasional article or book review making this clear, the way before him is not entirely smooth.

Jacob Korg[6] sees this book as a study of intellectual nihilism: to him, Godwin Peak (like Dostoyevsky's Raskolnikov) is saying 'if I believe in nothing therefore I should have no qualms about pretending to believe'. Since Gissing was familiar with Dostoyevsky, this theory is ingenious—but, I believe, misguided.

One should also, perhaps, resist a still closer comparison with Basarov, the anarchist family-rejecting young man in Turgenev's *Fathers and Sons* who also also falls in love with a middle-class woman. Essentially Peak, like Gissing himself, is at the opposite pole from nihilism: guilt, introspection, doubt, and weak, human hopes are his natural element. The guilt hitherto ascribed unconvincingly to the coffee-shop episode, now becomes centred, more plausibly, on the fact of faked belief: he is extremely conscious of his lack of integrity and tries to justify it to himself, not by intellectual arguments, but by attempting to think himself into the state of mind in which some form of belief really *is* compatible with previously expressed views—a typical Gissing manoeuvre.[7] Godwin Peak is one of a series of characters who compromise their integrity, not—or not only —with cold calculation, but with a blinkered attempt to readjust their own personal sights to fit the new goal. There is Richard Mutimer in *Demos* who discards Emma Vine: 'It never occurred to him . . . that in forfeiting his honour in this instance he began a process of undermining which would sooner or later threaten the stability of the purposes on which he most prided himself.' There is Dyce Lashmar, who puts on political fervour and borrowed opinions like new garments: there is Alma Frothingham who attempts to use her slight musical talent as a means to social advancement, and counts on the fact of being a lady to get away with much—a neat reversal of Gissing's usual preoccupation.

I think that if the rather baroque choice of theme in *Born in Exile* 'means' anything in terms of Gissing's own life, then it relates to a dilemma he did *not* have to face but might very well have done had he continued in his academic career. Although college dons or other distinguished members of the teaching profession did not have to take Holy Orders after 1871 most of them in fact continued to do so till at least the turn of the century, and not to do so was to handicap oneself professionally. One may assume that Gissing, when in his teens, saw this problem looming, and that it surfaced years later in *Born in Exile* as a never-resolved dilemma of his past transposed into a new setting.

As a footnote, one might add that some three years after the publication of this novel, Algernon Gissing apparently toyed

with the idea of getting himself ordained. Perhaps the novel
suggested the idea to him!

An interesting, concentrated treatment of the theme of com-
promised integrity crops up in a short story which may be a
key one, *A Poor Gentleman*, written in the 1890s. Educated,
amiable but untrained at forty for any profession, the poor
gentleman—Mr Tymperley—is, like a number of Gissing's
more sympathetic characters, the victim of speculation. Reduced
from previous comfort to a pittance, he leaves his country
home and comes to hide himself in shabby Islington lodgings—
Islington, that already-declining inner suburb where Gissing
himself had passed many grey hours. Indeed in many respects
he is the archetypal Gissing-hero, *homo solo*:

All this time he was of course living in absolute solitude.
Poverty is the great secluder—unless one belongs to the rank
which is born to it; a sensitive man who no longer finds himself on equal terms with his natural associates, shrinks into
loneliness, and learns with some surprise how very willing people
are to forget his existence. London is a wilderness abounding
in anchorites—voluntary or constrained. As he wandered
about the streets and parks, or killed time in museums and
galleries (where nothing had to be paid), Mr Tymperley often
recognized brethren in seclusion; he understood the furtive
glance which met his own, he read the peaked visage, marked
with understanding sympathy the shabby-genteel apparel . . .

In Middleton Murry's phrase, this man, whom Gissing would
have us believe is merely hard up, 'seems frustrated by something more (and less visible) than poverty'. He also shares other
of his creator's weaknesses:

Perforce a vegetarian, he found that a vegetable diet was good
for his health, and delivered to himself many a scornful speech
on the habits of the carnivorous multitude. He of necessity
abjured alcohol, and straightway longed to utter his testimony
on a teetotal platform. These were his satisfactions. They com-
pensate astonishingly for the loss of many kinds of self-esteem.

Many kinds?

Notably, Mr Tymperley's chief satisfaction—like Gissing's at a
period—lies in presenting himself to such middle-class acquaintances as he has retained from his past as a man of democratic

principle, acting on this principle to relieve suffering among the working classes. The same obsession with philanthropy which Gissing ascribes to other characters, he makes Tymperley use insincerely as an excuse for his presence in Islington: ' "I live among the poor",' he explains, ' "and as one of them, to obtain knowledge that cannot be otherwise procured".' Did Gissing, one can't help wondering, ever use this excuse himself? Certainly, with his perpetual tendency to keep different sets of acquaintances in different compartments, he was not invariably truthful, even with friends, about his domestic circumstances, past or present. He adds, by way of comment: 'Thus was Mr Tymperley committed to a singular piece of deception, a fraud which could not easily be discovered, and which injured only its perpetrator.' So the original secret—merely that of poverty— is compounded with something worse, a hidden dishonesty.

The moral crisis comes to Tymperley (as to Hood) in the form of a temptation to expropriate money. A middle-class woman to whom he has been talking of his fantasy charity, sends him a cheque for five pounds, asking him to use it for the good of 'his' needy poor. Like Hood, Tymperley wars with himself, at moments almost convincing himself that the donor has in fact guessed his secret and really means the money for him. With a curious mirroring of Hood's action, he rushes out in the morning and buys himself a new pair of boots—but with the difference that he cannot and therefore does not use the cheque for this purpose. Indeed as it is a crossed cheque and he has no bank account, there is no simple way for him to cash it; reflection sets in, and thus he is saved, after a frightful night of bad dreams in which he seems to be walking all over London in creaking, painful new boots, which 'ever and anon screamed at him a terrible name'. He hands the cheque to a local clergyman and two days later writes the donor a letter admitting his deception in abject terms. Thus the rather sad little story ends. But perhaps, for its writer, its theme of confession and painful honesty—by which Tymperley gains nothing but his own peace of mind—was a consoling exercise.

It is evidently the *secrecy* of guilt which corrodes, as much as the guilt itself, and occasionally elsewhere Gissing touches on this aspect of the situation. Yet the reasons for secrecy in itself are sometimes obscure. In *Will Warburton*, his last novel (not counting the historical fantasy *Veranilda*, on which Gissing was engaged when he died), Will, the central character, actually has no misdemeanour to reproach himself with: his suddenly penniless state is the result of others' incompetence. Yet he again, like Godwin Peak, behaves like a guilty man: he cuts himself off from all his friends and enters the grocery business with a small shop in Fulham. An honest, realistic and praiseworthy effort to rebuild his life, a modern reader might think. But Will Warburton seems to see his expedient as a type of capitulation, a betrayal of standards on a fundamental level. Shop-keeping almost invariably figures in Gissing's novels as a dreary life-sentence; Bernard Kingcote's retreat, in *Isabel Clarendon*, to a stationers in Norwich, represents that depressed person's final defeat; Godwin Peak's various relatives put themselves beyond redemption by being contented shop-keepers—it might be better, Gissing seems to be suggesting, if they at least hated the life. Evidently on this subject, Gissing, the son of a chemist (who both is and is not 'a shop keeper') was not entirely rational. Hence, the awful burden of secrecy, as Will attempts to keep his way of life unknown even to his mother and sister: 'And in those endless hours of solitude there grew upon him a perception of the veritable cause of his illness. Not loss of station, nor overwork, not love; but simply the lie to which he was committed . . . Slowly, dimly, he groped toward the fact that what rendered his life intolerable was its radical dishonesty.'

The misery inherent in keeping important facts secret from those one loves occurs again, more crucially, in *Denzil Quarrier* (1892). This is not one of Gissing's most 'important' books: the main theme—the adoption of a political career from motives of egoism—is more directly treated in *The Charlatan*, and the background is a bit laboured and obtrusive: it is as if Gissing took a too-conscious decision to write a 'political' novel as a Good Subject. But it is a well-constructed book, and there are many incidental passages of keen observation. The guilty secret of the would-be politician, Quarrier, is that he is living with a girl, Lilian, whom he has not married and indeed cannot marry since her previous husband is living—another example of Gissing's personal obsession with the subject of ill-favoured, unconventional or otherwise occult unions, and an interesting prefiguring of the union formed with Gabrielle Fleury some half-dozen years *after* the novel was written. Just as Gissing was to do with Gabrielle, Quarrier and his Lilian live a loving but socially isolated existence; Quarrier, in the very words his creator was later to use, declares to his friend Glazzard: ' "She is my wife, in every sense of the word that merits the consideration of a rational creature".' But Glazzard (as one might have suspected, from his slimy name) proves a false friend and schemes to expose Quarrier in his constituency out of a sheer, malevolent lust for power—a Zola-esque concept which sits rather oddly in this otherwise very English novel; indeed an intermittent reference to a man wrecking a train merely in order to feel powerful suggests that Gissing had Zola's *La Bête Humaine* in the back of his mind.

When he realizes what Glazzard is up to Quarrier's only possible course of action is to brazen the matter out in public by pretending to have been 'married' to Lilian all along—a new development which causes the girl much pain: 'What was now before her? . . . the elaborate deceit, the perpetual risk, weighed upon her heart . . .' Her unhappiness is compounded by the reappearance of her legal husband, Northway, a man with whom she has never actually lived (the delicacies of Mudie's Library* readers seem to be being regarded here) since he was arrested for forgery outside the church. In fact it is Northway, in this book, who carries the dark stigma of a prison sentence, but the unmistakable Gissing-agony-of-mind on the subject is all transposed onto Lilian: she is the outcast, the betrayer of her family, the one who has eaten the seeds of the pomegranate. Northway, at Glazzard's instigation, is trying a little blackmail:

In these nights of sleepless misery she thought of her old home. The relatives from whom she was forever parted—her sister, her kind old aunt—looked at her with reproachful eyes; and now, in anguish which bordered upon delirium, it was they alone who seemed real to her; all her recent life had become a vague suffering, a confused consciousness of desire and terror. Her childhood returned; she saw her parents and heard them talk. A longing for the peace and love of those dead days rent her heart.

It is arguable that, for a respectable woman in those days, to be exposed as living in a 'free union' was the equivalent to the male

* See Appendix.

disgrace of fraud or bankruptcy (and Lilian is not made of the theoretically tough, New Woman material of Rhoda Nunn in *The Odd Women*, with her brave new talk about that very thing). But all the same Lilian's 'confused consciousness of desire and terror' seems a slightly inappropriate and excessive reaction when she had lived peaceably with Quarrier for a couple of years already. I think that Gissing was here, once again, so carried away by the personal emotions associated for him with the theme of guilt and secrecy, that he was writing without strict relevance to the fictional situation he had created.

Lilian cannot bear her burden and eventually drowns herself. But Nancy Lord in *In the Year of Jubilee* (1894) is made of sterner stuff and is able to use her predicament as a means of growth and personal strengthening. She suffers, not from a pretend marriage which must convince others, but from an actual marriage which (for elaborate reasons connected with an arbitrary Will) must be kept secret, and which indeed for several years involves no cohabitation at all, though a child is born to her. Indeed her situation, as she herself remarks, is in practice exactly like that of an unmarried mother, and one is inclined to think that this is how Gissing saw her—she is seduced before marriage, and the ceremony itself, which makes little difference to the plot, was, perhaps, put in to make sure that the novel would recommend itself sufficiently to the powerful Mr Mudie—once again. By a coincidence (but coincidence is not really the word, since when several writers light on the same theme independently at the same time they are not so much coinciding as all picking up the same social drift) Thomas Hardy's *Jude the Obscure* first began to appear in instalments the same year as *In the Year of Jubilee* was published. Hardy, in making Jude cohabit and have children by a woman to whom he is not married and cannot marry, did indeed, draw considerable public odium on himself.

An actual illegitimate child crops up in *Sleeping Fires*, published the following year (1895): in fact it is the central theme of this one-volume work. Langley, one of Gissing's rather tiresome *Ryecroft* characters with private means and a cultivated melancholy, has spent many years doing very little but 'finding satisfaction in the society of a liberal-minded circle' and 'soothing his leisure with studies utterly remote from any popular or progressive programme'. However he has a secret guilt: in youth, he had an affair with a working-class girl and had a child by her; this came to light and caused the break-up of his engagement to a suitable middle-class girl. Years later he re-meets this lady, now a widow, who asks him, in the course of fuller explanations about the past, if he had never 'offered to marry' his working-class sweetheart. Langley answers with an asperity in which one can read all Gissing's own previous agonies and changes of opinion on the subject: ' "Thank heaven, no! Are you determined to echo the silliest cant? What sort of marriage would that have been? Have we not known of such?" '

Over the years, Langley's guilt has changed, not its essential nature, but its focus: 'He grew to an understanding of the wantonness with which he had acted so lightly in abandoning his child.' (It may be noted in passing that by this time Gissing had already had one son, Walter, by Edith Underwood, and loved 'the little man' dearly, bitterly as he had come to regret the marriage itself.) There is an interesting suggestion in this book—no more than a suggestion, though the title bears it out also—that sin, immorality, error (or whatever word one wants to use) goes on having its effect for years, being 'paid for' in different ways and changing its appearance with the course of time. Langley refers to 'Fate . . . a conventional word for all the mistakes we live to be ashamed of'. One could wish that Gissing had written a longer and better book on this theme.

Gissing rarely made use of illegitimacy as the secret in itself —rather surprisingly, since one might think that it provided a perfect fictional cipher[8] for his own diffused personal sense of unworthiness and deception. In *In the Year of Jubilee* the robust advertising agent Luckworth Crewe was a foundling but his history does not seem to oppress him particularly. Among Gissing's actual heroes only Piers Otway in *The Crown of Life* (1899) is illegitimate, and this circumstance takes the place which more conventionally humble origins have for the central characters of a number of other books. The result is the same; Piers Otway has a sense of being undesirable. Since this novel is all about love (unkindly, though not wholly unjustly, stigmatized by Wells as 'love in a frock coat') this sense becomes con-

centrated into the feeling that he is undesirable as a marriage
partner: 'He stared forward into the coming years, and saw
nothing that his soul desired. A life of solitude, or bitter frustration. Were it Irene, were it another, the woman for whom he
longed would never become his. He had not the power of in-
spiring love.'

Exactly why Otway should feel like this is not entirely clear.
His illegitimacy has impeccably romantic and even decorous
sources of the sort that, in reality, and even in the 1890s would
have been more likely to make him an object of interest to
young women than otherwise.[9] In this book there is no un-
couth previous wife, no blatantly common old uncles or brothers.
Yet Gissing, once again, carries real-life attitudes over in the
fictional context with questionable appropriateness. Moreover,
though Otway has in fact, unlike many Gissing heroes, no
guilty past of his own to reproach himself with, this novel
several times touches on the subject of men's pasts in general:
it is as if this is an undercover theme which relates, not to the
logistics of the plot as it stands, but to the emotional roots of
it in Gissing's own life. Take this description of Irene Derwent,
the book's heroine:

A hint of things forbidden with regard to any male acquaintance caused her to turn away, silent, austere. That such things
not seldom came to her hearing was a motive of troubled reflection, common enough in all intelligent girls who live in touch
with the wider world. Men puzzled her, and Irene did not like
to be puzzled. As free from unwholesome inquisitiveness as a
girl can possibly be, she often wished to know, once and for
all, whatever was to be learnt about the concealed life of men;
to know it and to have done with it; to settle her mind on that
point, as on any other that affected the life of a reasonable being.
Yet she shrank from all such enquiry, with a sense of womanly
pride, doing her best to believe that there *was* no concealment
in the case of any man with whom she could have friendly
relations.

The subject is picked up again by Eustace, Irene's brother, in
discussing her engagement to Arnold Jacks—a cold-blooded
politician of the Dalmaine, Lashmar variety:

"Girls haven't quite a fair chance, you know. They can't
see much of men."

"If it comes to that," said Irene merrily, "men seem to me in much the same position."

"Oh, it's so different. Girls—women—are good. There's nothing unpleasant to be known about them."

Eustace approves of Arnold Jacks: his remarks should not be read as a warning about that person, but rather as an allusion to a theme which was clearly running through Gissing's consciousness. He was writing this novel in 1898, when he had separated from Edith and was living virtually in hiding at Dorking while corresponding in the warmest tones with Gabrielle Fleury. It may be worth noting here—though I shall return to the subject in the next chapter—that, despite his apparent desire to persuade both Gabrielle and himself that she was the love of his life, the one true relationship, he did not by any means tell her everything about himself. There is in fact no evidence that Gabrielle ever knew about Nell at all during Gissing's lifetime.

One may, of course, feel that the 'concealed life', as typified by an association with someone like Nell, was by no means peculiar to Gissing himself but was a characteristic of middle-class Victorian males in general. It is a truism of social history that the extensive Victorian Underworld was largely created by the existence of the Victorian idyll of family life centred on the irreproachable wife: had well-brought-up Victorian girls been more approachable, the Nells of society would have been less necessary. Certainly Gissing's books display a worldly awareness of this in addition to his more personal concern with the subject. To some extent, men of his generation were forced to compartmentalize their lives and keep certain areas of them secret, unless they wished to live like curates—and significantly, the curate was the traditional butt of the *Punch* jokes of the period, a wet and sexless creature something less than a proper man. The Victorian doublethink deplored any specific peccadilloes on the part of a young man, yet implicitly countenanced *in general* the concept of the double standard. As Rhoda Nunn says in *The Odd Women*: 'What man lives in celibacy? Consider that unmentionable fact.' In the same book Everard Barfoot tells an old (male) friend of his about an incident in his own past, something he regrets but refuses to feel guilty about. Here is the authentic

note of male conversation, allusive yet frank, something far more
often found in letters of the period than in novels. Amy Drake
is a shopgirl who has been befriended, with high-minded intentions, by the Goodall family:

'It happened that by that very train which took me back to
London, when my visit was over, this girl also travelled, and
alone. I saw her at Upchurch Station, but we didn't speak, and
I got into a smoking carriage. We had to change at Oxford, and
there, as I walked about the platform, Amy put herself in my
way, so that I was obliged to begin talking with her. This
behaviour rather surprised me. I wondered what Mrs Goodall
would think of it. But perhaps it was a sign of innocent freedom
in the intercourse of men and women. At all events, Amy managed to get me into the same carriage with herself, and on the
way to London we were alone. You foresee the end of it. At
Paddington Station the girl and I went off together, and she
didn't get to her sister's till the evening.'

The Odd Women is one of the novels in which Gissing's own
obsessions interfere least with the full play of his intelligence and
his capacity for observation, and Everard Barfoot is one of the
fairest portraits we have of the ordinary man, neither monster
nor angel. (Another is Cyril in *The Whirlpool* who, like Barfoot,
got into a 'scrape' with a girl when young and pays an exaggerated
price for it.) Years before, in *Workers in the Dawn*, he had drawn
a picture of a man with a past in much less favourable terms.
Waghorn, the railway director who marries Maud Gresham
(and who later in the story is to foreclose on his late partner's
loan to Mr Tollady) is presented from his first appearance in
a far more sinister light: 'The countenance excited in him [Arthur
Golding] feelings of intense repulsion, though he had no idea
why. He felt instinctively that beneath that smooth outside of
immaculate respectability lay hidden secret depths of foulness
and all impurity.'

Those are strong words, suggesting more than is actually made
explicit in the book—though we learn that Waghorn is a crony
of Augustus Whiffle, the immoral ordinand who has seduced
Carrie, and ultimately we see him as a brutal husband too (though,
to be fair, Maud fires miniature pistols at him, a degree of pro-
vocation even for a milder man). His murky business enterprises
also fail. Clearly there was a strong association in Gissing's mind,

possibly a well-founded one, between turpitude in the public sphere and in the private one: at least once (in *Demos*) this association is spelt out: 'A suggestion that domestic perfidy was in the end incompatible with public zeal would have seemed to him [Richard Mutimer] ridiculous.' In the same book, Rodman, the con-man and false democrat who takes in Mutimer among others, and marries Mutimer's sister Alice, is ultimately shown as committing matrimonial offences as well as legal ones. He is physically violent, verbally sadistic, philanders with other women —and is in fact a bigamist. Another unfaithful and generally bad husband, Reuben Elgar in *The Emancipated* (1890), causes his wife, Cecily, first to grieve and then to revolt against the whole concept of the double standard: 'She asked no liberty to be vile, as her husband made himself; but that she was denied an equal freedom to exercise her powers to enrich her life with experiences of joy, this fired her to revolt . . .'

Man as 'vile', as 'foul' and with a 'concealed' life, or at the very least with (like Kirkwood in *The Nether World*) memories of 'passions from which he had suffering years ago . . . affecting him with a sense of unworthiness, almost of impurity'—such references, multiplied over Gissing's novels, suggest at any rate a degree of specifically sexual neurosis on the subject. The sexual puritanism and hence shame of even a profligate Victorian is a by-word, and Gissing, despite some brave theorizing about free unions, noble prostitutes and the like, does not seem to have been immune from the national epidemic of sexual guilt. Possibly he did show signs of a genuinely original, unconventional approach to the matter in wanting to marry Nell—though such an act seems more guilt-denying than guilt-free: a truly amoral, unworried spirit would not have felt any need to justify his passion by giving it the name of 'love'. But in any case the awful results of his passion for Nell were enough to implant sexual guilt even in a much more robust personality than Gissing's. Once planted, this guilt of the flesh was undoubtedly fed by Nell's sluttish habits, which became more and more pronounced on every level. Morley Roberts describes his first visit to their rooms: 'The front room in which he received me was both mean and dirty . . . There were signs in it that it had been occupied by a woman, and one without the common elements of decency and cleanness. Under a miserable and broken sofa lay a pair of dirty feminine boots.' Meanwhile, the wife lay drunk in the back room, arguing with the servant, and every so often rapping on the wall to summon her husband to her. A similar scene indeed takes place in *The Unclassed*. Add this to the fact that, while Gissing and Nell were living together, he had every reason to suppose that she was associating with other men, and it is hardly to be wondered that, in spite of all his high hopes and his flaunting of conventional prejudice, he came to see Nell as simply contaminating. A number of years later, in *Thyrza*, he lends this attitude to the widower, Bunce: 'To a man of any native delicacy, the memory of bondage to a hateful woman clings like a long disease which impoverishes the blood.'

The metaphor pulls one up short: another, still more specific possibility becomes apparent. Could Gissing have believed that Nell had infected him permanently with a sexually transmitted disease? And could this, in fact, have been true?

It is impossible to be sure about this. Certainly syphilis was a scourge in the nineteenth century, and doubtless many of the Victorian moralist references to prostitution as 'the hidden evil in our midst' carried overtones, to the informed mind, of a physical evil as well as a spiritual one. Indeed it has been suggested that the prevalence of venereal disease was one of the underlying reasons for the Victorian phobia about sex. The proliferation of world trade, and the greatly increased speed, as the century drew on, in the rate at which ships could move from one part of the world to another, provided opportunities for the spread of infection from one Continent to another far surpassing those of previous centuries. Then, in England itself, the vast new urban complexes which had sprung up in the wake of the industrial revolution acted as permanent nurturing grounds for infection: it was not just typhoid and cholera which flourished in London's overcrowded alleys and lodging houses. There were as yet no very certain cures for syphilis and other venereal infections, and there was a conspiracy of silence on the matter, at least as far as literature went. Ibsen's preoccupation with the subject—see *Ghosts*, and also *The Doll's House*—was the reason that in England this author rapidly got the reputation of being scandalous, though this fact in itself could not be made clear. Nevertheless one cannot doubt that, among men on their own, the subject was discussed—indeed Black's letters to Gissing when they were both at Manchester prove that it was. Black wrote,[10] without preamble:

The irritation continued growing worse, and on examination I found the prepuce swollen, and on turning it down, I found the whole of the inside salmon-coloured, as you called it, only little spots as though the skin had been eaten away so as to show the flesh and it almost looked as though it was bleeding. I applied a little of the subtilissimus, but the end continues to be irritated. The prepuce is a little hard as well; and there was a drop or two of yellow matter near the red spots.

I don't know what an ulcer should look like. Are these anything like the symptoms of soft chancre? Or is it like your inflammation? Or do you think it is only balanitis?

Please answer by return—I hope this will find you—and excuse me thrusting this frightful communication on you in a time of felicity. But answer instanter, for I tremblingly await my doom!

Give me Waltuch's private address.

Yours, non hilariter
J.G.B.

Quoth the raven, 'Never more'.

Should the subtilissimus go a bright green after being applied?

This disarmingly graphic communication speaks for itself.

Nine years later, writing to Algernon in May 1885[11] from his flat in Cornwall Mansions, Baker Street, which was his headquarters for several years between his two marriages, Gissing said: 'By the bye, I pursue investigations on the basis of Milton's Hygiene. Cold water I have entirely abandoned, and with astonishing results.' It is impossible to tell exactly what this refers to but, in the light of the evidence from the Manchester years, it is rather suggestive. In addition, the rest of the letter has been cut away in an odd shape, as if to censure some further remark on the same subject. Presumably this deletion is the later work of a member of the Gissing family.

There are several other pointers. Nell's 'scrofula' and skin disease have already been referred to. In October 1880, when he and Nell were living together, Gissing wrote to Algernon[12] that the doctor had said—'she was afflicted when quite a child with a form of scrofula, and that it still clings in her system'. 'Scrofula' was then an imprecise term used to cover a variety of things, many of which we should now diagnose rather as dermatitis. But the reference to Nell's 'affliction' 'clinging in her system' since childhood is also vaguely suggestive.

What can be said unequivocally is that, whether or not Nell was infected with syphilis or any other venereal disease when she and Gissing were actually living together, she was when she died and had been at an earlier date also. Morley Roberts ends the section on her death with a reference which, to those accustomed to the euphemisms of the period, admits only one interpretation:

We arranged the funeral together, and she was buried. If only all the misery that she had caused him could have been buried with her, it would have been well. She died of what I may call, euphemistically, specific laryngitis. Once he told me a dreadful story about her in hospital. One of the doctors at St Thomas's had questioned her, and after her answers sent for Maitland [Gissing], and speaking to him on the information given him by the wife, was very bitter. Henry [Gissing], even as he told me of this years after, shook with rage and indignation. He had not been able to defend himself without exposing his wife's career.

Again, many years later in 1901, when Gissing had settled with Gabrielle Fleury at St Jean de Luz, in the extreme south-west of France, the place where he was eventually to be buried, he wrote to his old friend Hick[13] (that same Hick who had known him in childhood and had later become a doctor), that after suffering for two years from a 'patch' on the forehead he had finally cured it with Iodide of Potassium. He added jovially: 'I am thinking of substituting I of P for coffee at breakfast and wine at the other meals. I am also meditating a poem in its praise.'

In the typewritten copy of these letters which is held in the British Museum, Henry Hick has added a note: 'I wrote suggesting that much he said about Potass Iod would lead the half-educated to diagnose syphilis.

'At no time when I saw George Gissing did he show signs of any specific disease.'

The very fact that Hick felt it necessary to state that point categorically suggests that some hint that Gissing was syphilitic had become part of the myth that gradually accrued round his name, particularly after the publication (1912) of Morley Roberts' book and, in the same year, of Swinnerton's uncomplimentary critical biography.[14] This is a curious work for, though Swinnerton actually said a number of complimentary things about Gissing's books, the overall impression is that he disliked and despised his subject—which was certainly not the case with Morley Roberts. Apparently the idea that Gissing *was* syphilitic was held by Swinnerton—he stated the fact, not in that book, but in another, *Background with Chorus*, written in 1956.

In the last analysis, whether Gissing did or did not harbour any such infection is probably less important than his personal belief that he might do so. It is possible that towards the end of his life, when consulting Hick and other doctors about the lung condition that finally killed him, he managed to voice half-buried fears on this other subject and that Hick or another was able to reassure him. It may even have been such reassurance which enabled him, in 1898, to form his relationship with Gabrielle Fleury and to write *The Crown of Life* which ends happily with Otway marrying a lady—the thing which Gissing himself had felt mysteriously unable to do. Clearly *some* sort of mental liberation occurred at that point in time since, on the rational level, the timing of Gissing's decision that he was, after all, fit to 'make love' (in the phrase of the period) to a well-born woman, makes no more sense than his earlier refusal to believe the thing was possible. The excuse he always gave for his marriage to Edith Underwood, and for all the similarly ill-advised marriages between social inequals that spot his books, was lack of an adequate income. But nothing in his situation in 1898 could have led him to believe that his problems in this direction were about to be solved; true, he was now experiencing a modicum of professional success but he complained how little this was reflected in monetary terms, and by then his commitments—eldest son lodging at Wakefield, younger son and Edith to be kept in lodgings elsewhere—were greater than ever. If he now at last felt free to form an association with the cultured, hyper-sensitive Gabrielle—assuming that they did actually enjoy the intimacies of marriage, which has not actually been proved beyond doubt either—that sense of freedom must have come from other reassurances than financial ones.

Was it a half-acknowledged fear of carrying some lasting 'taint', from Nell, the deepest secret of all then—that frustration that was 'something more (and less visible) than money'?[15] He ascribed this mysterious and illogical sense of unworthiness to a number of his heroes—illogical, because elsewhere, as I have said, he depicted men like Jasper Milvain, Dyce Lashmar and Godwin Peak trying to 'marry well' precisely *because* they are penniless and therefore disinterested romantic passion is something they cannot afford. Indeed in Godwin Peak one finds the two things, the sense of unworthiness to approach a lady and the determination to do just that, bizarrely combined. I shall discuss further this matter of Gissing's objective perceptions being at variance with his deepest emotional prejudices in the next chapter.

As a general conclusion, one might say that even the faintest *suspicion* on Gissing's part that, by associating with Nell, he had rendered himself undesirable as a mate for a 'nice' woman, would have been enough to reinforce the overall social insecurity and more realistic anxieties about the practical aspects of marriage which troubled him in any case. Wells, who knew nothing precise at first about Gissing's early experiences, readily perceived soon after meeting him that he was neurotic on this point, but ascribed this to his lower-middle-class upbringing—which was doubtless a factor also:

His home training had made him repressive to the explosive pitch; he felt that to make love to any woman he could regard as a social equal would be too elaborate, restrained and tedious for his urgencies, he could not answer questions he supposed he would be asked about his health and means, and so, for the second time, he flung himself at a social inferior whom he expected to be easy and grateful.

Expanding on the theme of Gissing's tendency to compartmentalize his life, keeping one friend apart from another, Wells continued:

He kept his own family also, the custodians of those strangling early standards, out of our way, just as he kept his wife out of our way. He was terrified at the prospect of incompatibility. His sensitiveness to reactions made every relationship a pose, and he had no natural, customary *persona* for miscellaneous use.

Although I think myself that Wells (himself the determinedly profligate son of lower-middle-class parents) exaggerated the 'strangling' effect of Gissing's upbringing, I believe that he did

here hit on an important truth about his friend: Gissing's social
chameleonism, and his accompanying need to keep each different
relationship in his life to some extent a 'secret' from others. His
secrecy about his marriage with Nell, his semi-secrecy (to his
acquaintances) about his marriage with Edith, and eventually his
secret union with Gabrielle, may all have been rational in context,
but they typified a tendency in him which had deep emotional
roots.[16] Whatever genuine or fancied guilty secrets he did harbour, there also seems to have been an overall and irrational fear
of being unmasked—or just of being found with the wrong
mask in the wrong place.

To some extent, this insecurity is a concomitant of the writer's
situation. In the last analysis, the novelist is a charlatan, an actor.
He puts on masks, he thinks himself into the skin of this or that
character whose experiences do not coincide with his own; he
invents situations which make use of the circumstances of his
own life but in a disguised and transposed form—he lives with
creations which his readers, if he is any good, accept as real but
which he knows to be mere fabrications of his own brain. In
addition, he is called an Author and a 'professional', words which
imply an official identity, yet in his own experience he is just a
man sitting alone in a room. The way he spends his time is
essentially secret, in that most people do not know how novel-
writing happens, and many of them have ideas on the matter
quite as silly as those of Amy Reardon's family in *New Grub
Street*, who can't think why Reardon doesn't 'try harder'. Writing
is a confidence trick. This is the simple, but extremely fundamental, 'guilty secret' that Gissing and Reardon share; a crippling
sense of the fragility of their own identity. It is this perception
that makes *New Grub Street* (1891) not just the key book of
Gissing's entire work, but a key-book in the development of the
novel away from the Dickensian theme of individual versus circumstances and towards the twentieth-century image of the
individual grappling with himself.

4   The Woman-Question

The Fatal Pattern

When one thinks of Gissing, one thinks of women; one cannot write for long on any of the dominant themes in his life without finding the theme exemplified or paralleled in his emotional and sexual relationships. It has been said that English fiction is mostly about Sex or Class, but in Gissing's case it is impossible to separate these two things from one another. His attitudes to the opposite sex were imbued through and through with an awareness of class, whether he showed his heroes reaching up in vain towards ladies or stretching downwards to lift the humble or the fallen. In the same way, his attitudes to class were permeated with sexual awareness, so that the class struggle, depicted in books like *A Life's Morning*, *Demos* or *Thyrza* becomes a sexual conflict, and class-prejudice is inextricably mixed with sexual aversion (*In the Year of Jubilee*). Paradoxically, this man who tried so hard at times to keep different bits of his life separate from each other, and different personalities among his circle unknown to one another, seems to have had the greatest difficulty in compartmentalizing within his own mind.

I have already said that, in my view, he displayed a rather feminine inability to separate sex from love; another way of putting this would be that he seems to have lacked the typically masculine ability to have an affair 'on the side' which does not influence the main stream of life or express the nature of that life. When, being a man with normal masculine needs, he found himself involved in a classically 'on the side' affair (with Nell) which certainly should have been allowed to remain there, he hastened to incorporate it centrally into his life—indeed, to sacrifice the rest of life to it. Years later, with the pertinacity of a lemming apparently bent on its own destruction, he did very much the same thing with Edith Underwood. Edith was more respectable than Nell (which was not difficult) but, since Gissing and she apparently picked each other up on the street or in a teashop their relationship hardly started out on a very exalted plane: no one, including Edith herself, can have supposed it to be the sort of encounter likely to lead to marriage. Yet Gissing forced it into this pattern: moreover it was as if he had elevated this obscure emotional need in himself into a principle. Morley Roberts tells a revealing story about a time when another acquaintance of theirs was living with a girl he had met in a pub and Gissing believed that he—Roberts—had given this man cause for jealousy: 'Without asking my view of the affair he wrote to me angrily, and declared that I had behaved badly—He added that he wished me to understand that he considered an affair of that description as sacred as any marriage.'

It is clear from this that the usual explanation given for Gissing's disastrous second marriage—the pressures of sexual desire—just will not do. Obviously this must have been a factor in it, and certain abrupt references in Gissing's diary (e.g. 'Feel like a madman at times. I know that I shall never do any more good work until I am married'*) may be read in this light. But sexual desire in itself could have been eased just by Edith visiting his flat (which, against all social canons of the period, she apparently did quite willingly) or by a series of Ediths. Most witnesses agree that women found Gissing attractive. Alternatively, if it was truly marriage that Gissing felt he needed, why the extraordinary choice of person? There were other more suitable women to whom he had been drawn, including a couple of literary ladies (the Miss Sichels) and an acquaintance of his sisters whom he had met in Wakefield a few months before and briefly declared himself 'in love' with (to his sisters and his diary). There had also apparently been a bizarre suggestion on Morley Roberts' part that he—Roberts—should introduce Gissing to a couple of well-educated girls with the intention of match-making openly expressed to all parties. But by this time Gissing had made such overtures to Edith Underwood that he considered himself bound by them. It is apropos of this that Roberts remarked: '. . . like all weak people, he was peculiarly obstinate, and nothing that could be urged had the least effect on him. I have often thought it was

* Written in September 1890 about a week before finding Edith.

his one great failure in rectitude which occurred at Moorhampton that made him infinitely tenacious of doing nothing which might seem in any way dishonourable, however remotely.' But Roberts was still baffled as to what special attraction Edith Underwood could *ever* have held for him:

'My first impression of the girl was more unfavourable than I had expected. She was the daughter of a small tradesman but little removed from an artisan, and she looked it.'[1] (Actually Mr Underwood, over-romantically described by Gissing in letters to his family as a 'working sculptor' seems to have been a monumental mason, a flourishing and commonplace trade in the late Victorian era.)

I disliked the young woman at first sight, and never got over my early impression. From the very beginning it seemed impossible that she could ever become in any remote degree what he might justifiably have asked for in a wife. Yet she was not wholly disagreeable in appearance. She was of medium height and somewhat dark. She had not, however, the least pretence to such beauty as one might hope to find even in a slave of the kitchen. She possessed neither face nor figure, nor a sweet voice, nor any charm—she was just a female. And this was she that the most fastidious man I knew was about to marry.

Ideas on what Gissing 'saw' in Edith to make him go through with a marriage which, even at the time, was clearly against his better judgement (his diary makes this plain) must forever remain on a conjectural level. One might speculate on a strong, initial, sexual tie—indeed, this may have operated between them for a number of years, for even when the relationship was patently in ruins, in 1896, a second child was born to them. One might also suggest that, though Edith at first appeared to Gissing as very 'docile', he had even then at a sub-conscious level perceived in her the neurotic unbalance which was later to become so alarmingly obvious, and that this in a curious way had an attraction for him. It is observable in life that the neurotic call to the neurotic; it is as if each senses, without realizing it, that they inhabit the same world of loaded images: their mutual isolation from the commonplace habitat of the amiably placid seems to them like a precious intimacy. Perhaps it was precisely because Edith Underwood was evidently *not* 'just a female', but a highly unstable person with her own secret problems, that Gissing felt, in a limited way, at home with her.

Moreover there is a consistent pattern here. Anyone may marry one highly neurotic woman by accident, so to speak, but to embark on something like a marriage with three argues a particular emotional taste. We have already seen that Nell was extremely neurotic: she was not the coarsely robust girl of the streets, she was disturbed, tearful and 'ill' even when Gissing first met her. Edith, though superficially calm—indeed, ominously quiet—seems to have come from a somewhat odd family: the first several occasions on which Gissing visited her home in Camden Town he met no one but her, though other members of the family including a sister were in the small house at the time. These were not the typical respectable-tradesman manners of the period; nor, come to that, was Edith's willingness to be picked up and her subsequent visits alone to Gissing's flat: indeed one might justifiably regard the whole nature of her relationship with him as evidence of her own oddity and social isolation—as well as his own. (Gissing later made use of this very circumstance, in a transposed form, in *The Odd Women*, to hint cleverly at the innate oddity of Widdowson long beore the full extent of his inadequacy becomes explicit: though gentlemanly, he picks up Monica Madden in the park, a circumstance which should have warned Monica—and the reader—that there is something not-quite-right about him.) When, in wretched marriage, Gissing had come to understand at a conscious level the extent of Edith's insecurity, as manifest in her incompetence, her grumbling, her violence and her obsessional jealousy, he commented bitterly on the fact that she had never once received a letter—that, in fact, she was totally friendless even at her own social and intellectual level. Evidently the significance of this had not earlier struck him—if indeed, in his own self-absorption, he had noticed it at all. One might fairly say that, in several respects, Edith seems to have displayed in herself Gissing's own worst features, without having any of his better ones as compensation.

The form Edith's neurosis ultimately took is not, now, entirely clear: the references of the period to 'insanity' (leading to an asylum in 1902) and a final death from 'organic brain disease' in 1917, do not commend themselves to present-day attitudes to-

F

wards mental health.[2] It seems rather significant that Gissing
made the same sort of charges against Nell, and even arranged at
a period for her to be looked after, just as he did for Edith.
Are we to believe that Gissing managed to marry two women,
both of whom 'went mad' while living with him, and that this
was a total coincidence? 'Mad' is a somewhat meaningless term;
one would like more evidence on Edith's insanity (at least one
short letter, written from the asylum in 1910, reads quite sanely,
if sadly); one may doubt whether a present-day Edith, even
without modern drug-therapy, would find herself in an asylum
at all. She lost both children permanently, first one then the
other; modern sympathies would tend to say that she was made
to pay a terrible price for her unbalanced behaviour and indeed
was possibly victimized and subjected to degradation in a way
she would not have been had she come from a more influential
family. But, in fairness to those responsible, one should say
that she ended by antagonizing everyone, not just her hyper-
sensitive husband, that she uttered paranoid threats against those
who attempted (perhaps rather patronizingly) to help her—and
that she was eventually taken into police custody for, among
other things, systematically ill-treating her younger son Alfred.*

The real 'truth' about Edith Underwood is probably now irre-
coverable. Those interested view her only with hindsight; she
has no one to speak for her; our view of her is contaminated by
the obsessional loathing with which her husband eventually came
to regard her. Yet one must recognize that all viewpoints are
relative. There *were* moments, at the beginning, however brief
and misguided, when she appeared to Gissing in quite another
light: 'Saturday, 28 September. Fine, hot. In afternoon with Edith
to Richmond; thence walked to Kew, and had tea there. Back
by bus. Exquisite sunset beyond the river from Kew Bridge,
rich dusky scarlet and no clouds. Opposite, the rising of a full,
red moon, a wonderful sight. When we got back, Edith came
to sit with me here for an hour.' This is the archetypal, simple,
lovers' outing—the genteel excursion, the poetry of a sunset, a
quiet intimacy. A month or so later he was writing 'Edith
came at 4 o'clock. Read to her "The May Queen" and "Pied
Piper of Hamelin".'[3] Here, at least, was one of those 'hours
wrested from fate', 'the moment worth living for' never mind

* See Chapter 6.

what would come after, the instant when to love (and read aloud) was everything, and objective assessments did not count.

Posterity has cast Edith in the role of evil genie while it has turned Gabrielle Fleury, whom Gissing met in 1898[4] shortly after tearing himself away from Edith and the younger child who remained with her, as the Good Fairy, the love of his life, the 'woman to go through fire for' (Gissing's words, to Roberts). Personally, I think that a degree of distorting hindsight is in operation here, too, though in this case the distortion is benign. Because Gissing had only a truncated period with Gabrielle, and because he himself was so determined from the outset that this was to be the great love-experience of his life, his 'crown of life', the strains that are all-too-apparent in the plentiful letters that have survived have never been realistically analysed.

The fact that Gissing was unhappy living with Edith in a drab little house in Worple Road, Epsom, and that he complained of domestic chaos there and of inadequate food, has been adduced as evidence against Edith. Much less has been made of the fact that he expressed himself almost as forcibly on occasions about the discomforts of life in the Parisian flat where he went to live with Gabrielle Fleury and her mother in 1899. ('A flat, as you know, is not a human abode, and with difficulty we lodge ourselves here.'[5] 'Gabrielle is in poor health, and likely to be so, owing to the ceaseless work and agitation caused by her mother's illness. Never a day, nay not an hour, of tranquillity.'[6]) The fact that he came to revolt against the food served in the Fleury ménage is well known. As I have said in Chapter 3, I am inclined to regard this complaint as a generalized expression of homesickness rather than a realistic viewpoint. True that a French diet is very different from an English one even today, and certainly was even more different from the stodgy, meat-and-pudding-laden fare usual for the British middle classes of the Victorian period. But Gissing himself was used to French food, and had in the past been enthusiastic about it: in view of the Gallic national preoccupation with eating it seems unlikely that the Fleury ladies' housekeeping, even if limited by economy and adapted to the delicate feminine stomach, was really so inadequate. (Gabrielle herself always furiously denied that it was.) In any case is one really expected to believe that a man in his forties, however polite and considerate, should really be incapable of saying to the woman he claims to love better than anyone else in the world: 'My dear, dinner has left me still feeling a little hungry: could we not keep a good supply of cheese in the house?'

The proposition is ludicrous on any reasonable level. Yet such was the state of traditional and deeply rooted hostility between England and France at that period that Gissing, when he came to England on a visit in 1901, had no difficulty in finding an English doctor to sustain his ominous neurosis on the subject. The Wellses also supported England rather than France in this misplaced wrangle; it was from their house that he wrote to Clara Collet in the June: 'I saw Pye-Smith, and his opinion was—the French diet thro' the summer means death next winter . . . I was simply—so Pye-Smith says—*starved* in Paris, and largely owing to the fact that not Gabrielle but her mother rules the house, in the maddening Gallic way.' Gabrielle had gone back to Paris to wait on ailing *maman* (who incidentally survived for another decade): she had expected Gissing to follow her but he did not; instead, encouraged by the Wellses, he settled in a sanatorium in England for the summer. Gissing entreated Clara Collet to write 'words of encouragement' to Gabrielle to pacify her lively resentment and distress at this situation—Clara Collet, who only three years before, he had asked to mediate in the same way between himself and Edith.

The point does not need labouring: clearly there was a pattern here that transcended personalities and details of circumstance—a pattern in which Gissing had a deep-seated need to kick against cramping domestic circumstances into which he himself had entered and to escape, physically, to some other habitat. Miss Collet herself seems to have been aware of this for she evidently surmised that all was not well between Gissing and Gabrielle. To this letter Gissing hastily replied: 'Between G. and me there is no shadow of difficulty, but the mother-in-law question has become very acute . . . Don't picture domestic rows. Everything has been under the surface, but it is just this suppressed irritation which has so exhausted me.'[7]

In Epsom with Edith it had been the open quarrelling which had distressed Gissing, now, in the 'perfect intellectual companionship' of the Fleury ménage, it was the opposite. Gissing was evidently heavily committed to the idea that everything must be perfect for ever between himself and Gabrielle, and this was having its own predictable results. Gabrielle, who could be almost morbidly perceptive about Gissing on occasions, despite her overall tendency to self-dramatizing sentimentality, possibly glimpsed the fatal pattern for herself; certainly her protests, to the Wellses, about Gissing's stay in England, which she perceived as a desertion of herself, had a frantic note—unjustified by the immediate circumstances but perhaps justified in terms of Gissing's long-term instability. Possibly she saw, without properly admitting the facts to herself, the constitutional flaws in Gissing's relationship with her, possibly she was at some level aware of the artificiality, the sentimentality, the degree of sheer posing in many of Gissing's love letters to her.

To sneer at a man's love-letters may seem unpleasant and uncalled-for: at times most of us sound maudlin, whimsical or less than entirely honest. But, this said, it is only fair to comment that Gissing's letters to Gabrielle[8] do not strike one, on the whole, as the letters of one adult in loving accord with another. There is a forced note about them: Gissing seems far keener on presenting himself, in a more or less favourable or at any rate romantic light, than on really being frank with his beloved. Naturally most of the letters date from the early days when they were not actually living together, but the impression is not so much of a man profoundly in love with a true mate, but of a man determined to be 'in love' and determined that both the emotion and the object of it must be exceptional in every way. 'Darling,' he wrote. '*I hope to know you as perfectly as one human being was ever known to another. I hope to make myself understood by you in the fullest sense possible to human nature.*'[9] Even supposing this questionable ambition to be a laudable one, it is not one to be achieved by a statement of intention. And the spectacle of this pair working each other up thus at long-distance into a state of ecstatic agitation over a trifling misunderstanding[10] does not, as one reads, seem to augur well for their future union. Gissing died at the end of 1903 after less than four years' cohabitation with Gabrielle, and that interrupted. I am by no means convinced that, had he lived on, their self-consciously beautiful relationship would not have floundered almost as badly as his previous ones did—if less dramatically and obviously.

Choice of woman is also, of course, relevant. While one could

not possibly pretend that cultured, refined, amiable, French
Gabrielle bore any obvious resemblance either to a Manchester
prostitute or to the taciturn daughter of a London tombstone
maker, I suggest that she was not the utterly different type that
Morley Roberts and others have made her out to be. The voluminous letters from her which have survived, mainly letters to the
Wellses,[11] the Robertses,[12] and to Clara Collet, show her to have
been difficult on occasion—to put it mildly. Roberts' picture of
her was evidently romanticized—perhaps deliberately and mercifully, since of course she was still living when he wrote his book,
and she had become in her loneliness hyper-sensitive concerning
any reference to herself and Gissing. At any rate it provoked
Wells into writing to him: 'Your estimate of Gabrielle is ridiculous. She was a tiresome, weak, sentimental middle-class French
woman who wrote her letters on thin paper.' One may feel
inclined to dismiss such a condemnation as a mere example of
flippancy, spite and Francophobia. However his more considered
judgement of her, in *Experiment in Autobiography*[13] gives rather
the same picture: 'She was a woman of the intellectual bour-
geoisie, with neat black hair and a trim black dress, her voice
was carefully musical, she was well-read, slightly voluble and
over-explicit by our English standards, and consciously refined
and intelligent.'

One might also add that when she met Gissing she was almost
thirty, had little money of her own and few prospects. Her father
died shortly after she met Gissing. Essentially she and her mother
fell into the category of the impoverished-genteel Gissing knew
well from his own background—though, as they tended to make
rather a lot of their vaguely aristocratic connections, it is probable that he himself did not ever realize the extent to which he
had merely exchanged one cramped lower-middle-class setting
for another, in another country, with different dishes served at
table. Foreign social nuances are notoriously difficult to perceive
accurately. It would probably be true to say that he was as
romantically captivated by the idea of a 'free union' with an
'intellectual', cosmopolitan woman who spoke several languages,
as she was by the idea of becoming the more-than-mistress of a
'great writer'.

Someone[14] who knew her when she was an old lady has told me
that, in his view, though she was not truly intellectual, she made

a good companion for an intellectual man by virtue of her enthusiasm and her capacity for interesting herself in a wide range
of things. This is no doubt a fair assessment. But many other
characteristics are all too evident in her letters—self-absorption,
morbid sensitivity, lack of common sense, a tendency to depression, hypochondria, emotional demandingness, what Wells (who
eventually refused to answer any more of her interminable
screeds) called 'the peculiar Latin capacity for making copious
infusions of simple situations'. None of these traits would have
been at all helpful to Gissing: for one thing they were all failings
he himself shared.

Once again, the neurotic was being attracted to the neurotic,
albeit in a different version. And, once again, his choice had
fallen on a woman who was to some extent 'forbidden' and therefore must be kept in semi-secrecy. She did not have the total unsuitability of a Nell; she did not have the intellectual and social
unsuitability of an Edith. But, in that he was unable to marry
her, and in that her own practical and emotional limitations
demanded both that she remain in France and that she *appear* to
be married to him, a situation was once again created of bluff,
subterfuge, compartmentalization and a degree of social isolation. Once again, as on the marriages to Nell and Edith, many
social relationships were arbitrarily severed; once again Gissing
seems to have fallen into the trap of imagining that a marriage (or
marriage-situation) is somehow a self-sufficient, essentially private
state which can dispense with the support of society. It was not,
as Wells and others supposed, that he could not 'make love' to
a lady: Gabrielle was the very essence of ladylikeness, and, rather
significantly, shortly before meeting her Gissing had been making
love to another unmistakable lady whom he met at Dorking—a
Mrs Williams;[15] clearly he was on the look out for the love-of-his-
life even before she arrived. No—it seems rather as if he could
not make any sustained approach to *an ordinary person*, taking
'ordinary' to mean the sort of person he might most normally
and suitably have approached, a middle-class English girl of some
education if small means: one of that multitude of 'odd women'
of the late Victorian era of whom he himself wrote so sensibly
and knowledgeably. On this as on other topics, there was a
message for him in his own writings. But he apparently could
not read it.

The Real Situation

The principal novel in which Gissing displayed his intellectual
awareness of what his era called 'the Woman Question' was *The
Odd Women*, published in 1893. This book, together with *New
Grub Street*, published two years earlier, are widely regarded as
his finest works. (Between them came *Denzil Quarrier* and *Born
in Exile*.) To me, they are superb books, which merit reading
and re-reading: if he had written nothing else they would still
assure him a permanent place in literary history. Indeed, his
reputation might have been better had he *not* written some of
his less good works—a circumstance of which he himself was
uneasily aware. One reason that I have, till this point, quoted
less from these two books than from many of the others is that,
being complete and successful in themselves, they do not seem to
demand explanation and dissection in the same way. Although,
when one comes to analyse them, long-term themes and obsessions of the writer once again become apparent, they are not
obtrusively and inappropriately so: art triumphs, the writer's
personal perceptions do not dominate or distort the work but are
made use of in the proper sense of the phrase. Both novels are,
to be sure, saturated with Gissing-concepts and the Gissing
world-view, but the result is what—to pursue the metaphor—is
called in chemistry a 'saturate solution', that is, the personal is
fully dissolved in the chemical liquid of creative fiction.

This is particularly remarkable when you consider that *New
Grub Street* was written—very quickly, after numerous false
starts—just as Gissing was painfully deciding to marry Edith;
and that *The Odd Women* was 'scribbled' in seven weeks (Gissing had no reason to lie about this in his own diary) during the
year when he had become a father for the first time. The house
was in dismal turmoil; the baby cried; Edith—or Gissing—or
both—had quarrelled with the nurse, and Gissing found himself
having to stop work to prepare the baby's bottles. By all the
laws of common sense—laws to which Gissing himself subscribed,
believing passionately in his own need for 'peace'—neither period
should have been at all propitious for the production of literature.
Yet the fact is that it was; and, furthermore, the years Gissing
spent with Edith, years which he himself regarded as 'wretched'
even at the time and which he viewed afterwards as wholly dis-

astrous, were the period when most of his best and most enduring work was done. Once he had gone to live with Gabrielle
Fleury, the grand escape which was supposed to transform his
life so much for the better, he wrote little of comparable worth.
There may be various reasons for this—his failing health was
undoubtedly a factor—but it still seems significant. Writers themselves do not always recognize under what conditions they really
perform best; once again, what suits the man may not suit the
writer. The subtle interaction between *New Grub Street* and
what was happening in his life while he was writing it is a subject to which I shall return presently. As to *The Odd Women*, it
is a shining example of the extent to which a writer may feel
depressed and limited by his personal circumstances and yet be
capable on paper of rising to heights of disinterested lucidity and
sympathetic characterization.

That 'the Woman Question' had begun to interest Gissing intellectually was not in itself surprising.[16] With two unmarried
sisters, genteely educated but with no specific training and no
money of their own, he could hardly fail to be aware of the social
problem such women presented even had his personality not led
him to understand and sympathize. But in any case the subject
was becoming a fashionable one; the 1870s and '80s had seen a
number of advances in the field of women's education and general
emancipation: the word 'emancipation' was itself being used—
Gissing's choice of *The Emancipated* as the title for the novel
he published in 1890 probably reflects the topical appeal of the
word. In fact that novel is only partly concerned with feminine
emancipation as such, and in a not entirely convincing manner,
but it does incidentally betray a considerable understanding of
the women's position in life—the limitations and constraints imposed as much by nature as by society. It is as if Gissing was
then feeling after 'the woman problem' but had not yet got to
grips with it. He was at heart too honest, too intelligent and too
subtle to become a partisan propagandist for Women's Rights.
Nevertheless as a thinking man of the time, and one with a considerable journalistic flair which he never properly exploited, he
took an informed interest in the New Woman, that figure of
popular fancy who had her heyday in the 1890s.

There is evidence, in *The Odd Women*, of Gissing having done
solid homework on the subject. We know that he went to Ethical

Society lectures on the topic. Two of the main characters, Mary Barfoot, a good Fabian type, and Rhoda Nunn her more distinctive friend, are unmarried women between thirty and forty who have pledged themselves to help other educated women toward financial and mental independence. To this end, and with Mary's money, they have set up a training school in Great Portland Street to equip educated girls to become secretaries. Today shorthand-typing may hardly seem a pinnacle of emancipated freedom, but at the period clerking jobs were nearly always done by men and therefore for a woman to take one on was a way of showing that she was, in Mary's words, 'a rational and responsible human being'. Mary makes an excellent speech on the subject, which could have come—and possibly in essence did—from a contemporary pamphlet. As she says, the one underpaid, overcrowded 'profession' for which all half-educated gentlewomen seemed to feel that they were minimally equipped was teaching: private governessing was the one ill-chosen resort of a poverty-stricken unmarriageable legion. To underline the point, two other women in the book, the elder Madden sisters, are both struggling along unsuccessfully and unhappily in this way. Rhoda Nunn suggests to them that they should at least try to organize themselves better and, instead of hoarding their tiny capital, use it to found a proper school, but it remains doubtful if they ever manage to follow this advice: Rhoda herself, for all her rather dictatorial enthusiasm, perceives their basic incapacity—'Impossible perhaps, she thought, to inspire these worn and discouraged women with a particle of her own enterprise.'

Inevitably one suspects that Alice and Virginia Madden, with their ill-health, their combination of maddening, ladylike feebleness and stoic endurance, and their touchingly unselfish regard for each other and for their cherished younger sister Monica, must have been to some extent suggested to Gissing by his own sisters: Ellen Gissing was a governess who went in for poor health and 'nerves' for some years, and Madge, like Alice Madden and also like Myriam Baske in *The Emancipated* was solaced in her unmarried state with a rigid and old-fashionel piety. However in fairness to the Gissing sisters one should add that they *did* succeed in starting a proper school, in Wakefield, and that it flourished with apparent success for many years. So often the originals who have suggested feeble characters in novels are tougher, more successful or at any rate more complex than their apparent portraits, because the characters are not truly 'them' at all but simply specific, if recognizable aspects of them. By the same token, Gissing himself had a great deal more to him than the enfeebled and partial version of himself which is Reardon in *New Grub Street*, and yet it is inevitable that Reardon the writer has come to be regarded as a self-portrait.

It is tempting to imagine that an original for Mary Barfoot or Rhoda Nunn 'was' Clara Collet, the lively, independent woman who befriended Gissing in the 1890s and for long years after his death continued to take an interest in his sons and in Gabrielle. Miss Collet who had got herself to London University by her own efforts, had been a teacher at the North London Collegiate School and later became a Civil Servant; with her fine common sense, her outspoken views and her travels with a Baedeker, she was an archetypal New Woman. However Gissing only met Miss Collet (as he always called her) in 1893, the year after *The Odd Women* was written, so this is a false trail—or is it? One thing that his relationship with Clara Collet does seem to make clear is that he simply was not sexually attracted to her type of woman. When they first met he was living in the greatest gloom with Edith and she became one of the few friends he felt he could invite to their home. He was in his mid-thirties, she was two or three years younger and by no means bad-looking; a contemporary photograph shows a short but comely figure with a certain sedate, womanly prettiness. Her kindnesses to Gissing were numerous; although her own resources were limited she readily (and very early) offered financial help; she also offered to act as guardian to the sons should anything ever happen to their father and this offer was eventually taken up. When the inevitable marriage-break came she spent a considerable amount of time attempting, apparently in all honesty and unselfishness, to patch matters up and to persuade Edith into a more reasonable frame of mind. True, her help was probably somewhat officious (her nephew remembers that, though she was a genuinely good person, she always had to be right about everything—and the trouble was that she usually *was* right): presumably, like many altruistic people she was an egoist. (Gissing himself, as we have seen, came to recognize this as a general truth, whether or not he noticed the fact about Miss Collet herself.) But it seems not unreasonable to suppose that Clara Collet was also attracted to Gissing, and may well have nurtured secret or suppressed hopes that he might be attracted to her. Indeed, why shouldn't he have been? They had much in common intellectually; he admired her and liked her: there was no rational reason why, in 1898, it should not have been sensible, courageous modern-minded Miss Collet who took up a place at Gissing's side rather than the newcomer Gabrielle Fleury.

However there seems to have been no thought of this in Gissing's mind. Susceptible as he undoubtedly was to many women, evidently Miss Collet was too basically sensible, too matter of fact—too suitable, even—to attract him. This fact in itself throws significant light on so much in his life which otherwise does not stand up to logical scrutiny. And Miss Collet, of course, behaved admirably. After what seems, from his letters to her, to have been a brief cooling in their relationship shortly after he left Edith for good, she rallied, and loyally made a friend of Gabrielle. Indeed she was the *only* one of Gissing's friends who managed to remain in that lady's good books all through her later years of increasing touchiness.

Whoever did suggest the idea of Mary Barfoot and Rhoda Nunn to Gissing—it may have been the Sichel sisters, the two literary acquaintances whom he dropped when he met Edith, or it may have been a combination of people—it is clear at any rate that he knew, or knew of, quite enough 'odd women' to think of seeking one of them in marriage, had he only been so minded. *The Odd Women* itself provides, almost as if on purpose, a whole gallery of types whom a man like him might reasonably have wooed. They are not idealizations, like Thyrza or Emma Vine or the other dream-figures from his earlier books; they were clearly real. Many of them were, like the Madden sisters, brought up by old-fashioned parents in a bumbling, lady-like futility, with 'sordid' money cares unmentionable and marriage held out as the only suitable career. Indeed it is part of the pathos of Alice and Virginia Madden that even when time and humiliation have made them reliquish any hope of finding husbands themselves, instead of turning their energies in other and more useful directions they continue to cherish the same hopes but at one remove from themselves: they cannot marry themselves—but Monica surely will. Monica is so young and pretty that she must! They are so reduced, mentally and spiritually, that even the marriage of their young sister appears to them as a raison d'être for themselves, a type of salvation. (Which, in the end, it turns out to be, but not the way they dreamed.)

But, as Rhoda Nunn explains carefully to Monica, not all *can* hope to marry, however willing and docile they make themselves:

'. . . do you know that there are half a million more women than men in this happy country of ours?'

'Half a million!'

Her naïve alarm again excited Rhoda to laughter.

'Something like that, they say. So many *odd* women—no making a pair with them. The pessimists call them useless, lost, futile lives. I, naturally—being one of them myself—take another view. I look upon them as a great reserve. When one woman vanishes into matrimony, the reserve offers a substitute for the world's work. True, they are not all trained yet—far from it. I want to help in that—to train the reserve.'

'But married women are not idle,' protested Monica earnestly.

Rhoda is trying to give Monica a glimpse of her own ideal, but Monica is not the stuff of which independent women are made; she is one of Gissing's most attractive yet pathetic creations: 'She had no aptitude whatever for giving instruction; indeed, had no aptitude for anything but being a pretty, cheerful, engaging girl, much dependent on the love and gentleness of those about her.' With a painful combination of clear sight but a limited field of vision she sees that, whatever the Rhodas of life may choose, she *must* marry:

She thought of her sisters. Their loneliness was for life, poor things. Already they were old; and they would grow older, sadder, perpetually struggling to supplement that dividend from the precious capital—and merely that they might keep alive. Oh!—her heart ached at the misery of such a prospect. How much better if the poor girls had never been born.

Her own future was more hopeful than theirs had ever been. She knew herself good-looking. Men had followed her in the streets and tried to make her acquaintance. Some of the girls with whom she lived regarded her enviously, spitefully. But had she really the least chance of marrying a man who she could respect—not to say love?

The simple shortage of men, rich *or* poor, to marry all the surplus middle-class girls of the period is underlined in this book again and again. Widdowson, the man who Monica does in fact marry, disastrously, is told of it by his sister-in-law:

'Do you seriously tell me,' asked Widdowson, with grave curiosity, 'that there are ladies in good society who would have married me just because I have a few hundreds a year?'
'My dear boy, I would get together a round dozen in two or three days. Girls who would make good, faithful wives, in mere gratitude to the man who saved them from—horrors.'

Monica herself later points out the same thing to him when they have been visiting a match-making widow called Mrs Cosgrove:

'They never *will* marry!' said Monica to her husband, rather thoughtfully than with commiseration.
'Why not? They are nice enough girls.'
'Yes, but they have no money; and'—she smiled—'people see that they want to find husbands.'
'I don't see that the first matters; and the second is only natural.'

Widdowson is right about the girls in question—the Bevis sisters—being 'nice enough'; by no means all the surplus women in this novel are down-trodden like the elder Maddens. More competent, cheerful spinsters—yet involuntary spinsters none the less, one is given to understand—figure among the girls from the Barfoot training establishment. Mary Barfoot herself is presented as a sympathetic, womanly person, and with private means, yet she too has been thwarted of love in youth. In writing this novel Gissing perceived, accurately and sympathetically, a real problem of the time, the ignoble and silent tragedy of half a million lives.

This would be mildly interesting, but no more, if this perception were similarly apparent in his other novels or was borne out in any way in his personal life. But, as we know, the reverse is true. Not only did he fail to marry any of the suitable 'odd women' languishing in the England of the late nineteenth century; he strenuously denied, in his life and elsewhere in his work, that such women existed at all.

The illogicality of this was noticed even by a contemporary reviewer (not always the most perceptive of commentators) who remarked that, in reality, Reardon (in *New Grub Street*) would have been far more likely to have had a devoted helpmeet by his side than a critical and ambitious Amy . . . 'but to give him such a wife would not be Realism'.[17] In that book one fortuneless man of letters *does* achieve such a mate; the Micklethwaite ménage is blissful, and the only reason it is not set up till both partners are on the verge of middle age is that the wife herself has crushing family commitments; there is no suggestion that she was, at any time, unwilling to live simply in a cottage— Gissing's favourite idyll, and one to which he returned unsatisfactorily again and again. In the end of *The Odd Women* itself Dora Milvain is quite prepared to throw in her lot with the financially insecure Whelpdale. It seems clear that, provided a girl without snobbish or unrealistic social ambitions was picked, marriage with a desirable equal *was* possible for all but the most destitute of educated men. Indeed Gissing's own friends and contemporaries had successfully made such marriages: Morley Roberts, H. G. Wells and Gissing's brother Algernon (whose own literary career was a highly precarious business) all achieved happiness with wives of suitable education who loyally supported them.

Gissing's persistent idea that no girl of 'refinement' would possibly be prepared to marry him in his circumstances was presumably related to elements in his character and previous experience discussed in earlier chapters; at all events, as is the way with obsessions, it seems to have maintained its place in his mind in isolation from rational and conscious knowledge. Shortly before meeting Edith he wrote to his German friend Bertz, in a well-known letter: 'This solitude is killing me. I can't endure it any longer. In London I must resume my old search for some decent working-girl who will come and live with me. I am too poor to marry an equal, and cannot live alone.'[18]

You would imagine, from this, that Gissing was still living in the one-room near-slums of his earliest London years. But in fact he had left all that behind him, and for good. Austin Harrison, whom at one time he tutored, declared later that, in his view, Gissing was never in real want after 1882. By 1890 he had lived for several years in 7K Cornwall Mansions, a small flat in a gloomy but decent block just off Baker Street, and, though of course never secure from financial disaster (what writer is?) had every prospect of continuing to live at this same modest but sufficient level. He lent this flat, more or less, as a habitat to

several of his impecunious but decidedly middle-class characters:
the Bevises (brother and two sisters) live in a similar block in *The
Odd Women*, so does Everard Barfoot; in *New Grub Street* the
Reardons inhabit it. True, they fail to keep up with the rent—
but then Gissing was not Reardon; he was a good deal more
successful. True too that Gissing could probably not have kept
up with the social ambitions of an Amy, but his marriage to
Edith went to the opposite extreme; far from being the doggedly
practical step which he maintained, it did not fulfil even one
social advantage. Arguably, married to Edith, Gissing could have
done what Reardon could not do: he could have taken his bride
to 'two rooms in Islington' and renounced all pretension toward
keeping up middle-class appearances. Indeed some sort of renunciation of this type seems to have been in his mind when, shortly
before the marriage, he sold his dress suit since 'I suppose I shall
never again sit at a civilized table again.'[19] But subsequently his
behaviour lacked logical consistency. He carried Edith off to
Exeter where they lived in lodgings with 'attendance'; later
the pair returned to the London area and, after a spell in South
London, settled in the red-brick villa in Worple Road, Epsom.
It was hardly a dream home, but it was very far from being
a working man's tenement or yet the simple cottage of the elusive
idyll: it was a commonplace middle-class abode complete with
front room, dining-room and the other appurtenances of a minimally gentlemanly existence, necessitating at least one full-time
servant. Indeed one of Gissing's grievances against Edith soon
became that she was incapable of managing servants: it does not
seem to have occurred to him that if you marry a simple girl
on purpose to avoid upper-class pressures, you cannot expect her
to behave in an upper-class manner.

The notion that poverty alone prevented him from approaching a suitable woman was lent to many of his characters. This is
part of Kingcote's trouble in approaching Isabel Clarendon,
though Gissing himself seems semi-aware, in writing the book,
that this cannot be the whole of the story. He several times makes
the point that Kingcote's love has a quality of submissive entreaty in it which does not, in practice, inspire Isabel's confidence:
'There was nothing masterful, no exaction, no distinctly masculine fervour.' That is, not only does Kingcote have no money
himself, a practical lack for which the plot in fact provides a

remedy; he behaves like a humbly penniless man, and this is where his real disadvantage lies. In contrast Eustace Vincent, though penniless and even of dubious respectability, makes himself socially acceptable through sheer nerve. Such characters give one a powerful sense of the shaky nature of much Victorian society, behind the imposing façade. The same novel contains one of Gissing's vignettes of impoverished literary men—Thomas Meres, a widower with two daughters who lives in Chelsea; he is a forerunner of the galaxy of shabby intellectuals who grace *New Grub Street*:

> The difficulties of a man in Mr Meres' position, with two girls to bring up, were naturally considerable. Mrs Clarendon had constantly advised him to marry again; at which he always shook his head and maintained silence. The woman who may with safety be taken in marriage by a poor man given to intellectual pursuits is so extremely difficult of discovery that Thomas Meres might well shrink from beginning the search . . .

That embodies Gissing's standard prejudice on the matter, one to which he reverts again and again. Add to it that poor Thomas Meres cherishes a hopeless passion for Mrs Clarendon, whom he sees as a star far above him (as Biffen in *New Grub Street* does for Amy Reardon) and the picture is complete. Yet a few pages further on Gissing states, apparently without realizing the discrepancy of view: '. . . no position is harder than that of educated girls brought up in London in a poor household. A bachelor is not necessarily shut out of society on account of his poverty; but a family must give and take on equal terms or be content to hold aloof.' One might reasonably suppose that all the Thomas Meres of the period could have married the equally numerous 'educated girls brought up in London in a poor household' and that after that, even if costly entertaining were out of the question, at the very least they could have gone to tea with each other. This probably is what did happen. But such a comfortable solution to the problem evidently did not commend itself to Gissing, who, for his own reasons, needed to see the problem as virtually insuperable.

The poor man's sense of inferiority which is, in itself, fatal, is lent even to the brazen Jasper Milvain of *New Grub Street*, but Jasper—unlike his creator!—has the acumen to analyse his own feeling and thus deal with it rationally: ' "Perhaps you don't know how I suffer in feeling myself at a disadvantage. My instincts are strongly social, yet I can't be at my ease in society, simply because I can't do justice to myself. Want of money makes me the inferior of the people I talk with, though I might be superior to them in most things".' Jasper is another of Gissing's basic types, most perfectly realized in this novel but rehearsed in earlier ones and later caricatured in *The Charlatan* and in Arnold Jacks the politician in *The Crown of Life*: he knows that, to get where he wants to be, the best course of action is to marry a rich woman. Without being totally cynical, he nevertheless takes care *not* to fall in love with penniless girls, and is ready to persuade himself into a state of genuine fervour over a girl with money. He explains his carefully-nurtured theory on these matters to Whelpdale, another free-lance journalist like himself:

'I haven't much faith in marrying for love, as you know. What's more, I believe it's the rarest thing for people to be in love with each other. Reardon and his wife were an instance; perhaps—I'm not quite sure about *her*. As a rule, marriage is the result of a mild preference, encouraged by circumstances, and deliberately heightened into strong sexual feeling. You, of all men, know well that the same kind of feeling could be produced for almost any woman who wasn't repulsive.'

(Here, incidentally, is one Gissing speaking, the susceptible and rather unstable sexual being who strove hard to be a realist. In life, this personage was combined with the Reardon–Otway–Kingcote type of romantic idealist, and the two personages warred with one another in Gissing's over-strained frame.)

Jasper feels slightly guilty about his theory, and excuses it, to himself and to others, on the grounds of honesty and clearsightedness; he makes use of the rather spurious excuse that Marian Yule, the poor girl who may or may not be going to inherit money, is a modern woman to whom a man can be open about these things—refusing to allow that pure emotion may count with her, since he is not letting it count with himself: ' "Now all this I have frankly and fully explained to Marian. I dare say she suspects what I should do if she came into possession of money; there's no harm in that. But she knows perfectly well that, as things are, we remain intellectual friends".' Meanwhile he is paying attention to a contralto in Chislehurst; his sister Dora recounts this to the other sister, Maud: ' "He says she is about thirty, and rather masculine, but a great heiress. Jasper is shameful!" '

When Marian does get left £5,000 he speedily proposes to her. He is genuinely attached to her; but when the bequest proves void he does indeed behave shamefully, jilting her by slow means which indicate that he is ashamed of himself but makes the situation worse. Eventually—this is the prime irony of this most bitterly ironic book—he marries Amy Reardon (Reardon being by then dead) who is Marian's cousin and whose own legacy has remained intact. Right at the end of the book he recalls the Marian episode in an intimate moment with Amy:

'Her image is very faint before me,' Jasper pursued, 'and soon I shall scarcely be able to recall it. Yes, you are right; she nearly ruined me. And in more senses than one. Poverty and struggle, under such circumstances, would have made me a detestable creature. As it is, I am not such a bad fellow, Amy.'
She laughed, and caressed his cheek.
'No, I am far from being a bad fellow. I feel kindly to everyone who deserves it. I like to be generous, in word and deed. Trust me, there's many a man who would like to be generous, but is made despicably mean by necessity. What a true sentence that is of Landor's: "It has been repeated often enough that vice leads to misery; will no man declare that misery leads to vice?" I have much of the weakness that might become viciousness, but I am now far from the possibility of being vicious . . . Happiness is the nurse of virtue.'

One may doubt if men like Jasper actually speak thus to their wives, even if they do make a fetish of plain-speaking, but quite certainly they think such things, and Jasper's reflections sum up a major theme of the novel. Meanwhile the weak and obstinately honourable, Reardon and Biffen, have gone to the wall.

Born in Exile was written about the year after *New Grub Street* and makes use of the same theme of a man wooing a woman richer than himself, with genuine feeling but also with the idea of social advancement: in fact in Godwin Peak's case the attraction Sidwell Warricombe has for him is so inextricably bound up with her image as a lady that he cannot separate true emotion from

ulterior motive: 'The sense of social distinction was so burnt
into him, that he could not be affected by any pictured charm
of mind or person in a woman who had not the stamp of gentle
birth and breeding . . . the ideal which possessed him was merely
such an assemblage of qualities as would excite the democrat to
disdain or fury.'

Such an ideal was by then beginning to be Gissing's own; the
image of the pure-hearted working-class girl which dominates
the novels he wrote during the '80s was fading, to be replaced
during the '90s by the *Crown of Life* ideal and the ultimate
attempt to realize it in the person of Gabrielle. It is interesting,
and typical, that, in *Born in Exile*, he was apparently able to perceive the innate flimsiness of the ideal and yet continued to cherish
it in life. Indeed one of Peak's male friends remarks to him: 'At
forty—well, let us say at sixty—you will have a chance of seeing
things without these preposterous sexual spectacles'—that is,
without the obsessional belief that he can never win the woman
he wants.

Peak (like Kingcote) is provided with a final solution to his
economic insecurity, but his halting affair with Sidwell gradually
falls to bits anyway. As Middleton Murry remarks: 'Lack of
money is hardly more than a symbol of a deeper cause of frustration . . . It would be truer to the impression made by these books
to say that the ideal woman is made unattainable by the nature
of things, or by some inexorable and hidden law which either
forbids fruition or turns it to ashes in the author's imagination.'[20]
One feels that, in the course of writing *Born in Exile*, Gissing
came right to the edge of realizing this, and perhaps it was this
half-realization that his heroes' problems were not only circum-
stantial but also self-afflicted, which gave him the insight to turn
next to *The Odd Women* and its radically different view of
things. Indeed, though certain women in his later books continue
to be mysteriously unattainable (the tiresome Eve in *Eve's Ransom*
is a case in point) he never again makes such heavy use of the
lack-of-money theme alone as an excuse for his heroes' failure.
In *The Crown of Life* the role of the penniless and sensitive outcast is apportioned to the minor character Kite, another illegitimate son—who, significantly fails in the end in both health and
will-power. Piers Otway has private means, and though reveal-
ingly described as 'one of those men who cannot live without

a woman's image to worship' is allowed in the end to achieve his Irene. The cynical reader cannot help wondering if, since 'a woman's image to worship' was apparently necessary to him, he would really find the daily round of married life so suited to his temperament; one can imagine him, after a year or two of commonplace intimacy, beginning to wilt at his wife's side and wonder if this was really what Great Love was supposed to be like. One may also permit oneself to wonder if this, in fact, is what Gissing began to do with Gabrielle.

Only in *Will Warburton*, Gissing's last proper novel, written slowly while he led an invalid's existence in France, is the central character allowed to marry suitably and affectionately but not his dream girl. Will falls 'in love' (or what Gissing considers to be love) with Rosamund Elvan. In his fervour he feels himself to be 'a mere erratic chaos, a symbol of Nature's prime impulse whirling amid London's multitudes'. One might think this was a description of desire rather than love, and by the end of the book, after assorted imprudences committed in the name of this 'love', Will (and Gissing) seem to be fumbling toward this conclusion: '. . . his common sense, his reason, his true emotions, were defeated by an impulse now scarcely intelligible.' As Will tells Bertha Cross, the nice, quiet girl he finally decides to marry: 'The fit of madness from which I suffered is very common in men.' No doubt Gissing believed this to be so.* He adds elsewhere, apropos of Will's mad excursion to the south-west of France to look for Rosamund: 'Yet this was how the vast majority of men "fell in love"—if ever they did so at all. This was the prelude to marriages innumerable, marriages destined to be dull as ditchwater or sour as verjuice. In love, forsooth! Rosamund at all events knew the value of that, and had saved him from his own infatuation.'

So much for the note of exalted love-fervour in which *The Crown of Life* had ended. In *Will Warburton* it is hard not to see some degree of disillusionment. If Gabrielle resembles anyone in that book it is the romantic and slightly pretentious Rosamund Elvan. There seems every prospect as the novel ends, that Will and Bertha will achieve sufficient happiness and satisfaction with one another; they will continue to keep the grocer's shop, but apart from basic social and educational compatibility

* See Chapter 2.

they share another quality rather rare among Gissing's romantic heroes and heroines—a sense of humour. However everyone is sorry for them, and Gissing does not wait to show us how their rather unusual life will work out in daily detail. Once again he seems to be affirming that it is one of the essential characteristics of an ideal that it *cannot* be attained, at least not in the form originally conceived. The idea expressed clearly in *Thyrza** that reality, however satisfying and worthwhile, is inevitably only an imperfect and second-best version of an abstract Possibility, a perpetual Might-have-been thus runs through Gissing's novels from first to last. It seems to have been one of his most fundamental constructs, and no doubt its absence from *The Crown of Life* is the real reason why that novel, for all its good moments, is peculiarly unconvincing. Whether or not people in life do actually fall wildly in love and form lasting happy marriages on that basis is not the point: the point is that, except for brief and untypical periods in his life, Gissing found it hard to conceive that they did. The theme of *The Crown of Life* may have corresponded to his mood at the moment of writing, but it contradicts his deeper beliefs and thought-patterns and is thus, ironically, unworthy of him.

The novel in which, more than in any other, Gissing set out to prove that if you pursue your ideal it turns to ashes, was *New Grub Street*. I say 'set out to prove', for the marriage of Edwin and Amy Reardon, which begins with such high hopes and exalted emotions on both sides and founders so utterly on poverty (and Reardon's weaknesses), had no counterpart in Gissing's own experience. The study of this collapse is one of the most painful and realistic things he ever wrote; it transcends the best descriptions of the Arthur–Carrie relationship in *Workers in the Dawn*—yet in life no Amy ever existed in anything approaching a marriage relationship with the writer. This needs to be remembered by those who, seeing that so much of what Gissing writes (including the personality of Reardon) is transposed from his own experience, are inclined to view him as a writer who always 'wrote from life' and had limited powers of creation. The Reardon ménage, complete with its sad details of cramped accommodation and economies on the laundry, is a triumphantly subtle and convincing creation from start to finish.

* See Chapter 2.

Yet clearly it had a personal meaning for Gissing also. It is as if, in creating a Mrs Reardon, and even bestowing on the couple the flat opposite Marylebone workhouse in which he himself lived at the time, he was busy trying to prove to himself that he would be utterly unwise to marry a middle-class girl. The final version of *New Grub Street* was begun immediately after Edith began to visit him. As we know from his letter to Bertz,* he had been playing with the idea of an Edith for a while; clearly now that the possibility that he might—for the second time—link his life with someone considerably below him socially and intellectually, was actually becoming real, he was in a ferment about it. His diary for the period expresses continual doubts; yet in spite (or perhaps because) of these doubts he felt impelled to rush the matter through without delay. They met in September 1890, and were married the following February. Indeed when Edith herself, left in London while Gissing went to the West Country to find lodgings, began to show signs of wanting to put off the wedding, he insisted it should take place at once or not at all. Perhaps this was in part a devious attempt to break with Edith without doing anything himself that could be called dishonourable,[21] but if so it did not work. On 24 February 1891 Gissing returned to London for one night; they were married at St Pancras Registry Office first thing in the morning, drove to Paddington in a fog and caught the train to Exeter. Gissing's diary does not record that any friend or relative from either side was present at this highly unnatural alliance. He did however note that the same day a letter of his on Greek metre appeared in *The Times*.

It would seem that in order to get through this period of his life at all, Gissing had to convince himself that any more suitable and attractive choice of marriage partner would be disastrous. Amy Reardon is a carefully drawn portrait. It would have been easy to make her into a stock-type of vain, snobbish, selfish middle-class girl—her mother in fact belongs in this category. But Amy is not like this; she is intelligent, and quite capable of sincere love; she is not even as 'base' as Jasper Milvain, but she is his counterpart in that she is a woman who, given adequate means and the realization of her justified expectations, would treat everyone kindly and appear in perpetuity as a loving wife and mother. Being very young, she has married Reardon in the belief

* See p. 175.

that he is on the threshold of a career as a distinguished author
—a career that can only progress from good to better. Like
Rosamund Elvan, she is attracted to the idea of marrying a
'creative person'. When it is gradually borne in on her that Reardon's career, far from progressing from success to success, is not
even standing still but is going rapidly backwards, she is utterly
consternated. In all honesty, she cannot separate her image of
Reardon the man from that of the Author; to her it seems that,
in failing her on the second count, her husband has transformed
himself into someone other than the man she married. 'I am not,'
she declares, 'the wife of a clerk who is paid so much a week.'
What Reardon means by wifely love—a love that would follow
him to a slum if necessary—is simply alien to her personality
and general outlook. She is no Adela Waltham from *Demos*. His
bitter reflection—'He had won the world's greatest prize—a
woman's love—but could not retain it because his pockets were
empty'—is not entirely accurate. The truth, revealed only when
the pockets empty, is that he had not won 'love' in quite his sense
of the word; significantly the happy start of their marriage is
shown only in retrospect as if in acknowledgement that it was not
quite soundly based. Yet had Amy not been tested by exceptional
circumstances, this emotional defect in her character, if defect
it really is, would never have come to light. Gissing remarks with
a good deal of perspicuity as well as irony that characters in
novels are always supposed to be prepared to sacrifice all for love,
but that this is a higher standard of morality than we normally
demand in real life: later, Amy herself comes to despise novels
for their unrealistic emphasis on the part love plays in living,
and develops a taste for what we would now call popular
sociology. Without abandoning her basically middle-class outlook,
with its emphasis on emotional and financial security, she begins
to hold views on life in general and women in particular: 'She
was becoming a typical woman of the new time, the woman who
has developed concurrently with journalistic enterprise'—journalistic enterprise of Jasper Milvain's hard-headed sort. The trials
and final breakup of her marriage have turned her from an im-
pressionable girl into a determined adult. At the same time she
has a faculty, regarded by her creator as typically feminine, for
living in the present and shutting her eyes to unpleasant facts.
She is genuinely agonized when her little boy dies from

diphtheria, followed a few days later by Reardon who is reunited
with her at the last; however within a year she is happily married
to Jasper Milvain.

This, then, was one of the private uses of *New Grub Street*:
for its creator it was a make-believe exploration and rejection
of the idea that a really desirable girl might be for him, and thus
a rationalization for the marriage he himself was actually making.
But there is another marriage which is just as significant both in
the context of the novel and the life of the author: the grim
little household on the respectable fringes of Camden Town
where Alfred Yule lives with his despised wife and his much-
tried daughter Marian. Yule is an ageing free-lance writer of a
type already becoming obsolete in the 1880s; he has little faculty
for articles on 'subjects of the day' or for writing about real
life itself at all; his work is always writings about writings, more
prose on English Prose, literature on Literature—'I have done a
few admirable things. You remember my paper on Lord Herbert
of Cherbury? . . . Swept aside in the rubbish of the magazines.'
His genuine ability and disinterested scholarship have long ago
been warped by the struggle to earn a living; he is petty, obsessional, suspicious, malevolent—and at the same time poignantly
and unrealistically optimistic in his conviction that he could run
a successful review if only he had the chance. One cannot, I
think, improve on the description of him by John Gross as the
sort of person who today would be 'a disgruntled Senior Lec-
turer caught up in a permanent feud with the head of his department. Eighty years ago the competition was keener, the
alternative outlets fewer.'[22]

One of Alfred Yule's grudges against life is that he has married
a wife who cannot be any sort of intellectual companion to him,
still less a hostess to his acquaintances. It is implied that he took
this step, long ago, from loneliness and sexual need—the very
reasons Gissing was giving, to himself and to his intimates, for
his impending marriage with Edith. Mrs Yule is a simple, kindly
person who drops the occasional 'h' and has disreputable relatives
in Holloway. She tries her best to please her tyrannical husband,
and has suffered twenty years of consistent humiliation punctuated
with outbursts of abuse. The marriage, in short, has been a
disaster, warping two lives which should never have been joined
and laying a burden of divided loyalty on Marian, the one child

of this mis-union. Furthermore, not content with giving one such graphic example of the perils of marrying an Edith, Gissing supplies additional evidence in a chapter surveying other literary men whose choice of partner has been unfortunate. To quote John Gross again—'when he indicates that *all* Yule's friends have been unable to fulfil their early promise chiefly on account of the "unpresentable wife", it is hard not to feel in the presence of something like a mania'. In the light of this mania—which makes itself apparent in other books also, both those written long before his marriage to Edith and those written after—one is inclined to ask with still more bewilderment what on earth Gissing thought he was doing? Surely if the Yule household 'means' anything in terms of Gissing's personal voyage of discovery, it can only be a most explicit warning to himself against the very step he was then about to take?

I believe that in part it is just this: the most classic example of all of the writer knowing with his pen what he could not put into practice in his life. But, to complicate the issue, it seems to me that an element of consoling fantasy was also at work. Alfred Yule, to be sure, is presented as having made his own life and his wife's wretched. But he is also presented as a harsh character. Whether Gissing himself actually had capacities for destructive harshness is a debatable point, but certainly he *believed* himself to be a kind and long-suffering man. The only possible conclusion is that he enjoyed drawing a picture of Yule's unfairness to his working-class wife in order to fantasize how far more gently and fairly he would treat his own. Mrs Yule is, in her own limited way, a paragon, a Patient Griselda; no doubt Gissing, wrongly believing that he had found such a 'peculiarly gentle and pliable'[23] creature himself, was able to persuade himself for much of the time that all would be well—or at any rate well enough. His novel, in fact, showed how *not* to manage the marriage with a social inferior; such evocations are, to the writer, a way of feeling that he has gained control over the awkward subject by nailing it between the boards of a book, and can now go on to manage better himself in reality. Unfortunately, the feeling of control is largely spurious. To have envisaged a disaster beforehand is by no means a reliable form of insurance against it.

It is perhaps worth adding that the house the Yules lived in in St Paul's Crescent, off the Camden Road, was the house where Edith's family lived; just as the Reardon's flat in Marylebone was actually Gissing's own. It is hard to believe that Gissing himself was unaware that he was, in this novel above all others, trying on different guises for himself, accepting, rejecting and qualifying. If he had really scrutinized the results of this self-examination with the care and scrupulousness he applied in writing the book, he surely would have drawn back from his marriage to Edith in time? But self-scrutiny, except at a fictional remove, was the one intellectual torment in which he did not specialize. A sense of urgency, part real and part fabricated, possessed him; he was running out of money. The manuscript went off to the publishers and he went off to Exeter. Another decade of suffering was thus assured to him.

Another novel of the Edith Gissing period, *In the Year of Jubilee* (1894), provides a striking example of a central character doing just what, in fact, Gissing himself was later to do. In this novel Arthur Peachey, a Camberwell builder's clerk, is goaded beyond bearing by his wife's quarrelsomeness, incompetence and violence, and finally leaves home taking his small son with him. He leaves the boy with relatives of his own in the country. This is exactly what Gissing himself was to do with Walter, his eldest boy, three years after the time of writing.* But when he wrote *In the Year of Jubilee* Gissing himself was already regretting the marriage in which he was entrapped; one may suppose that, in exploring in fiction the possibility of a father retreating with his child away from an unstable mother, he was quite consciously turning over in his own mind the possibility that one day he might do just that. This section of the book has little to do with the rest in terms of plot: its function appears to be purely illustrative. Gissing's views on the innate quarrelsomeness of the lower classes, particularly lower-class women, are discussed in Chapter 5. But there is another significant marriage in the novel, the bizarre union of Lionel Tarrant and Nancy Lord, which embodies, more than any other of his fictional marriages, the fantasy of the faithful wife with whom one doesn't actually have to live—something which might have suited Gissing's own temperament well had he ever been able to achieve it.

While he was always ready to express himself admiring and

* See pp. 216–20.

envious of others' wedded bliss, and on one occasion was surprised because Morley Roberts left his young wife to make a
long voyage abroad, his own domestic history leaves one in little
doubt that he tended to find *any* cohabitation, whether with
wife, sisters or even with another male, a strain on his nerves.
At the same time he was peculiarly unfitted for solitary existence,
and knew himself to be. In life, he ricocheted from one state to
the other, exchanging a life of ignoble domesticity for one of
hermetic solitude, then back again into a cramped and claustrophobic union, then off again into solitude, then once again into
sequestered intimacy . . . The exhausting cycle never seems to
have achieved any satisfactory compromise between two
extremes. The Nancy–Lionel Tarrant marriage, though it weakens
an otherwise good novel by its essential unlikeliness, may well
represent his nearest approach to recognizing the conflict in
his own emotional nature which he could not face fully in
life.

I have already said (in Chapter 3) that Nancy's secret marriage
is, for most of the book, no real marriage. Lionel Tarrant reflects
at one point, when she is visiting his rooms, that he loves her as
one loves a mistress but not quite as a wife: she herself, later, after
their son is born, has the same reflection, bitterly. Yet married
they are. The plot mechanism is this: Nancy Lord's father is
seriously ill and, anxious about his daughter's good sense, has
made a Will directing that if she marries before the age of
twenty-six she will lose all claim on his estate. Both these facts
are unknown to her. On holiday at a seaside resort, she falls in
love with Lionel Tarrant, a young man of no occupation several
cuts above her in the social scale. Carried away by her emotions
she lets Lionel make love to her in the present-day sense of the
word, at the end of a powerful scene between them in an idyllic
country spot; a scene which, in spite of some rather consciously
Keatsian overtones (see *Ode to Beauty*) is remarkably frank for
the period simply in its admission that two essentially intelligent
and well-bred beings can get carried away by sexual passion
just like the lower classes. At all events one supposes that passion
must have pushed itself to the limits, since Lionel Tarrant apparently feels it necessary to make 'reparation' by marrying her at
once by special licence, despite a good many qualms on his part:
he is not a 'blackguard' and Nancy Tarrant (unlike Amy Drake

in *The Odd Women*) is evidently not the sort of girl one merely sleeps with, even though she is not precisely the sort Lionel had envisaged marrying either.

Nancy returns home intending to announce her marriage as a *fait accompli*, only to find that her father is dead and that the provisions of his Will make it essential the marriage should remain secret. Since Lionel himself has no money to speak of (his expectations in that direction are rudely disappointed) he and she embark upon a course of secrecy. Lionel presently goes to the Bahamas in a vain quest for a fortune (the pattern of escape again) leaving Nancy to bear alone and in secrecy the child she has meanwhile conceived. For a while things look extremely black for Nancy, and she is inclined to think the worst of Lionel whose behaviour, though understandable, has hardly been admirable or in the romantic tradition of the hero of a novel. However he at last returns, after various trials of poverty and disillusionment, and eventually succeeds in convincing Nancy (who has been matured by her ordeal) that he himself is a stronger and better man than he was before. Meanwhile her secret has been betrayed, her lonely attempts to retain her inheritance have been in vain. No reason remains, one might think, why the pair should not acknowledge their marriage to the world and set up house together in the normal way, particularly since Nancy has now gone up greatly in Lionel's estimation. Instead, however, the novel ends with Nancy and her child established in a cottage in Harrow with one faithful female retainer (a favourite Gissing idyll) and Lionel visiting her like a lover just when the spirit moves him but otherwise enjoying all—or almost all—the freedom of a bachelor existence.

I have already observed that the hasty marriage ceremony seems to owe more to the prejudices of Mr Mudie's library system than to strict necessity in the context of the plot. The plot would still have worked in the same manner—and been far more intrinsically likely—had Lionel merely promised to marry Nancy without delay and then found his honourable intention frustrated by Mr Lord's Will before it could even be carried out. But in any case the ending of the book makes it plain that the plot mechanisms have been no more than a device for setting up a situation which corresponded less to specific circumstances than to a deep-seated Gissing fantasy. Even at an early stage in their odd marriage Lionel is already consoling Nancy with his personal view of marriage in general.

'We ought to regard ourselves as married people living under exceptionally favourable circumstances. One has to bear in mind the brutal fact that man and wife, as a rule, see a great deal too much of each other . . . People get to think themselves victims of incompatibility, when they are suffering from a foolish custom— the habit of being perpetually together . . . The common practice of man and wife occupying the same room is monstrous, gross . . .'

One might put this down to special pleading in particular circumstances, and to Lionel's selfish immaturity, but at the end of the book, when he is supposedly much changed, he is still of the same view. Regarding their continuing lovers' relationship he firmly tells Nancy, who has been hoping that their marriage can now be a real one: 'With a little more money, this life of ours would be as nearly perfect as married life ever can be.' It is a point of view which has a certain amount to recommend it, but neither Lionel Tarrant nor George Gissing seems to have examined it with much care. Tarrant shares both Gissing's fondness for cerebral principles, and his tendency to be swayed by circumstances. The lack of any editorial comment (so to speak) from the author suggests that the view was one he himself held at that moment, or at any rate held in certain moods, and its essentially subjective nature is betrayed by Lionel's subsequent ill-founded assertion that 'there is not one wife in fifty thousand who retains her husband's love after the first year of marriage'. Here, it would seem, we are in the presence of another Gissing mania—indeed one closely related to the 'unpresentable wife' one; at all events Gissing's failure to analyse Lionel's viewpoint or to explore the possible future tensions of the separationist idyll he advocates, severely weakens a novel which in other respects contains excellent writing. Contrary to his own expressed principles,[24] the author seems to be proselytizing, with emotional vehemence but without much insight. Moreover Lionel's view of his style of marriage does not even have the theoretical coherence of the sort of free union proposed to Rhoda Nunn at one point by Everard Barfoot. He, at least, suggests a mutual independence, while Lionel Tarrant quite shamelessly urges the double standard and expects his wife to stay quietly in her corner while he roams abroad. What's more, he even exerts a male domination to stop Nancy publishing the novel she has written to while away her lonely existence—a situation Gissing also made use of in a short story, *The Honeymoon*. There is no suggestion that Nancy should reasonably protest about this, and on the whole this novel does not greatly reassure one as to the essential fairness of Gissing's own view of the role of women, despite his numerous protestations to Bertz and others on the desirability of feminine emancipation. One is inclined, rather, to see Nancy Lord, who is of course Lionel Tarrant's inferior in education, as well as socially, as the culmination of the long line of more-or-less Patient Griseldas, running through Ida Starr, Thyrza and Jane Snowden. She is perhaps the nearest thing Gissing ever created in fiction to a really suitable mate for himself—but, despite many naturalistic touches about her, one is inclined to doubt whether she could ever actually have existed. As Gissing himself once remarked to a book-seller acquaintance: [25] 'One puts into literary form hopes which are not very likely to be realized.'

The theme of a husband exerting control over his wife, the counterpart to the termagant-wife theme, is one which crops up again both in Gissing's life and in his work and is worth exploring.* It is one of several themes in *The Whirlpool*, Gissing's last really ambitious novel and the last one he wrote while living with Edith. Harvey Rolfe marries Alma Frothingham; she (like Nancy Lord and Monica Madden) is an interesting example of the *woman* of irregular social status, as opposed to Gissing's more usual man: her guilty secret is a bankrupt and suicidal father. Not essentially vicious or ill-tempered, she is yet sufficiently insecure and flighty to cause her rather dour middle-aged husband considerable trouble. In some respects her story is a further working out of the Amy Reardon theme: the folly of a studious husband marrying a conventionally ambitious middle-class girl. Harvey thinks that 'the educated man who marries on less than a thousand a year is either mad or a criminal' but does not stick to his principles: he marries Alma and there follows a protracted tussle between them on suitable modes of life. Harvey is for a simple life in the country, Alma for the West End and success

* See Chapter 5.

as an amateur singer—with emphasis on the success rather than on the singing. They compromise on a red brick villa in Gunnersbury which suits neither of them, and Alma is presently devoured by the evil associations of her London life—the 'whirlpool' of the title.

Gissing penned this novel while actually living in a red brick villa in Epsom, though, as we know, Edith presented quite different problems from Alma. Much of the misogynism in the book is strictly speaking irrelevant to its theme and transparently relates to Gissing's own experiences with Edith rather than to anything discernible in Harvey Rolfe's experience. ('I hate a dirty, lying, incapable creature, that's all, whether man or woman. No doubt they're more common in petticoats.') It would seem that, in detailing the other and more subtle horrors of the Rolfe establishment, Gissing was once again trying to assure himself that there were worse things even than being married to a social inferior.[26] But because Alma, unlike Amy Reardon, is dishonest and rather unbalanced (she kills herself in the end with an accidental overdose of sleeping draught) the picture of their marriage does not have the same force as that of the Reardon marriage. One cannot help feeling that Rolfe, like several other of Gissing's heroes (Arthur Golding, Julian Casti, Arthur Peachey) has been so exceptionally unfortunate in his choice that no general message can be drawn from it—and moreover that the choice itself casts much doubt on the man's essential sense and intelligence. There is something fundamentally improbable in these mésalliances. To know that Gissing's own alliances were equally—indeed more— improbable, explains them in terms of his creativity, but does not excuse them in a fictional context. Truth is, notoriously, stranger than fiction, but to say that is not to justify the appearance in a fictional setting of what Coleridge called 'an improbable possibility'. When you have said that Gissing's books are often flawed by behaviour on the part of the characters which, despite much exposition, the plot never quite manages to explain, you have named the peculiar quality in Gissing's own story also.

5 Studies in Conflict

So many otherwise distinguished male novelists, notably Dickens, have been inept at entering the female consciousness, that Gissing's own talent for this is all the more striking. A bookish boy is almost inevitably a home-loving boy, who spends more time than many boys by the fireside with his mother and sisters; presumably this circumstance helped to foster Gissing's awareness of the feminine world at an early age, but much of his capacity for this must have been innate. His empathy toward women is evident in his earliest works—as indeed it is in the events of his life—but his insight into their emotions became much more incisive as he gradually shed his artificial distinction between Good women and Bad ones. The woman with both vices and virtues, who develops and changes as the book progresses, first appears in the person of Adela Waltham in *Demos*; then, more centrally, in the characters of Miriam Baske and Cecily Doran in *The Emancipated*; it is a distinctive feature of almost all his later novels. But in most of his books, both early and late (*The Odd Women* is the exception), this understanding of women exists as if in isolation from his less rational obsession about being unable to win the desirable woman, and the effect is bizarrely disjointed: it is as if the male and female characters, while involved with one another, are actually inhabiting slightly different sorts of novel.

Presumably the rather strong feminine principle in Gissing's nature led him to understand intuitively the passive and masochistic elements in female nature, and also the defences and self-preservation devices which are erected. As Mrs Ormonde in *Thyrza* says to Walter Egremont: ' "Remember how often I have told you that you have much that is feminine in your character. You have little real energy; you are passive in great trials; it is easier to you to suffer than to act. Your idealism is

often noble, but never heroic . . ." ' Suffering is certainly the
keynote of Gissing's diary, and though, when he finally got
to work on a novel, he worked in a concentrated way for many
hours a day, each book was punctuated with months of indeci-
sion, false starts, self-doubt, time-consuming escapist trips here
and there, and, in fact, with what in a less intense and distressed
man could only be called idleness. A novelist is not a man of
action, and the guilty knowledge of this 'failure' in manhood
seems to have oppressed Gissing. He undoubtedly did find it
difficult to act, in any respect, in an efficient and decisive manner,
with the result that when he *did* manage to galvanize himself he
overdid it, substituting for speed and decision a blinkered rashness
and obstinacy. The effect on these occasions, such as his marriages,
is of a person consciously playing 'a man's part' in a way unsuited
both to his temperament and to circumstances. His talents were
rather for endurance and for being of service to people. He
wrote in his diary on 14 October 1888:

> Strange thing that I, all of whose joys and sorrows come from
> excess of individuality, should be remarkable among men for my
> yieldingness to everyone and anyone in daily affairs. No man
> I ever met *habitually* sacrifices his own pleasures, habits, intentions
> to those of a companion, purely out of fear to annoy the latter.
> It must be a sign of extreme weakness, and it makes me the slave
> of men unspeakably inferior . . .

Gissing wrote this while irritated by the companionship of one,
Plitt, whom he had allowed to accompany him to Paris, but it
seems true of his life in general, and since Gissing himself stigma-
tizes it as 'weakness' there is no reason to suppose he is priding
himself on an imaginary virtue. In any case his sister and Roberts
both draw very much the same picture.

He created, besides Walter Egremont, a whole gallery of men
who, though possessed of a man's ambition and a man's sexual
propensities, are otherwise of rather pliable, hyper-sensitive
feminine caste: Julian Casti, Hubert Eldon, Bernard Kingcote,
Wilfrid Athel, Godwin Peak—and, most of all, Edwin Reardon.
One unkind critic has said that these men have ' "please kick me"
suspended round their servile necks.'[1] When he needed to draw
a more sturdy, extrovert all-of-a-piece male character he went
to work with conscious artifice, and the result is usually convinc-

ing, but seldom is the reader expected to identify with him in the same way—Robert Asquith in *Isabel Clarendon* is a good example of the type.

Morley Roberts remarks:

It is a curious fact, although it was not always obvious even to himself, and it is not now to anyone but me, that I stood as a model to him in many of these books, especially, if I remember rightly, for one particular character[2] in 'Bond and Free' [*The Emancipated*]. Some of these sketches are fairly complimentary, and many are much the reverse. The reason of this use of me was that till much later he knew very few men intimately but myself; and when he wanted anybody in his books of a more or less robust character,[3] and sometimes more or less of a kind that he did not like,[4] I, perforce, had to stand for him. He owned this to me, and once he was not sure how I should take it.

One should perhaps add that at least once, in a now forgotten book, *Maurice Quain*, Roberts himself drew a portrait of Gissing.

The Jealousy Theme

What makes *The Odd Women* a remarkable book is that in it Gissing managed to free himself from his ubiquitous suffering-male figure—or at any rate from identification with such a figure—and thus was able to demonstrate the problems of women's existence without contradictory undertones. The long-term frustrations and tensions of the elder Madden sisters and also of Mary Barfoot are well done (the portrait of Rhoda, to which I shall be returning by and by, is more questionable) but the real tour de force is the marriage between Monica Madden and Edmund Widdowson. It holds the self-evident seeds of its own destruction right from their first unorthodox encounter on a bench in Richmond Park, yet it is so subtly done that for quite a while the reader, like Monica herself and like Mary and Rhoda, is misled into half-believing that this marriage with an older man may, after all, be the best thing for the girl.

Monica's position is difficult, as was Gissing's own. Almost without money, and without an effective family background, she has been reared as 'half a lady and half a shop girl'. Born in more fortunate circumstances, her gentle amiability and basic common sense would have stood her in good stead; she is by no means one of those under-bred young women who lack both moral foundation and self-respect, like the French sisters in *In the Year of Jubilee*. But, in her unprotected situation, her natural desire to give and receive pleasure already places her at risk, and her ladylike distaste for the large drapery store where she works and lives makes her a ready prey to the first man who seems to promise escape into a more congenial *and suitable* life for herself. The built-in irony in her relationship with Widdowson is that she meets him in a way in which no upper-class girl of the period (or even today) is supposed to meet a husband, but is attracted to him precisely because he appears so gentlemanly and is able to promise her a highly conventional and sheltered way of life. Widdowson, for his part, is correspondingly isolated and insecure socially—why otherwise should he need to seek a serious relationship in a casual encounter—and it is just because of this that he places such emphasis on social conformity. Distinctions of the period are blurred slightly for us now, but to the 1890s Widdowson must have appeared very much the would-be gentleman (dressed with care but with subtle errors such as a lack of gloves) bent on proving his social position by adopting what were then in fact dated, mid-Victorian attitudes to women, books, foreign travel and most other subjects. (Ruskin is his favourite author.) From his first meeting with Monica he shows a significant nervous tension about her taking the district railway alone, which soon develops into a full-blown neurosis about the undesirability of her going out alone in the evening, and a tendency to hang about her lodging spying on her. Driven to find a wife by unorthodox methods, at the same time he cannot tolerate the idea that his prospective wife is the sort of girl one meets in that way.

Monica senses this inherent strain in their relationship and is worried by it. She is also uneasily aware that, in the name of 'love', Widdowson is trying to pressurize her into marrying him against her better judgement. But inexperience gets the better of her: as she reflects later, in the claustrophobic boredom of his villa at Herne Hill:

Before marriage, her love-ideal had been very vague, elusive; it found scarcely more than negative expression, as a shrinking from the vulgar or gross desires of her companions in the shop. Now that she had a clearer understanding of her own nature, the type of man correspondent to her natural sympathies also became clear. In every particular he was unlike her husband.

Her understanding of her own nature has come about through her need to oppose her husband, who, like all petty tyrants, becomes worse when he gets what he wants, rather than better. His recently acquired private means have made him occupationless. He does not go to work, and his ideal of married life soon reveals itself as a grisly travesty of the Victorian love-nest:

Monica soon found that his idea of wedded happiness was that they should always be together. Most reluctantly he consented to her going any distance alone, for whatever purpose . . . Never had it occurred to Widdowson that a wife remains an individual, with rights and obligations independent of her wifely condition. Everything he said presupposed his own supremacy; he took it for granted that it was his to direct, hers to be guided. A display of energy, purpose and ambition on Monica's part, which had no reference to domestic pursuits, would have gravely troubled him . . .

The irony of it is that Monica is essentially a docile type with no particular desire to exert herself in spheres outside the home; after all, she has rejected Mary Barfoot's offer of help toward independence in order to marry this man. It is only her husband's megalomaniac possessiveness which drives her to rebel at all:

'Now why can't we always live like that? What have we to do with other people? Let us be everything to each other, and forget that anyone else exists.'
'I can't help thinking that's a mistake,' Monica ventured to reply. 'For one thing, if we saw more people, we should have so much more to talk about when we are alone.'
'It's better to talk about ourselves. I shouldn't care if I never again saw any living creature but you. You see, the old bear loves his little girl better than she loves him.'

Widdowson reveals himself as obsessionally jealous. Like all such jealousies, his is essentially irrational and feeds upon itself—indeed it *must* feed upon itself, since, at least for a long time, it has nothing else to feed upon. Monica's very honesty and good sense ensure that Widdowson's morbid suspicions can only fix them-

selves on trivial social encounters and commonplace manifesta-
tions of personal freedom which she cannot and will not forgo:
'Any other man would deem her a model of wifely virtue. Her
care of the house was all that reason could desire. In her behaviour
he never detected the slightest impropriety. He believed her
chaste as any woman living. She asked only to be trusted, and
that, in spite of all, was beyond his power.'

Eventually, however, Widdowson's paranoia comes near to
bringing about its own fulfilment, as is the way of paranoias.
Monica is so wearied with his company and his obsessions about
a wife's duty that she is driven more and more to seek relief in
other society. At first this is innocent, but presently her air of
unhappiness and emotional need brings her to the attention first
of Everard Barfoot and then of an amiable, sentimental rather
irresponsible young man called Bevis. So undermined is she by
her husband's neurotic nagging, and so completely has he killed
her affection for him, that she yields to Bevis's protestations and
is all set to run away with him—only he, belatedly taking fright
at the step, withdraws at the last moment. Meanwhile Widdowson
has employed a private detective to watch Monica and now all is
lost: he has made his own nightmare come true—or more or less
true. A fearful scene of violence takes place, particularly horrific
in the context of Widdowson's normal obsession with respectability.

'Have you been out this afternoon?'
She was prompted to a falsehood, but durst not utter it, so
keenly was he regarding her.
'Yes, I went to see Miss Barfoot.'
'Liar!'
As the word burst from his lips, he sprang at her, clutched her
dress at the throat, and flung her violently upon her knees. A
short cry of terror escaped her; then she was stricken dumb,
with eyes starting and mouth open. It was well that he held her
by the garment and not by the neck, for his hand closed with
murderous convulsion, and the desire of crushing out her life
was for an instant all his consciousness.
'Liar,' again burst from him. 'Day after day you have lied to
me. Liar! Adultress!'
'I am not! I am not that!'

Eventually she escapes from his clutches and from the house into
heavy rain. All is over between them. Widdowson refuses to

believe that the child she is carrying is his (which it is) and she in any case refuses to return to him. The one great desire of her life—for emotional and financial security—lies in ruins; Bevis has failed her, and in any case how could she have gone with him pregnant with the child of her hated husband? She makes up her mind to die during her confinement and does; a rather mid-Victorian conclusion which has, nonetheless, its own psychological validity.

There are several elements in the Widdowson affair which crop up rather frequently in Gissing's work: a marriage which is in some way socially awkward and unnatural, a situation in which one person sees another in an unrealistic light, in effect creating that person out of their own subjective need, a consuming jealousy and violence between men and women. All are worth pursuing in relation to Gissing's own existence. The first, the mésalliance, I have already dealt with to some extent, though it is perhaps worth pointing out that the Widdowsons' union is a particularly subtle version of the type, since it superficially appears so suitable that these two socially isolated persons should come together. This brings us to the second element: Widdowson wants to see Monica as his ideal of submissive wifehood and more or less manages to turn her into that, but, failing to sustain his essentially unrealistic image, he concocts instead an image of a lying adulteress and in fact very nearly turns her into that, too. Monica for her part wants to see Widdowson as a protective and even dominating male, but the extent to which he overplays this role makes her revise her concept of her own needs. In her desperation she turns to the nearest man who seems to be all that her grim husband is not; this person happens to be Bevis but, once he has left her and gone abroad she realises that their 'passion' was little more than a projection of her own need:

. . . she took out the French stamped envelope and tried to think that its contents interested her. But not a word had power of attraction or repulsion. The tender phrases affected her no more than if they had been addressed to a stranger. Love was become a meaningless word. She could not understand how she had ever drifted into such relations with the writer. Fear and anger were the sole passions surviving in her memory from those days which had violently transformed her life, and it was not with Bevis, but her husband, that these emotions were connected.

Bevis's image stood in that already distant past like a lay figure, the mere semblance of a man. And with such conception of him his letter corresponded; it was artificial, lifeless, as if extracted from some vapid novel.

The fragility of such love-images, to which women—and men— cling was a subject on which Gissing's own life had made him something of an expert. I shall be returning to this at the end of the chapter, with an examination of what, for me, is the best short story he ever wrote, *The Foolish Virgin*. But for the moment, while we are still with *The Odd Women*, it is worth taking a look at the jealousy theme. So cerebral is this novel in some ways, and so much use does it make of then rather advanced questions concerning women (the nature of feminine independence, 'free unions', women's possible need to 'sow their wild oats' as well as men) that it is not readily apparent at first reading that it is crammed with studies of a much older and more primitive problem between the sexes.

At first jealousy presents as a lower-class problem only. Miss Eade, an unattractive girl working in the same drapers as Monica, is furiously jealous because Monica is being pursued by one of the shop men, Bullivant, and refuses to believe that Monica doesn't care for him. This girl's emotional irrationality is blatant; it is easy to expose it to derision; but with the advent of Widdowson we have jealousy of a rather more refined kind, dissembled under an air of concern that Monica should observe ladylike proprieties and also 'truly love' him. Just so, in Gissing's first novel, Arthur Golding's jealousy concerning Carrie is cloaked in his laudable desire to 'save her from bad company'. Still, one may be inclined to view Widdowson's obsession as being in part (perhaps like Arthur's) a sign of his social insecurity. But by the time he wrote *The Odd Women* Gissing had evidently developed beyond the stage of believing, like Thyrza, that real ladies and gentlemen don't suffer from such base emotions. He gradually reveals that, when younger, the pre-eminently ladylike and reasonable Mary Barfoot has suffered bitter jealousy over her cousin Everard, and that in fact this, rather than rational disapproval, is the basis of her refusal to forgive him his behaviour over Amy Drake.* Finally it becomes apparent that even the

* See p. 150.

forcefully independent and unusual Rhoda is not immune from
this craven emotion: she becomes covertly jealous when it
appears (misleadingly) that Barfoot has been associating improperly with Monica Madden, and conceals this feeling under
a show of demanding 'on principle' that Barfoot should justify
himself to her—a demand which in fact loses her any possibility
of marriage with Barfoot. Finally, like a grotesque popular chorus
to round the book off, Miss Eade appears again, running into
Monica on a station platform, where (she says) she is due to meet
her brother, and still anxious to know whether the latter had
anything to do with the shopman Bullivant. This sections ends:

Miss Eade moved sullenly away, not more than half convinced.
Long after Monica's disappearance she strayed about the platform
and the approaches to the station. Her brother was slow in
arriving. Once or twice she held casual colloquy with men who
also stood waiting—perchance for their sisters; and ultimately
one of these was kind enough to offer her refreshment, which
she graciously accepted. Rhoda Nunn would have classed
her and mused about her: a not unimportant type of the odd
woman.

It is possible that when Gissing wrote *The Odd Women* Edith's
own tendency to make jealous scenes had already shown itself.*
But there is also the undeniable fact that Gissing himself was capable of burning jealousy, and that this shared weakness may have
been one of the several under-cover emotions that drew him to
Edith in the first place. He lends the emotion of sexual jealousy
to too many of his characters for this to be mere chance. In
Workers in the Dawn not only does Arthur feel frantically jealous
about Carrie—who reciprocates this by developing a corresponding jealousy of the portrait of Helen Norman she finds among
his things—but Helen Norman herself suffers much when the
existence of Carrie becomes known to her: 'Thus she passed one
of those nights which work upon the human body and mind with
the effect of years.' That is a sentence for the initiate, those who
know what such nights are like. In *The Unclassed* Harriet Smales
becomes obsessively jealous of Ida Starr; in *Thyrza* the good
Lydia struggles with the same emotion, as does Gilbert Grail.
In *Isabel Clarendon* Kingcote is painfully jealous of anyone close

* See pp. 215–18.

to Isabel, a feeling much exacerbated by lack of occupation, as is the equally insecure Godwin Peak's jealousy of Bruno Chilvers in *Born in Exile*. Peak's feeling toward Chilvers begins when they are both at school and he is the poor scholarship boy when Chilvers is not, but later the presence of Sidwell Warricombe gives it a more specifically sexual focus. In the same way Edwin Reardon is fundamentally jealous of Jasper Milvain because he, Reardon, feels professionally lonely and inept while Milvain is always proclaiming his gregarious and businesslike methods of success, but this emotion crystallizes in the belief that Milvain has been influencing Amy against him. These male jealousies are essentially impotent, but in *Denzil Quarrier* the ambitious jealousy of the mysteriously corrupt Mrs Wade leads to tragedy, just as Harriet Smales' threatens to; in *The Nether World* the same emotion is turned to more openly murderous intent in the rather unconvincing Zola-esque figure of Clem Peckover.

By the time of writing *In the Year of Jubilee* such melodrama has been toned down to a merely lower-middle-class petty spite, but the results of such a version of jealousy in Ada Peachey, in Beatrice French and in Jessica Morgan—a particularly vicious picture of the 'respectable' female who will stoop low to get what she wants—are devastating.

Gissing seems to be of the opinion that the female of the species is more deadly than the male. Some might say that he simply recognized the truth that rampant jealousy is more of a female characteristic than a male one, though his particular understanding of it was due to the fact that it was a characteristic he himself possessed in abundance. But at all events the appalling effects of the emotion achieve their fullest and most perceptive illustration in Widdowson, and with this ultimate in jealous husbands Gissing seems to have to some extent exorcized the bogey in so far as it related to his own experience. Otway, in *The Crown of Life*, does not suffer from the corrosive jealousy of his literary forerunners (perhaps Gissing, wanting to portray him as a winner rather than a loser, hesitated to give him such an ignoble characteristic); and Rolfe, in *The Whirlpool*, though mistrustful of Alma in all sorts of ways, never develops a specifically sexual grudge about her behaviour, though he might well do so. Instead, the role of jealous husband is given to the essentially simple and good-hearted Hugh Carnaby who, in his passion, kills a man by accident and goes to gaol for the crime—a late reappearance of the prison-theme in Gissing's work.

It seems to me that the reason Widdowson is so thoroughly convincing is that he is a caricature of certain aspects of Gissing himself. The author would probably have repudiated the idea with indignation. But Widdowson has, in fact, a number of the characteristics of both his creator and the Gissing-figures in other books. He is socially insecure and lives a lonely existence; his private means make it unnecessary for him to join the normal men's world of work outside the home, just as Gissing's earnings from writing did, and this is bad for him—as it was for Gissing. His life '. . . has always been full of worrying problems . . . I can't take things the simple way that comes natural to other men'—a Gissing admission if ever there was one. He is shy of women, and has somewhat old-fashioned and sentimental ideas about their 'place', and at the same time is physically passionate; indeed his desperate idyll of married life is like a horrible travesty of Gissing's own rather unrealistic ideas on the subject when he set up a home with Gabrielle: he even tries to remove Monica from the 'temptations' of London to the security of a country retreat, just as Rolfe removes Alma and Gissing himself removed Edith. Possibly, in his meticulous analysis of just what a man like that can do to a perfectly ordinary woman, Gissing came as near as he ever would to suspecting what part his own un-reasonableness had played in ruining his relationship with Nell and would play in ruining his marriage with Edith.

Mrs Grundy

Because the phrase 'odd women' has a suggestive ring to the modern reader, and may even have had to the reader of 1893, one should perhaps not dismiss the book without asking whether another element may be present in it. Henry James' *The Bostonians*, the earliest unmistakable treatment of lesbianism in fiction, had been published five years earlier and probably read by Gissing (he and James were to meet later in the decade) so it does not seem likely that either he or his more sophisticated readers should have been totally unaware of the interpretation that could be put upon a relationship such as that between Mary Barfoot and Rhoda Nunn. Rhoda not only works for Mary but lives in her house and is apparently subsidized by her to some extent. She is about ten years younger than Mary, but, if one were to see them as lesbians, one would have no hesitation in casting Rhoda in the 'masculine' role; she is also the one whose views on men, marriage and so forth seem more rooted in her essential nature than in her circumstances. Mary merely wishes to provide those surplus women who cannot hope to marry with a fulfilling alternative existence, while Rhoda (as her surname suggests) is positively anti-marriage. She has a masculine aggressiveness, and exercises attraction for feebler women such as the Maddens. There are various other hints. On her first appearance Rhoda is described as 'an unfamiliar sexual type'; later we hear that she has never been loved by a man and has never—since an immature passion for a father-figure in her teens—been in love herself. When Everard Barfoot first makes a physical approach to her she finds it extremely disturbing. He, for his part, regards her as a 'challenge' in a way that is not really adequately validated by references to her cerebral 'principles'. True, she becomes more receptive, and she and Barfoot even enjoy an idyll in the Lake District during which she actually disappoints Everard by being 'like a woman' and wanting to be offered marriage rather than a free union, but as a picture of two people in love this section is most unconvincing even by Gissing standards: both seem to be striking self-conscious attitudes; the whole thing is a veiled contest between them, and passion readily turns to anger and obstinacy on both sides. The reader is inclined to feel that, at some level, Rhoda knew all along she could never play a female role and that Everard knew this too. Finally, when hard-hearted Everard has disappeared abroad—from whence he writes letters saying how well he is getting on with the marriageable daughter of another family—Rhoda has 'persuaded herself not only that the thought of Everard Barfoot was hateful to her soul, but that sexual love had become, and would ever be, to her an impure idea, a vice of blood'.

One wonders if Mary Barfoot's jealousy when Rhoda appears to be leaving her for Everard is, in strict truth, not based just on her own long-ago association with her cousin, but in a homosexual resentment that Rhoda should desert her for any man. Did Gissing himself secretly see it this way, but feel unable, in the shadow of Mr Mudie, to make his view more explicit?

One perhaps should not be too sure about this. The social conventions of feminine friendship (and male friendship, for that matter) vary a lot from one period to another: what, to one century, may be normally affectionate behaviour between two persons of the same sex, is, to another generation, an embarrassing display of ambiguous sexuality. Particularly in the Victorian era, when social relations between men and women outside marriage were subject to so many constraints, it must have seemed quite natural for women to develop, in compensation, overtly sentimental attachments to one another which we would now tend to regard as 'odd'. But in at least one other novel, *Demos*, Gissing paints a picture of a woman—Stella Westlake—who seems to push romantic attachments to other women beyond the bounds of convention and sense; at one point she almost appears to be physically seducing the unhappy Adela, whose own experiences with Richard Mutimer might well have put her off male sexuality. The point is interesting, but disputable.

It was not only the description of unorthodox sexual emotion that was taboo in Gissing's era. Whether one regards Mr Mudie and the proprietors of other nineteenth-century lending libraries* as the evil gaolers of self-expression and frankness, or whether one thinks that their rigidly imposed standards of propriety were simply an expression of society's own wishes, which Mudie himself maintained, the fact is that till well past the turn of the century English writers did not enjoy anything like the freedom of speech of their continental counterparts. Indeed it is only in about the last decade that this cultural gap has finally been closed. Mudie's famous rule-of-thumb was that no novel bought by the library system should contain anything unfit for reading aloud in the family circle. As Gissing and certain others pointed out, with increasing irritation, this meant in effect that truth had to be subordinated or euphemized into matter then suitable for the ears of a fifteen-year-old schoolgirl. Or, as Kipling expressed it in an anonymous poem in the Saturday Review, in 1897 when the economic stranglehold of the three-volume library edition had finally been broken:

We asked no social questions—we pumped no hidden shame—
We never talked obstetrics when the Little Stranger came:

* See Appendix.

We left the Lord in Heaven, we left the fiends in Hell.
We weren't exactly Yussufs, but—Zuleika didn't tell.

Gissing chafed resentfully under the Mudie-yoke from the
beginning of his career. In the end of *Workers in the Dawn* he
makes his 'shocking' woman character, the divorcée Maud
Gresham, say: 'I cannot tell how much or how little you know
of my story, which really I may some day be tempted to present
to you in the familiar three volumes. I think it might go down
excellently with the patrons of Mudie's, especially if the character
of the heroine were a trifle idealized.' As if to pay the author out
for this gibe, his next novel was in fact rejected by the publisher,
Smith and Elder, on the grounds that it would *not* appeal to Mr
Mudie or to his subscribers. This book, whose title, *Mrs Grundy's
Enemies*, indicates that Gissing had wanted to tackle the whole
subject of propriety and prudery, was actually set up in type
by another publisher, Bentley, but never published, and no copy
has ever been found. Those interested in Gissing dream of un-
earthing it in some dusty cache of manuscripts.

One should not imagine that Gissing would necessarily have
been ready to avail himself of the verbal freedom of a Zola or
a Maupassant, had such a chance been offered to him. He himself
was a product of his own times, and was moreover too fastidious
to feel that total explicitness was either desirable or even
possible in English. He also understood that precisely because of the tradition of Grundy-ism in English no acceptable English vocabulary existed for conveying a number of
things. Of George Eliot's *Adam Bede* he noted in his Commonplace Book:

The fact of sexual intimacy between Donnithorne & the girl . . .
is rather revolting to me, & I remember that in my first reading
of the book it came as a sheer surprise. This of course is explained
by the utter inadequacy of the representation of passion. English
prudery, by forbidding adequate treatment of the subject,
results in its presentment possessing a sort of indecency, of baseness.

His attitude to frankness both in prose and in speech is probably
summed up in his note (also in the Commonplace Book): 'My
ideal of conversation between men is that it should be such as

could go on in the presence of a sensible & educated woman. Often enough it would be offensive to a daughter of Mrs Grundy.' In other words, he disliked equally both the coarseness of exclusively male conversation of the period and the artificial prudery of mixed social intercourse (the two things presumably go together). But as time went by socio-literary restrictions were lifted slightly and Gissing's own standards of what might reasonably be offered to the public without scandalizing them underwent corresponding modification. Towards the end of his life it seemed to him odd to reflect how much the sheer subject-matter of *The Unclassed* had scandalized a large number of people, including his own brother, when the book first came out: the world of the '90s had in some respects altered a good deal from that of the early '80s. Certainly it is the absence of almost any hint of the true nature of sexual passion which makes *Workers*, *The Unclassed* and even *Demos* read slightly oddly; whereas, by the time *In the Year of Jubilee* was published (1894) Gissing could include an actual scene of seduction which would have been unthinkable ten years earlier. But even then there was a great deal which could not be said, or even hinted, except by way of a kind of metaphor. The metaphor he adopted a number of times for sexual relations was the depiction of violence between husband and wife.

Domestic Strife

It may be objected that violence only expresses bad or at any rate disturbed sexual relations between married partners, not satisfactory ones. This is true, and it is unfortunately also true, as I have already commented, that Gissing seems to have had a remarkable blind spot about the nature of happy marriage. Marriages even between incidental characters in his books tend to be presented either as essentially strife-ridden—Everard Barfoot produces a whole catalogue of these in *The Odd Women*—or, more rarely, as unrealistically and self-consciously ideal. (The Micklethwaites in the same book, or Lionel and Nancy Tarrant in *In the Year of Jubilee*.) Marriage is seen either as a curse or as an extravagant blessing: it never seems to have occurred to Gissing that, for large numbers of people, marriage is not happy or unhappy except in so far as life itself is happy or unhappy.

The Mortons' comfortable wedded life in *The Whirlpool* is an attempt to present a good, medium happiness without hysterical proclamations of high-minded ecstasy, but even that is somewhat idealized. Elsewhere, in *The Emancipated*, he produces, apparently in all unconsciousness, the remarkable spectacle of a supposedly happily married couple (the Spences) who are constantly, for the space of several years, accompanied by a third person, Miriam Baske! And indeed this novel (written the same year as *New Grub Street* but greatly inferior to it) is heavily flawed because, despite much incidental insight into marriage as it can affect women, it entirely fails to present a lifelike picture of an ultimately successful and solid union—the very thing it sets out to do. Miriam Baske begins the book as a pinched, puritanical spinster-in-all-but-name (actually a widow, but Madge Gissing thought, probably rightly, that the character was modelled on her) and ultimately grows into a suitable wife for Mallard, a roving, middle-aged Morley Roberts type* with certain Gissing characteristics tacked onto him. The basic literary conception (which one critic[5] has called the 'rescue into love' theme) is an interesting and ambitious one, but here the execution simply does not convince. It is not thus, via such contortions and struggles of principle, that compatible couples are formed. One may suppose that the death of his own father when Gissing himself was barely in his teens robbed him of his home model for wedded comfort just at the time when he would otherwise have been able to perceive it in an adult way, and that this is one reason why he apparently failed to carry any image of this over into his future life or to reproduce it in any of his three relationships.

The married couple which grips Gissing's literary imagination is the couple locked in conflict. It is as if he knew well himself, and needed to convey to others, the demands of sexuality (as well as those of law and convention) which bind people to one another and give them such power to hurt each other. But only by implication could he express this. This is the description in *The Emancipated* of Miriam Baske's early marriage with a wealthy man far older than herself:

Most happily, the man died. Had he remained her consort for ten years, the story of Miriam's life would have been one of

* See note 3.

those that will scarcely bear dwelling upon, too repulsive, too heart-breaking; a few words of bitterness, of truth, and there were an end of it. His death was like the removal of a foul burden that polluted her and gradually dragged her down.

Hardly less pregnant with unsaid things is the description, in the novel of that name, of Isabel Clarendon's previous marriage —also to a man considerably older than herself:

His manners were a trifle frigid, and his eyes wandered absently as he talked with you, but it was said he could make himself excessively agreeable when he pleased. Probably he did so to Isabel. He was much addicted to politics, and had all his life nourished political ambition; his failure to reach anything was perhaps responsible for a certain sourness of visage, a certain cynicism of tone, at times . . .

They were married, and lived together for five years. Outwardly there was nothing whatever to suggest that they were not as happy as married people ordinarily are. They had no children, and Mr Clarendon was said to be vexed at this, but such little vexations a wise man philosophically endures. And Mr Clarendon laid claim to a certain kind of philosophy. In these latter years of his life his cynicisms of speech became rather more pronounced, but they were of a kind which with most people earned him credit for superiority. One favoured phrase he had which came to his lips whenever he happened to be talking of his worldly affairs; it was 'Après moi le déluge'. He seemed to mean something special by this. Isabel grew to hate the sound of those words, as if they had been a formula of diabolical incantation.

Clearly Isabel is living with an enemy. She makes the best of it, consoling herself with the pleasures which money could buy, particularly with the physical pleasure of riding to hounds—

She entered into the joy of hunting with almost reckless abandonment . . . Mr Clarendon stayed at home these days, and was in the doorway to receive her when she returned. They were not seen to greet each other.

Then Mr Clarendon fell ill of the disease which was to kill him. It was horribly painful, necessitating hideous operations, renewed again and again; an illness lasting for three years. He went to London, and Isabel began her work of tending him. To move about his bedroom, with that clear, cold, grey eye of his following her wherever she went, was a ghastly trial, but she bore it. Society was renounced; only occasionally she went to see intimate friends. One day her maid, a woman who loved her, begged

leave to tell her something—something of which she was not sure
she ought to speak.

'Whenever you leave house, ma'am,' she said, 'a man follows
you—follows you everywhere, and back home again.'

'Why, what man?'

'A man, ma'am, who—has been to see master several times,'
said the servant, with apprehension.

'You mean—a paid man? A man employed for this?'

It was enough. Isabel went out no more. A friend or two came
to see her, but at length she was deserted. Her mother died, and
she could not even attend the funeral. Then Mr Clarendon was
removed to Knightswell, where she tended him for yet another
year. At length he died after an agony of twelve hours. His last
words were: 'Après moi le déluge.'

It seems that Isabel has won a Pyrrhic victory in a fearful contest, where jealousy (again) is the presenting symptom, and the
root of the matter—impotence, like Casaubon in *Middlemarch*?
abnormal sexual tastes which she refuses to gratify?—remains
unmentionable.

More often the half-hidden aspect of Gissing's bad marriages
appears to be, more straightforwardly, a desire on the part of
the husband to strike the wife and a capacity on the wife's part
for provoking this approach. Sometimes this is suggested from
the man's point of view, sometimes from the woman's. So, in *A
Life's Morning*, we have a retrospective picture of the mill-
owner Dagworthy's previous marriage with a wife from a socially
superior but impoverished family. He rapidly discovers that his
wife does not possess the 'true refinement' he has been seeking
(a significant comment in itself) and they cannot 'speak half a
dozen words without irritating or disgusting each other'. In his
disappointment and frustration, Dagworthy brutally assaults a
groom who has displeased him and is brought to court. He
realizes himself that the groom was a substitute for his wife, and
indeed the incident gives rise locally to 'the very prevalent belief
that he had ruled his wife by similar methods'.

The Dagworthys are released from each other by the wife's
death, but already, in *Workers in the Dawn*, Gissing had depicted
a couple who eventually resort to divorce, something rare and
scandalous at that period. Maud Gresham marries Waghorn, the
smoothly villainous railway director whom Golding had already
suspected of 'secret depth of foulness'. Perhaps Maud suspects

this herself, since just before her marriage she buys two miniature pistols, an interesting comment on her expectations of conventional matrimony. Later we meet her deliberately provoking her husband, sitting reading *Madame Bovary* and rowing with him about a milliner's bill. He tells her his business affairs have failed; she refuses to support him financially, and launches into a long, ironic tirade against him; she fires her pistols at him and he, not surprisingly, beats her up. Afterwards, in keeping with her almost masculine level of physical aggression, she herself runs off with an immoral clergyman. This is the violence-within-marriage situation when both partners are much at fault and essentially vicious. But in *Demos* we have suggestions of a similar level of physical confrontation, though Adela is essentially blameless and it is specifically stated early in the book that Richard Mutimer is a cold personality. Nevertheless it becomes clear that their fundamental incompatibility, social and emotional, must inevitably express itself on an intimate level.

Why the ladylike Adela marries the essentially plebian Mutimer is not entirely clear, except that her family is living in genteel poverty and his new-found wealth is presumably (like Dagworthy's) a source of sexual attraction as well as a purely practical inducement. He woos her with Socialist theory, but the real attraction he holds for her is probably that expressed by the effusive Stella Westlake much later in the book: ' "He stands for earth-subduing energy. I imagine him at a forge beating fire out of iron . . . If he were more intellectual he would become commonplace; I hope he will never see further than he does now".'

If Mutimer is viewed (mistakenly) as some sort of Lawrentian male-principle, then Adela presumably seemed before marriage (equally misleadingly) the epitome of female receptivity. Her mother's comment on her is, of course, a satire on the viewpoint of the foolish mid-Victorian matron, but it is also a subtle indication of Adela's feminine function: ' "I can truly say . . . that Adela has never given me an hour's serious uneasiness. The dear child has, I believe, no will apart from her desire to please me. Her instincts are so beautifully submissive".'

In fact, as gradually becomes clear, Adela has plenty of will of her own and also integrity—that commodity which her apparently strong husband lacks. He also lacks her class-habit of putting a good face on things. When he is standing for parliament (like many of Gissing's characters he attempts to use this as a means to social advancement)—

Adela found it necessary to keep silence on political matters; once or twice he replied to her questions with a rough impatience which kept her miserable throughout the day, so much had it revealed of the working man. As the election day approached she suffered from a sinking of the heart, almost a bodily fear; a fear the same in kind as that of the wretched woman who anticipates the return of a brute-husband late on Saturday night.

Her fear is in fact justified. On the night he loses the election he returns home drunk and forces his way into her room, waking her:

When he had pulled the blind up he turned, propped himself against the dressing table, and gazed at her with terribly lack-lustre eyes. Then she saw the expression of his face change; there came upon it a smile such as she had never seen or imagined, a hideous smile that made her blood cold. Without speaking, he threw himself forward and came toward her. For an instant she was powerless, paralysed with terror; but happily she found utterance for a cry, and that released her limbs.

She runs away and locks herself in another bedroom, where she sits up wrapped in a counterpane till morning. Presumably, had he been writing a score of years later, Gissing would have made Adela's wifely predicament still more explicit. As it is, cryptic reference to Mutimer's 'instincts for domination' continue to crop up and he also becomes extremely jealous about Adela: in Gissing's mind this seems to have been almost an integral part of the male sexual-syndrome. She begins to look ill and he derives an unpleasant pleasure from this. However, in this covert sex-war the tables are turned. Adela finds a missing Will—symbolically she finds it through taking off her wedding ring in Church and dropping it—which disproves Mutimer's inheritance; she shames him into giving up the money. The two leave the large house at New Wanley and travel back to that smoky Islington from which Mutimer originally came. On the train Adela really studies her husband for the first time:

Perhaps he was asleep, perhaps only absorbed in thought. His lips were sullenly loose beneath the thick reddish moustache; his eyebrows had drawn themselves together, scowling. She could not avert her gaze; it seemed to her that she was really scrutinizing his face for the first time, and it was as that of a stranger. Not one detail had the stamp of familiarity; the whole repelled her. What was the meaning now first revealed to her in that countenance? The features had a massive regularity; there was nothing grotesque, nothing on the surface repulsive; yet, beholding the face as if it were that of a man unknown to her, she felt that a whole world of natural antipathies was between it and her . . . Suppose that apparent sleep of his to be the sleep of death; he would pass from her consciousness like a shadow from the field, leaving no trace behind. Their life of union was a mockery; their married intimacy was an unnatural horror. He was not of her class, not of her world; only by violent wrenching of the laws of nature had they come together . . .

Written by a man still in his twenties, of passionate but limited experience, who knew few middle-class women and none intimately, this seems to me a remarkable passage. The sense of the basic unfitness of the two for one another prefigures Gissing's own emotion when married to Edith—some ten years later.

The contest between Adela and Mutimer escalates, a further scene ensues in which he accuses her of infidelity, attempts to lock her in, and all but strikes her—'The thin crust of refinement was shattered; the very man came to light, coarse, violent, whipped into fury by his passions, of which injured self-love was not the least'. But of course Adela wins in the end: she has a secret weapon, she is essentially cold. This is something that mars her for the modern reader and mars Gissing's other early heroines also—the quintessentially suffering female Emma Vine in the same book; Emily Hood in *A Life's Morning* (she was meant to die unmarried, like Thyrza, but the publisher made Gissing change the end); Jane Snowden whose name speaks for itself; even Ida Starr —and this list leaves out of account obvious women-without-legs, like Helen Norman, or like Maud Enderby in *The Unclassed*, who palpably substitute religious masochism for sexual. It is as if, in spite of his interest in the theme of women developing and becoming stronger through experience, and despite his often-expressed view (lent to Mary Barfoot) that the women of his time needed to be educated into becoming people, not sheltered dolls, Gissing was unable for a long time to relinquish a sentimental attachment to the Victorian ideal of the essentially 'pure' lady. His working-class girls who have ladylike potential show it by the fact that they do not bestow their hearts (or bodies) easily: conversely, girls like Nancy Lord who *do* succumb, however understandably, are betraying a certain want of class.[6] This view of female nature was, of course, by no means peculiar to Gissing: what is interesting—and sad—is that it persisted despite his capacity for deeper and more objective insight into the female mind. Only exceptionally, as in *New Grub Street*, did he manage to *show* young women to be people just as men are, with their weaknesses, desires and vanities accompanying finer qualities also.

By the same token, Gissing seems to have believed when he wrote his early books—or pretended to believe—that male physical desires are proper to lower-class men rather than to gentlemen. I have already commented on Julian Casti's relationship with Harriet Smales in *The Unclassed* from this point of view, and on the improbable fact that Waymark does not sleep with Ida. Nor does Casti beat Harriet, as she deserves and perhaps wants, and all in all his gentlemanly attitude to her makes him seem rather weak and unmasculine. The equation in *Demos*—sexual desire = violence = underbred male—thus simply makes more explicit something already implicit in early books. In the same book the physical nature of the relationship between the con-man, Rodman, and Alice Mutimer is emphasized as if this were, in itself, a sign of baseness, and culminates in an ugly display of his physical mastery over her. Alice, incidentally, declares herself at this period to be quite determined not to have children, though she revises her ideas later after her bigamous husband has deserted her: evidently Gissing relied on his readers to see her lack of mothering instinct—and, by implication, her knowledge of birth control—as a sign of turpitude in her, later reformed through sorrow. (The same code is used by Tolstoy in *Anna Karenina*.) 'Malthusianism', as it was then called, was a new and daring topic much disputed in camera: Gissing, with his interest in 'the woman question' could hardly have failed to be aware of it though, typically, he seems to have half-clung to a rather old-fashioned concept of woman's duty. In point of fact the birth rate among the upper- and middle-classes declined dramatically from 1870 onwards. It was a pity Gissing never felt willing or able

to broach the subject more directly in a novel,[7] for it is one
he would have treated well, and many of his books express his
sense that, for the poor and genteel poor of the period, numerous
children were a threat and a torment. His attitude to his own
sons' births was extremely rueful.

That Gissing himself was aware of the close analogy between
sex and violence, in *Demos* and elsewhere, is shown by one brief
reference in *The Nether World*, a glimpse of the squalid home-
life of Bob Hewett and Pennyloaf: Pennyloaf tells a visitor that
if she hit Bob he'd do worse to her—'smirking, the good little
slavey.' But the book in which the topic is most openly tackled is
In the Year of Jubilee, in which, as already noted, the relations
between Arthur and Ada Peachey seem to reflect fairly closely
certain incidents in Gissing's own domestic life with Edith. In
the novel we read:

Arthur Peachey lived only for his child, the little boy, whose
newly prattling tongue made the sole welcome he expected or
cared for on his return from a hard day's work. Happily the child
had good health, but he never left home without dread of perils
that might befall in his absence. On the mother he counted not
at all; a good-tempered cow might with more confidence have
been set to watch over the little one's safety . . . On approaching
the house he suffered, as always, from quickened pulse and heart
constricted with fear. Until he knew that all was well, he looked
like a man who anticipates dread calamity. This evening, on
opening the door, he fell back terror-stricken. In the hall stood
a police-constable, surrounded by a group of women: Mrs
Peachey, her sisters, Emma the nurse-girl, and two other servants.

Emma is accused—rightly or wrongly—of stealing money, and
the house is in an uproar. The girl, sent upstairs to pack, attempts
unsuccessfully to cut her own throat. When Peachey reproaches
his wife with causing this disaster, Ada turns on him and accuses
him:

'. . . Oh you're a nice sort of man you are! Men of your sort
are always good at preaching to other people. You've given her
money—what does *that* mean? I suspected it all along. You
wouldn't have her sent away; oh no! She was so good to the
child—and so good to somebody else! A dirty servant! I'd choose
someone better than that, if I was a man. How much has she

cost you? As much, no doubt, as one of those swell women in
Piccadilly Circus—'
    Peachey turned upon her, the sweat beading his ghastly face.
'Go!—Out of this room—or by God I shall do something
fearful!—Out!'
    She backed before him. He seized her by the shoulders, and
flung her forth, then locked the door. From without she railed at
him in the language of the gutter and the brothel . . .

While Ada is at the police-station with Emma, Arthur Peachey
gets up his little son, tenderly dresses him and makes off with
him to a hotel for the night, preparatory to taking the child
down to his sister's in Kent in the morning.

    On returning from the police-station, haggard and faint with
excitement, but supported by the anticipation of fresh attacks
upon her husband, Ada immediately learnt what had happened.
For the first moment she could hardly believe it. She rushed
upstairs, and saw that the child was really gone; then a blind
frenzy took hold upon her. Alarming and inexplicable sounds
drew her sisters from below; they found her, armed with something heavy, smashing every breakable object in her bedroom—
mirrors, toilet-ware, pictures, chimney-piece ornaments.
    'She's gone mad!' shrieked Fanny. 'She'll kill us!'
    'That beast shall pay for it!' yelled Ada, with a frantic blow
at the dressing table.

Gissing could hardly have fabricated such a domestic scene from
nothing: it goes beyond any tradition of the whining, hostile
wife. While certain details may have been carried over from the
long-ago fiasco of his life with Nell, we do know that by the
time Edith was separated from Gissing she had become openly
violent, and may have begun years before; although Gissing's
diary for the period gives a less graphically horrific account than
the one quoted above, it is clear that there was much he never
wrote in his diary at any period of his life. On the whole, Edith
is conspicuous by her absence from this chronicle of books read,
pages written, letters received, weather enjoyed (or, more often,
not enjoyed): only from time to time did Gissing apparently
decide to make an entry giving chapter and verse for what, more
often, he simply referred to as 'domestic wretchedness'. For
instance, on 10 October 1894, i.e. about six months *after* he completed *In the Year of Jubilee*, he wrote:

As examples of the kind of torment I am silently bearing all these days and years, I will set down two stories, of recent date: (1) On coming to live in this house, which I have furnished with special view to E's wishes and vanities, I made it my one request that she would keep out of the kitchen, and not quarrel with the servant. A week after the servant's arrival (and she is very hard-working) I hear tumult from the kitchen. There stands E., cleaning a pair of boots, and railing at the servant in her wonted way —I had to put a stop to that by an outbreak of fury; nothing else would have availed, and this will only be effectual for a week. (2) Today the little boy* has not been very well, owing to wet weather. At eight o'clock tonight, as E. did not come down to supper, I went quietly to the bedroom door, to listen, as I often do, whether the boy was asleep. To my amazement, heard E. call out 'Stop your noise, you little beast!' This to the poor little chap, because he could not get to sleep. And why not? Because the flaring light of a lamp was in the room. I have begged—begged—again and again that she will *never take* a lamp into the bedroom, but she is too lazy to light a candle, and then uses such language as I have written.

But for my poor little boy, I would not, and could not, *live* with her for another day. I have no words for the misery I daily endure from her selfish and coarse nature.

While it is clear from this, and from similar scenes recounted nearer the break-up of their marriage, both in the diary and in letters, that Edith was neither kind, patient nor sensible, one may perhaps form the impression that Gissing systematically undermined such slight resources of confidence and stability as she may have had—without of course having the faintest realization that he was doing so. Not only did he refuse to introduce her to almost all the new literary friends he made in the '90s, on the grounds that she was unpresentable (she must have realized this, whether he expressed it to her or not) but he would not even allow that she was capable of looking after her own children adequately. He may well have been right—but one feels sorry for her, perpetually being nagged not to take a lamp into the bedroom. She was infuriatingly irrational; the culminating scene between them in which she accused him of hiding the top of a shaving brush and then lying to her about it (see Diary for 25 August 1897) makes this clear—but her reported behaviour suggests the enormous frustration and resentment of a woman

---

* Walter, then aged rather less than three.

forced to lead a lonely life (she complained of this) and denied all outlets for her self-esteem. Probably he took no trouble at all to conceal the fact that he habitually sought company, affection and intellectual sympathy away from her: if she did indeed make the sort of allegations against him that Mrs Peachey makes against Arthur, no doubt these were her only way of expressing a jealousy which on another level was justified. It is fairly clear that Gissing, like most people with a tendency to self-pity, had a quite peculiar capacity for driving others frantic with indignation while continuing to regard himself as the only sufferer. No doubt Edith wanted to hit her husband as often as he wanted to hit her.

That he did want to hit her—and maybe once or twice succumbed to the temptation, a thing which would have shamed and pained him—is suggested by his remarkable chapter on 'Women and Children' in his study of Charles Dickens, which he wrote in 1897–8, in Italy, immediately after leaving Edith for good. While this book is in many ways excellent, and the chapter in question shows a detailed knowledge and appreciation of all Dickens' more memorable female characters, literary criticism it is not: at this point Gissing's own preoccupation with the shortcomings of womanhood clearly loomed so large in his mind that he was unable to see this aspect of Dickens' work except as a vindication of his own experience and an accurate representation of Dickens' own. It was as if, for the time being, he himself was committing the naïve critic's sin of criticizing characters in a book as if they were real, ignoring the elements of caricature and selection so obvious in Dickens' books above all. He might as well have treated the master's novels as a considered indictment of the *male* sex, on the basis of all the unsympathetic male characters found in them. It seems a pity that he had to mar an otherwise perceptive study by using a selection of Dickens' women as a stick to beat his wife—or as substitutes for Edith whom he could bludgeon in print—and unbalance this chapter further with provocatively untrue remarks like: '. . . on the whole it was for men that Dickens wrote. Today the women must be very few who by deliberate choice open a volume of his works'—as if he thought all readers would read as he did, through the same spectacles of obsession. The description of Mrs Gamp, Snagsby or Varden is spattered with subjective adjectives like 'detestable' and 'hateful', and Dickens is even praised for somehow presenting these 'creatures' in a tolerant and humorous light, with transparent remarks like 'Women who might have wrecked homes are shown as laughable foils for the infinite goodness and patience of men about them', and '. . . we may be quite sure that many a primitive woman paid for it with a broken skull'.

Clearly, at this point, Gissing was not sane on the subject, and, in charity, one can only take this unbalance as a message of what he—in many ways a consciously fair and sympathetic man—must have suffered in his second marriage. But one suspects that the real situation was a far more complex one than just that of a long-suffering husband and a destructive wife. Already, in *The Odd Women*, another book which contains a catalogue of hateful wives, put into the mouth of Barfoot, Gissing had stumbled as if inadvertently into the fact that it takes two to make such a relationship:

'There's my friend Orchard. With him it was suicide or freedom from his hateful wife. Most happily, he was able to make provision for her and the children, and had the strength to break his bonds. If he had left them to starve, I should have *understood* it, but couldn't have approved it. There are men who might follow his example but prefer to put up with a life of torture. Well, they *do* prefer it, you see. I may think that they are foolishly weak, but I can only recognize that they make a choice between two forms of suffering. They have tender consciences; the thought of desertion is too painful to them . . .'

A similar hint that Peachey perhaps needs to suffer at his wife's hands (how, otherwise, can he have married her in the first place?) occurs in *In the Year of Jubilee*. Persuaded by his wife, first with threats and vilification, then with tears and promises of amends, Peachey capitulates and returns to her, though he still leaves his little boy in Kent: 'About a month after that the furniture was removed from de Crespigny Park to a much smaller house at Brixton, where Mr and Mrs Peachey took up their abode together. A medical man shortly called, and Ada, not without secret disgust, smilingly made known to her husband that she must now be very careful of her health.' Of course the lull does not last. The second child is born—

Naturally, the months preceding this event had been, for her husband, a renewal of martyrdom; his one supporting solace lay in the thought of the little lad at Canterbury. All the old troubles were revived; from morning to night the house rang with brawls between mistress and servants; in the paroxysms favoured by her physical condition, Ada behaved like a candidate for Bedlam, and more than once obliged her husband to seek temporary peace in lodgings . . . A month after Ada's confinement he once more acted a sane part, announced by letter that he would rather die than continue living with his wife.

This, in outline (though in a slightly different order), was exactly what happened between Gissing and Edith Gissing some three-and-a-half years *after* this novel was written, even to the birth of the second child.

Middleton Murry has suggested that Gissing felt a sense of horror and degradation because he had more than once been driven to use physical violence on a woman or women himself. This is possibly true—but I would suggest that he felt equally shamed by a conflicting awareness: the long-term knowledge that he perhaps failed to assert himself in more appropriate ways. His novels display a realization that a more benign and symbolic display of strength at an earlier point in a confrontation is traditionally part of the male role. For instance, Bernard Kingcote fails to win Isabel Clarendon not just because of his lack of money or social position, but because he will not play a masterful part, though she attempts to edge him into it. Gissing realizes this: 'If a man have not strength, love alone will not suffice to bind a woman to him; she will pardon brutality, but weakness inspires her with fear.' And again: 'Had he adored her less completely, had the brute impulse of domination been stronger in him, his power and her constancy could have defied circumstances.' The author seems to be regretting this state of affairs, in general, for he adds: 'It is the difference between practice and theory; the latter is pure, abstract, ideal; the former must soil itself with the world's conditions.'

Here is Gissing's usual trouble in reconciling common sense with an exalted dream. In his life, he never does seem to have worked out the extent to which he should, in kindness and consideration, 'yield' to women, and the extent to which this was foolish weakness; his time with the Fleurys in Paris found him still in the grip of this dilemma, unable to decide whether he could reasonably complain about camphor in the closets or a lack of bacon for breakfast, much resenting petticoat government but hating to make a fuss. The situation of the sensitive man, unable through very awareness, pride and desire to be considerate, to assert himself before a woman as a man should, is one to which he returns in several novels. Reardon is a classic example of the type. He waits till his sense of his own failure and uselessness as a man has undermined Amy's own image of him before he tries to summon up the determination to bear her off with him to cheaper lodgings—a show of strength that comes too late. She refuses out of hand, with contempt:

He had foreseen a struggle, but without certainty the form Amy's opposition would take. For himself, he meant to be gently resolute, calmly regardless of protest. But in a man to whom such self-assertion is a matter of conscious effort, tremor of the nerves will always interfere with the line of conduct he has conceived in advance. Already Reardon had spoken with far more bluntness than he proposed; involuntarily, his voice slipped from earnest determination to the note of absolutism, and, as is wont to be the case, the sound of these strange tones instigated him to further utterance of the same kind. He lost control of himself; Amy's last reply went through him like an electric shock, and for the moment he was a mere husband defied by his wife, the male stung to exertion of his brute force against the physically weaker sex.

'However you regard me, you will do what I think fit. I shall not argue with you. If I choose to take lodgings in Whitechapel, there you will come and live.'

He met Amy's full look, and was conscious of that in it which corresponded to his own brutality. She had suddenly become a much older woman; her cheeks were tightly drawn into thinness, her lips were bloodlessly hard, there was an unknown furrow along her forehead, and she glared like an animal that defends itself with tooth and claw.

'Do as *you* think fit? Indeed!'

Could Amy's voice sound like that? Great Heaven! With just such accent, he had heard a wrangling woman retort upon her husband at the street corner. Is there then no essential difference between a woman of this world and one of that? Does the same nature lie beneath such unlike surfaces?

He had but to do one thing: to seize her by the arm, drag her up from the chair, dash her back again with all his force—there, the transformation would be complete, they would stand towards each other on their natural footing. With an added curse, perhaps.

Instead of that, he choked, struggled for breath, and shed tears.

Amy turned scornfully away from him. Blows and a curse would have overawed her, at all events for the moment; she would have felt: 'Yes, he is a man, and I have put my destiny in his hands.' His tears moved her to a feeling cruelly exultant; they were the sign of her superiority. It was she who should have wept, and never in her life had she been further from such display of weakness.

We are back with the sex-war, in its most overtly physical form. But by now Gissing the writer seems to have discovered that men and women *are* all the same under the skin, whatever their class. In the same book, Marian Yule, though in some respects an archetypal Gissing suffering female, modest appearance and all, an intellectual Emma Vine, is a flesh and blood woman. She needs to be swept off her feet by Jasper and is disappointed when he does not do this. He is not even sufficiently demonstrative physically for her taste, apart from his lack of love-vocabulary. His preoccupation with expediency chills her, not just because it is somewhat slighting to her, but because it makes him seem too cautious to fulfil the lover's role to her satisfaction. This was evidently a female need which Gissing's own receptivity of temperament—his 'craving for sympathy'—led him to understand well. A similar disappointment is suffered by Monica in *The Odd Women*, when she realizes that Bevis, despite extravagent protestations of love, will not actually carry her off abroad with him, but prefers cravenly to wait and see.

Gissing continued to play with the theme of male domination: *The Whirlpool* is very much about this, as Rolfe and Alma skirmish uneasily about the type of life they ought to be leading, and Rolfe suffers from Gissing's own problem of not knowing where to draw the line. The same theme of a husband attempting, with right on his side, to curb the ambitions and the expenditure of an unstable wife, also appears in a short story from the same period—*The Tyrant's Apology*. Gissing's own attitude to his 'tyrant' (who is prone to make remarks about being master in his own house and women not being individuals) seems ambivalent: I suspect that it was a topic he never fully resolved himself to the end of his life, even in theory. There were too many contradictions within himself to permit of a settled view, even had he not been stuck, as he apparently was, with the idea that one must either dominate or be dominated. Intellectually, he inclined to enlightened views on 'the woman question', but emotionally he was attracted to the idea of an older, simpler mode of life in which women inevitably played a subservient role—this is his 'good housekeeper' daydream, as exemplified by Mary Woodruff in *In the Year of Jubilee* who is there as a contrast to all the modern women, and envisaged also in *Ryecroft*. (When he published *Ryecroft* he received a number of letters from correspondents who believed it to be an actual autobiography, including one from a gentleman who enquired if Ryecroft's housekeeper was now looking for a position because, if so, he would like to engage her!) However the defeatist dream of the woman reduced to an undemanding nanny ignored the sex-imperative, which was an equally important part of Gissing's make-up. As Middleton Murry remarked, in real life Ryecroft's housekeeper would have had to have shared his bed.

Perhaps one might sum up the irreconcilable problem by saying that Gissing's need to fulfil essentially aggressive, masculine desires was only equalled by his aversion to imposing on others or hurting them in any way. Far more than most men, he seems to have perceived his own capacity for inflicting pain on others and been appalled by it—his attitudes to male aggression in the wider sense are discussed in the last chapter. The times when he did screw himself up to play what he thought of as a conventionally dominating male role—as when he forced Edith into marrying him at once, or when he 'insisted' (poor Edith) that she breast-feed their second child[8]—the role sits oddly on him. His natural reaction was not fight but flight; and when he did finally fly from Edith's abuse, he was too unnerved by the experience to dare go back to retrieve a change of clothes: someone else (Clara Collet's friend Miss Orme) had to persuade Edith into sending them after him. The very word 'brutal' seems to have been a loaded one for him: sometimes in letters he used it quite inappropriately, as when he used to apologize to Algernon for delaying in answering a letter 'in my usual brutal way'. In point of fact, no one could have been a more regular, meticulous and considerate correspondent.

Suffering Women

His awareness of the vulnerability of women, and the unfairness of woman's lot, which in life alternately paralysed him and precipitated him into disasters, provided some of the most timelessly perceptive passages in his work. In *The Emancipated* Cecily Doran and Reuben Elgar fall in love with the irrational suddenness that characterizes such alliances in Gissing's novels. They marry, and Cecily comes to regret it, for Reuben is weak and spoilt: she first realizes that she has come to love him less than she did when she discovers that she does not want her child to be too much like him. Talking frankly about her to Mallard, an older man, Spence, remarks:

'In this respect there's no distinction between Cecily and the wife of a costermonger. Civilization is indifferent. Her life is marred, and there's an end on't.' Cecily herself presently reaches the same painful conclusion:

There came to her a sudden outbreak of passionate indignation at the unequal hardships of a woman's lot. Often as she had read and heard and talked of this, she seemed to understand it for the first time; now first was it real to her, in the sense of an ill that goads and tortures. Not society alone was chargeable with the injustice; nature herself had dealt cruelly with women. Constituted as she is, limited as she is by inexorable laws, by what refinement of malice is she endowed with energies and desires like to those of men? She should have been made a creature of sluggish brain, or torpid pulse; then she might have discharged her natural duties without exposure to fever and pain and remorse such as man never knows.

She asked no liberty to be vile, as her husband made himself; but that she was denied an equal freedom to exercise all her powers, to enrich her life with experiences of joy, this fired her to revolt. A woman who belongs to the old education readily believes that it is not to the experience of joy but of sorrow, that she must look for true blessedness; her ideal is one of renunciation; religious motive is in her enforced by what she deems the obligation of her sex. But Cecily was of the new world, the emancipated order. For a time she might accept misery as her inalienable lot, but her youthful years, fed with the new philosophy, must in the end rebel.

That seems as comprehensive a review of the situation of women in many periods as you may find anywhere, even to a reference to masochism as a natural part of the feminine make-up—something which present-day Liberationists prefer to ignore. When Cecily's husband has finally left her, her situation is desperate indeed. As Mallard feels like saying to her (but does not): 'You have missed your chance of natural happiness and it will only be by the strangest good fortune if you ever again find yourself in harmony with fate.' What he does say, to someone else is: 'I wish she were an artist, of whatever kind; then it wouldn't matter so much. A woman who sings, or plays, or writes, or paints, can live a free life. But a woman who is nothing but a woman, what the deuce is to become of her in this position?'

The near impossibility for most Victorian women of surfacing from a bad marriage to make a more satisfactory one (Amy Reardon was peculiarly fortunate in Reardon's death!) must have meant that many were forced to adjust to an unhappy fate. Add to this the fact that social conventions made it difficult for them to know a man well before marriage, and it will be apparent that Gissing's sympathy was far from misplaced—even though he seems to have believed that men were 'caught' unawares just as often as women. A nice vignette of a thoughtless and well-meaning girl entrapped into marriage with a petty tyrant, occurs in *Thyrza*: 'When Paula had been three or four days wedded, it occurred to her to examine her husband's countenance . . . She was rather in want of something to think of just then, feeling a little lonely, and wishing her mother, or her brother, or somebody whom she really knew, were at hand to talk to.'

In fact Dalmaine, her husband, soon makes it clear to her that now they are married she is to change in certain respects to conform to his wishes. Before marriage, her attraction to him has led her to talk socially of political issues. (He is a Radical MP.) Now her husband tells her bluntly that she has been making a fool of herself:

'. . . However, I have no wish to wrangle. Let it be understood that you gradually abandon conversation such as this as of to-night. For the sake of appearances you must make no sudden and obvious change. If you take my advice, you'll cultivate talk of a light, fashionable kind. Literature you mustn't interfere with; I shouldn't advise you to say much about art, except that of course you may admire the pictures at the Grosvenor Gallery.

You'd better read the Sunday journals carefully. In fact, keep
to the sphere which is distinctly womanly.'

Later we hear: 'He was fond of Paula in a way, but he had
discovered since his marriage that she had a certain individuality
very distinct from his own, and till this was crushed he could
not be satisfied. It was his home policy, at present, to crush Paula's
will. He practised upon her the faculties which he would have
liked to use in terrorizing a people.' In short, we have yet another
example of a man whose private actions are out of keeping with
his declared views. Poor Paula is not of the stuff of which Adela
Waltham is made, and by the end of the book she has become
a mere echo of her husband's views, garrulous and eager to please.
Equally tyrannous domestically is another of Gissing's gallery
of rogue-politicians, Dyce Lashmar the 'charlatan', but his particular device consists in misusing the letter of a declared principle
for his own ends: in the name of modern good-comradeship
and a no-nonsense attitude to women, he manœuvres the anxious
widow, Mrs Woolstan, into lending him money. Later, balked of
brighter hopes and in the belief that her modest income makes
her worth marrying, he marries her—only to discover that her
income has disappeared in the direction of an incompetent specu-
lator. One does not feel particularly sorry for foolish Mrs Woolstan since she, like everyone else in this cynical book, is to some
extent caricatured, but one cannot help knowing that Lashmar,
in his resentment, is going to make her life a misery. The background assumption throughout this novel (written while Gissing
was living with the Fleurys) is that hostility is the basis of the
relationship between men and women: as Connie Bride (who is
going to take good care not to become anyone's bride) says to
Lashmar: '. . . There are plenty of women, still, who like to be
despised, and some of them are very nice indeed.' Gissing
had come to see, by the end of the 'nineties, that the
emancipation of women was not the straightforward matter of
education and opportunity he had perhaps believed seven years
earlier.[9]

Some of Gissing's novels—presumably *Our Friend the Charlatan* and, in particular, *In the Year of Jubilee* with its curdling
picture of lower-middle-class women—gave him the reputation
of being a misogynist. The charge is made against the central

alter-ego characters in his two late novels, Harvey Rolfe and Will Warburton, and both repudiate it. Presumably Gissing would have repudiated it himself, maintaining that it was only certain all-too-prevalent aspects of certain all-too-common women which repelled him. Perhaps it would be fair to say that in that, by the latter part of his writing career, he saw more clearly and intimately into women's lives than most of his contemporaries, he was often bound to show them in a way that, while it did not necessarily condemn, did not flatter either. No man is a hero to his valet—and nor is the central woman character of a novel a 'heroine' to any author who attempts an adequate portrait of her. Take, for instance, this sardonic picture of Alma Frothingham when she is being propositioned by the stock-seducer Cyrus Redgrove; the suggestion that her 'honour' is largely dependent on her snobbish self-image does not shock now, but it would have when written:

. . . She imagined herself still illuminated by the social halo, guarded by the divinity which doth hedge a member of the upper middle-class. Was she not a lady? And who had ever dared to offer a lady an insult such as this? Shop-girls, minor actresses, the inferior sort of governess, must naturally be on their guard; their insecurity was traditional; novel and drama represented their moral vicissitudes. But a lady, who had lived in a great house with many servants, who had founded an Amateur Quartet Society, the hem of whose garment had never been touched with an irreverent finger—could *she* stand in peril of such indignity?

Nor are Alma's musical interests more kindly handled: 'It was not the first time that Alma affected to be absorbed in music when not hearing it at all . . . For Alma had no profound love of the art. Nothing more natural than her laying it completely aside when at home in Wales, she missed her sufficient audience. To her, music was not an end in itself . . .' The point about her nature is made further explicit: 'Without admiration she could not live, and nothing so severely tested her resolution to be content with the duties of home as Harvey's habit of taking all for granted, never remarking upon her life of self-conquest, never soothing her with the flatteries for which she hungered.'

Someone else, one might add, had a great need for supportive

admiration, and that was Gissing himself. He was simply paying
Alma, and several other of his 'heroines', the compliment of giving
them the same complex, egoistical natures he ascribed to many
of his male characters. Alma also shares her creator's tendency
to 'hypnotize her imagination with a new ideal of life'. But not
all women would appreciate this compliment. One can, for instance, see that the central character in *The Foolish Virgin*[10]
would shrivel up with embarrassment and resentment, her self-
image crucified, if she thought anyone perceived her as Gissing
did. And yet this story (1895) is, for its period, a masterpiece
of sympathetic insight into the female situation.

Rosamund Jewell, the 'foolish virgin' of the title—the phrase
is to be taken in its most obvious meaning rather than in its
strictly biblical one—is plain, socially pretentious, and lives in
one of those boarding houses at which Gissing excelled. Coming
down to breakfast one morning, she finds the other boarders talking meaningfully about news that an absent 'Mr Cheeseman' is
engaged: almost harder for her to bear than this information is
the fact that the other boarders see that she minds, since putting
up a front has become the main occupation of her empty existence. The same morning she receives a letter from her sister to
say that her brother-in-law is refusing to support her any more;
she must 'do something' like other women in her position. Alone
in her shabby back bedroom, surrounded by illuminated texts and
portraits of admired clergymen, she gives way to impotent rage
at 'the selfishness of people' and 'the perfidy of man':

It was hard to believe that her brother-in-law would ever with-
hold the poor five pounds a month. And—what is the use of
boarding houses if not to renew indefinitely the hope of
marriage?
She was not of the base order of women. Conscience yet lived
in her, and drew support from religion; something of modesty, of
self-respect, still clad her starving soul. Ignorance and ill-luck had
once or twice thrown her into such society as may be found in
establishments outwardly respectable; she trembled and fled . . .

The pathetic thing is that this 'starving soul', while priding herself that she has principles and standards and would not marry
just anyone, has in fact become attached to the one person
available, one of Gissing's oily shop-men, a person socially beneath

her. And now he has deserted her for someone else: 'Her affections suffered, but that was not the worst. Her pride had never
received so cruel a blow.'

Later that day she travels to Teddington to see an upper-middle-
class family with whom she has managed to remain on terms of
friendship. She wants to ask the young man of the family,
Geoffrey Hunt, for whom she has long nourished a hopeless
passion, how she is to earn a living, but pride again makes her
present the matter rather differently:

'. . . I want—I am trying to find some way of being useful in
the world. I am tired of living for myself. I seem to be such a
useless creature. Surely even I must have some talent, which it's
my duty to put to use! Where should I turn? Could you help
me with a suggestion?'
Her words, now that she had overcome the difficulty of beginning, chased each other with breathless speed, and Geoffrey
was all but constrained to seriousness: he took it for granted,
however, that Miss Jewell frequently used this language; doubtless it was part of her foolish, futile existence to talk of her soul's
welfare, especially in tête-à-tête with unmarried men.

It is interesting to see the aspirations presented seriously in *The
Odd Women* shown here vulgarized into something said for
effect. Clearly the New Woman had by then created her own
mythology. The same thing is shown in the person of Olga
Hannaford in *The Crown of Life*.

By way of a response, Geoffrey tells her about an impoverished
middle-class family he knows in which the wife does all her
own cooking and housework. (This was something of a secret
dream of Gissing's—see the next chapter.) He is simply trying
to talk her out of the mood of self-pity he vaguely perceives, but
Rosamund somehow takes the idea she thinks he has thrown out
as a kind of challenge, a chance to 'prove' herself to him: she
will go and work for this hard-up family. She does so, and at first
is buoyed up by a sense of self-sacrifice and heroism, but as time
goes by and Geoffrey Hunt makes no move in her direction she
begins to feel that she has been betrayed—into the tedious,
wearying existence of a domestic servant. She is in this mood
when a letter arrives from Mr Cheeseman, full of flowery protestations of Remorse for past behaviour. She allows herself to
be drawn into correspondence with him again but enjoys herself

playing a role of aloof condescension. Then one morning she hears via her employers that Geoffrey Hunt is getting married: her barely sustained bubble of hope and self-confidence explodes:

A passion of wrath inflamed her; as vehement—though so utterly unreasonable—as in the moment when she learnt the perfidy of Mr Cheeseman. She raged at her folly in having submitted to social degradation on the mere hint of a man who uttered it in a spirit purely contemptuous. The whole hateful world had conspired against her. She banned her kinsfolk and all her acquaintances . . . And her poor life was wasted, oh! oh! She would soon be thirty—thirty! The glass mocked her with savage truth. And she had not even a decent dress to put on. Self-neglect had made her appearance vulgar; her manners, her speech, doubtless, had lost their note of social superiority. Oh, it was hard! She wished for death, cried for divine justice in a better world.

Many of the feelings here lent to Rosamund are female versions of Gissing's own sense of the injustice of fate and the world's cruelty, as intermittently confided to his diary.

What she in fact does is seek out Mr Cheeseman, who obligingly comes up with a proposal of marriage. On the grounds simply that he is better than no one and she does not positively dislike him, she accepts, writes to tell her employers—and then receives another letter from him in which he calls the whole thing off.

She breaks down, and Gissing grimly hints at assorted degradations 'save only that from which there could have been no redemption'. At last, quite without money and broken in spirit, all pride and delusion over, she finds her way back to her employers, who take her in:

Halliday heard the story from his wife, and shook a dreamy compassionate head.

'For goodness sake,' urged the practical woman, 'don't let her think she's a martyr.'

'No, no; but the poor girl should have her taste of happiness.'

'Of course I'm sorry for her, but there are plenty of people more to be pitied. Work she must, and there's only one kind of work she's fit for. It's no small thing to find your vocation—is it? Thousands of such women—all meant by nature to scrub and cook—live and die miserably because they think themselves too good for it.'

'The whole social structure is rotten!'

'It'll last our time,' rejoined Mrs Halliday, as she gave a little laugh and stretched her weary arms.

We are back once again, in a new and more subtle form, with the individual suffering for the iniquities of society, Gissing's earliest theme of all. The road from Carrie to Rosamund has been a winding one, but the connection is there.

6 The Man and his World

One of the difficulties of creating any kind of comprehensive picture of Gissing is that, like most people interesting enough to write about at all, he changed as the years went by. Indeed, change, quite frequently involving a violent swing of opinion and the abandonment of a previously-cherished viewpoint, is one of the constant factors in his nature; he himself was aware of this, even to the point of exaggerating it. As time went on, there were a number of periods and events in his life which he wished to disown and about which he did not tell even close friends the exact truth; like many writers he disliked most of his earlier books, finding it painful to revise them. Writing to Bertz in November 1894, recalling the days when both of them had been penniless and unknown, he said: '. . . how strange a thing it is when, in walking about the streets of London, I pass the streets where I lived in those days of misery! Of course *that man* and *I* are not identical. He is a relative of mine, who died long ago; that's all.'

Already ten years earlier, in *Isabel Clarendon*, he had made Kingcote say: '. . . "there is nothing I hold more in horror than the ghost of my former self. I deny identity . . . how can one be held responsible for the thoughts and acts of the being who bore his name years ago? The past is no part of our existing self; we are free of it, it is buried. That release is the pay Time owes us for doing his work".'

One might add that the claim 'the past is no part of our existing self' is one few thinking and responsible men would make; indeed it is arguable that our past is *all* we are. The attitude is, however, understandable in a novelist, who has a special relationship with his own past. It is, after all, his stock of raw material; by using it piece by piece he does indeed 'get free of it'. The experience that is merely remembered tends to remain simply a source of static emotion, but the experience written about is thereby transformed into something else: it is to some extent distanced and externalized and therefore no longer has the same on-going effect on future behaviour. I do not mean that all, or even any experience can be rendered totally extinct by the therapeutic procedure of writing a novel; obviously certain ones, such as Gissing's Manchester affair and its sequel, bite so deep that they remain significant for ever, but the marks left are not the *same* as the marks left by an experience which has merely been 'buried', in Gissing's inept phrase, and not transformed into anything else. The curious remark 'That release is the pay Time owes us for doing his work' is meaningless, coming as it is supposed to from a non-creative person (Kingcote); Gissing can only have been thinking of himself and confusing the work he had done, as a writer, in processing his past experiences, with the mere effects of Time. In the same way, in the letter to Bertz quoted above, he seems to be suggesting that time alone had transformed him since the epoch when he lived in 'days of misery'; it does not appear to have occurred to him that it was the very act of putting those days into novels which had worked the transformation. Many people find it so difficult to understand how writing happens, tending to regard the novelist just as one of themselves but with an extra flap tacked onto his personality, that quite often writers themselves adopt this view of their own identity, failing to recognize that it is this extra dimension which makes them what they are, subtly altering and colouring all their reactions, endowing them with a peculiar double-vision.

Gissing suffered, as a writer, because writing is tiring, sometimes difficult, and often lonely, but he would certainly have suffered many times more had he not had this extra outlet, this characteristic which all the time made him something more than just another highly-strung, well-meaning personality lost in an uncaring world. He was not good at seeing himself, and among his most persistently cherished illusions was the belief that he only wrote novels in order to earn his bread and that, with a private income, he would have been able to fulfil his dream (see *Ryecroft*) of sitting in a country cottage reading Great Literature all day. In fact it is quite clear that, though monetary pressures often forced him to work when he was not feeling like it, he was basically a born writer,[1] who used his insatiable creative ability as the dynamic element in a life otherwise full of lassitude, uncertainty and frustration. Indeed his knowledge that he was really this, and that the *Ryecroft* dream, if tried, would have turned to ashes within six months, intermittently breaks through the consciously intellectual and quietist crust. The asphyxiating effect of reading for reading's sake is subtly indicated in *New Grub Street*, with the British Museum Reading Room figuring as the Valley of the Shadow of books in which all the literateurs congregate, endlessly manufacturing yet more commentaries on commentaries. And as early as *Isabel Clarendon* the solitary-country-cot is quite specifically denounced when Kingcote admits to a London friend that in this context he is losing all will-power and sense of purpose:

'I pass my days in a dream, which too often becomes a nightmare. It is very likely you are right, and that with every day thus spent I only grow more incapable of activity, instead of making advance by a perception of what I could and ought to do. I find myself regarding with a sort of dull amazement every species of active and creative work . . .'

Perhaps the image Gissing projected of the scholar-manqué, who would rather have been scanning Greek hexameters than penning English prose, was in part a persona for public consumption, for he knew in his own heart that his novels were more than mere pot-boiling and even, at rare moments, recognized that his viewpoint was a special one. He wrote to Algernon in July 1883,[2] just after he had managed to dispose of Nell more or less permanently:

In the midst of the most serious complications of life, I find myself suddenly possessed with a great calm, withdrawn, as it were, from the immediate interests of the moment, and able to regard everything as a picture. I watch and observe myself just as much as others. The impulse to regard every juncture as a 'situation' becomes stronger and stronger. In the midst of desperate misfortune I can pause to make a note for future use, and the afflictions of others are to me materials for observation.

That is a bit self-conscious, as if Gissing had suddenly decided to 'play writer', as earlier he had played 'scholar' and then 'mouthpiece of the advanced Radical party', but it at least indicates that he was aware of the *difference* between himself and the next man whom he so resembled—that subtle but all-pervasive difference which enables the writer to be a writer and at the same time makes him an unreliable interpreter of the non-writer's world: a dilemma which many writers fail to recognize at all and none ever solve completely.

The problem of identity is one which tends to dog writers; there is so little in their life which supports them, everything which makes them what they are must be drawn from within themselves, like the web of the spider. I have already touched on this at the end of the chapter on the 'guilty secret' theme, and in discussing *New Grub Street* in the following chapter. The lack of a supportive framework to his life is painfully apparent from Gissing's diary, though he himself never seems to have become fully aware of the nature of the problem, tending to diagnose it as being due to 'loneliness' or 'lack of intellectual companionship'—both of which *are* aspects of the writer's essentially solitary work-situation, but are not the core of the problem. Not only the writer's self-esteem but his very self-image requires regular recognition of the fact that he *is* a writer, and such recognition only spasmodically came Gissing's way. When things did not look hopeful he must often have felt, like poor Reardon, that he was some sort of fraud who would in a matter of time be exposed—perhaps even driven to abandon the tag 'writer' entirely and find himself back once more as a hack tutor or clerk. When his first book was published he wrote to Algernon with the innocent pomposity of a young man who believes in magic transformations: 'By the bye, I shall of course, in future always sign myself—Author.'[3] Ten years later, when he was at the Exeter Registrar's Office giving notice of his second marriage and gave his occupation as 'literary man', the Registrar—apparently an amiable person, anxious to please—said to his clerk 'Put gentleman'. Any writer will recognize the ironic significance of this for Gissing and understand why he recorded it in his diary.

There is a deeper problem in the writer's situation. I have said that the ability to create books was the one dynamic element in Gissing's otherwise erratic and fruitless life—but the fact is that the creation occurs while merely sitting at a desk. Moreover, although what is created may be perceived as important and enduring (both by the writer and by a sufficient number of readers) it may equally be perceived as just more Reading Room fodder. Reading, at every level from serious study to addiction to novels, is so widely regarded as an escapist activity in some ways, that the creator of reading matter may find it hard to avoid an implicit charge that he is simply encouraging the passive elements in human nature. Thus we have the paradox that what, for the writer, is his raison d'être, his one true activity, is associated with a lack of activity by everyone else. I think that this paradox is what *New Grub Street* is essentially about; the fact that the paths of the various characters tend to cross in the Reading Room is not just a practical aspect of the plot but is a subtle symbol for the hollow at the centre of the lives of people like Alfred Yule, Edwin Reardon and even Jasper Milvain— though Jasper, typically, deals with it by loudly proclaiming the uselessness and ephemerality of his literary work (except in monetary terms) before anyone else can. Add to this the figure of John Yule the old paper manufacturer, who appears at the beginning of the book like a sinister chorus to proclaim his philistine hatred of education in general and books in particular, and what you have is a book against books, a written treatise against writing—the first genuine anti-novel.

To the central (non-writing) character of *The Crown of Life*, Gissing lent a feeling that must have been his own, a 'habit of comparing, contrasting himself with other men, with men who achieved things, who made their way, who played a part in the world'. The knowledge that he himself had no set position, no power over others' lives, and that no external imperatives connected with business, profession or rank organized his days for him, led Gissing (as it has led many other writers) to invent artificial imperatives for himself which were often pointless and sometimes positively damaging. Although he was aware of his need, as a writer, to get adequate material for the novels he turned out one after another, he was perpetually deciding, in the name of work, to forego social engagements which contributed to his material—a particularly useless form of self-discipline. Thus, to take only one of many instances, in mid-June 1888 he was writing in his diary: 'Surprises me much that I have heard nothing from the Gaussens, who were to be in town at the end of May.' Several days later he went to look for them and (as

he put it) 'had to accept invitation for Wednesday afternoon.
Only got to work at six o'clock; did 2 pages. On Wednesday
I shall of course write nothing. What would become of me if I
had regular social intercourse?' The ambivalence of this is striking,
even if one does not look back (as no doubt he did not) to the
entry made only a week or so earlier when he wrote: 'I have
lived in London for ten years, and now, on a day like this when
I am very lonely and depressed, there is not one single house in
which I should be welcome, if I presented myself, not one family
—nay, not one person—who would certainly receive me with
goodwill.' Even allowing for a degree of exaggeration in this—
Roberts, Gissing's chief confidant, happened to be away at the
period—one may say that Gissing for some reason had enormous
difficulty in perceiving in his own life a simple cause and effect
situation here: if you habitually behave, as he did, in an elusive
manner, begrudging such time as you do give to fraternizing with
others, you are bound to be lonely, you are bound to have only
a narrow circle of acquaintances, let alone real friends, and to
suffer from a lack of stimulating companionship. And yet, as so
often, he does seem to have perceived this with his writer's hat
on. Already, in *Isabel Clarendon*, he had made Asquith, the competent male-figure for whom reading a book is an exceptional
activity seen as a self-indulgence, criticize Kingcote in these
terms:

'Something morbid about him, I suppose; he looks, in fact,
rather bloodless, like a man with a fixed idea. Ten to one he's on
precisely the wrong tack; instead of wanting more of his own
society, he ought to have less of it . . . The great preservative of
sanity is free intercourse with one's fellow men—to see the world
from all points and to refrain from final conclusions.'

The point is put more prosaically in *New Grub Street*. Amy
Reardon tells her husband, ' "We can't live in solitude, Edwin,
though really we are not far from it",' and she is not just referring to her own boredom but to Reardon's state of mind. Gripped
by the obsession that he must get his next book finished, bad as
it may be, and by a hyper-sensitive belief that they cannot accept
hospitality they are unable to return in kind, he has told her to
refuse all invitations. The unwisdom of this is put into the mouth
of a not particularly sympathetic woman character, Amy's friend

Mrs Carter, but one sees that Gissing was debating the point with himself, as he debated so much, through the medium of this key-book: ' "You know what you once told me, about how necessary it was for a novelist to study all sorts of people. How can Mr Reardon do this if he shuts himself up in the house? I should have thought he would find it necessary to make new acquaintances".'

In fact, after *New Grub Street*, and as the last decade of the century progressed, Gissing himself did make rather more worthwhile acquaintances, and indeed went out more at this period than at any previous one. By hardly ever introducing Edith to his friends—even Wells never met her—he achieved a social status quo, and was regarded as rather a mystery figure by those who knew him only socially, something he possibly enjoyed. This adjustment was upset again when he retreated to France and an exile's life with Gabrielle. He had a sociable streak in him; although Henry James, who met him briefly at a literary dinner, recorded, in a remark[4] that has become famous wherever Gissing is mentioned, that he appeared to be a man 'quite particularly marked out for what is called in his and my profession an unhappy ending', several people mention that he was 'charming, even suave'. An American who made his acquaintance in Rome in 1898 wrote afterwards: 'I look upon Gissing as one of the most cheerful, luxury-loving, witty people I have ever met.'[5] Wells (who first met him at a dinner in March 1896) described him as: 'an extremely good looking, well-built man, slightly on the lean side, bland, with a good profile and a splendid leonine head'. He said that he spoke 'in a rotund, Johnsonian manner, but what he had to say was reasonable and friendly'.[6] (One wonders if the 'rotund' manner was originally adopted as a cover for a provincial accent.) Wells also called him 'a damaged, joy-loving human being' but only the kindly banker Edward Clodd—in some ways a more loyal friend to Gissing than Wells was—seems to have realized that Gissing's private grief and public enjoyment were two facets of the same capacity for reacting strongly to everything—'Early misfortunes had increased a hypersensitiveness which was an unenviable portion of his mental endowment, yet this was in keeping with the joy and eagerness into which he flung himself when in the company of his fellows'.[7]

It was probably for the same reason that he showed throughout life an inability to delegate minor responsibilities to other people. He cared too much about everything. Although complaining frequently that he could not get proper service, first in the lodgings where he passed his early manhood, then from the servants who trailed in procession through his household with Edith, his personal writings give the impression of a man who would not in fact, leave others to do things in their own way but had to interfere. Wells said that he was a most impractical person, but his letters give the impression of a man who *believed* himself practical and would proffer advice on anything from the right sort of breakfast to where his correspondent ought to live to the times of trains to Italy. He also expected a lot from friends in return; at various times most of his friends had to put themselves out for him. It says much for his engaging qualities that they were willing to do so.

So much has been written about the various trials Gissing suffered, pecuniary, marital and physical, that one point needs making clearly: he undoubtedly was what is known clinically as a depressive personality. Like almost all depressives, he himself had difficulty in admitting the fact, and therefore was perpetually seeking for reasons beyond himself which he could blame. This was undoubtedly the source of much of his restless and impetuous behaviour—his perpetual delusion that somewhere else, or in some other country, or in a different type of air (a minor obsession with him) things would be better. A short story of his called *The Elixir* is an interesting example of this fantasy in fictional form: the central character is a man dogged by misfortune who reaches a state of despair. But then there is a sudden turn of luck, despair obligingly disappears, and everything is all right for ever. This, Gissing seems to be saying in code to himself, is how it would be if only life gave me a second chance by making me not a depressive any more. But it was only in code that he said it.

One is inclined to wonder if Gissing's tendency to pronounced and essentially irrational gloom was in fact *the* guilty secret he kept hidden even from himself, and the mysterious factor which inhibits so many of his heroes from realizing their potential. It was as if, though at moments glimpsing the subjective nature of his moods, he was unable to carry rationality through to its logical conclusion and realize that, if his pain was 'real' only

inside his own head, it was largely pointless to try to exorcise
it by external means. For at moments he undoubtedly did realize
his moods' cyclic quality. He once wrote to Algernon (August
1885): 'Depression is periodic, at least I find it so. Experience
helps one to face it, recollecting that it passes before long and a
time of rest ensues.' At other times he expressed the truth about
himself almost as clearly, but in a veiled form and with the
usual references to unfortunate external circumstances—for instance in this letter[8] written as early as 1881: 'I suppose a perfectly peaceful and intellectually active life is one of those
blessings I shall always only have looked forward to till there is
no time left for it, and, according to my favourite quotation,
"the night cometh when no man can work".'

To others, his unstable emotional make-up was obvious. Even
Ellen Gissing, always inclined to praise rather than criticize,
wrote: 'There is no doubt that Gissing was born with a strong
tendency to depression.'[9] Her further comment that this tendency was increased by 'too close study in his boyhood' may
seem naïve, but actually she and the various other people who
maintained that it was bad for Gissing to 'asphyxiate himself with
books' (the phrase is Roberts') were quite right: Gissing's un-
structured daily life was the worst possible one for a temperament which needed much controlling if it was not to rule him
completely. It is extremely noticeable in his diary that the times
when melancholy oppressed him most were not those times when
he was in fact wrestling with any of the circumstances on which
he used to blame his wretchedness; on the contrary, it was in his
peaceable moments that depression attacked. For instance, in the
year following Nell's death, the first for over a decade in which
he might have been supposed to be in relatively calm waters with
no immediately pressing problems, his diary is full of references
to his black mood. 'A magnificent day,' he wrote in June, 'but
cannot enjoy it. I never enjoy anything now—*never anything*.'

He seems himself at that moment to be suspecting that his
depression was not reactive but innate—that, in common terms,
there was 'something wrong with him'.

I have hinted a number of times in this book that I believe
Gissing positively sought unhappy or at any rate tensionful
situations. No doubt this was partly because, at one level, he felt
a need to excuse his melancholy tendencies, to himself and others,

so he deliberately gave himself good excuses for distress. There could also have been a further reason for it. A curious aspect of his type of depression is that it actually tends to disappear, temporarily, in a situation of external stress (intractable depressions that clear up in time of war or civil strife are well known to psychology). It could have been that the apparently masochistic wooing of misfortune was also, in Gissing's case, a devious means of escaping from his internal troubles into external ones which were, in fact, preferable to him.

Whatever the reason, or mixture of reasons, his restlessness was marked. Gabrielle Fleury wrote[10] to Wells in June 1901, while Gissing was in England at a sanatorium:

If I seem to you absurdly timid it is because I know how impossible it is to feel absolutely sure and safe with him, on account of what you call 'cowardice', with something else added to it: an extraordinary, terrible and perhaps morbid *unstability* in mind, views, decision, feelings (I at least mean in the things of ordinary life), a quite peculiar unability of being happy for a long time in unchanged circumstances, and surroundings. That, you can't fully realize, I think, without constantly living with him for a year or two. I had, however, detected and feared it already before becoming his wife, but I had tried to persuade myself that this dangerous disposition was one of the bad results of the peculiarly sad and miserable life he told me he had had all along and that it could be cured like everything else by what we both thought would be happiness for him. Now I have come to know that it is a constitutional feature of his quite in his blood, like his physical disease, and unfortunately uncurable—that.

At the same period she wrote to Clara Collet: 'George, with regard to practical, everyday life, is like a child. As soon as he meets one of the many little worries inevitable to every existence, he attributes it to the actual conditions of life—not to life itself—and imagines he would avoid it in changing his circumstances.' She went on, bravely and rather over-optimistically, to attribute this febrile quality in Gissing's nature to his poor physical health—'I have come to think it is a physical want which recuperates in moral nature.' Evidently she had not read, or had not noted, the passage in *Born in Exile* in which Gissing made Godwin Peak's mother say to her son: ' "You are very like your father, Godwin . . . He couldn't rest, however well he seemed to be getting on. There was always something he wanted, and yet he didn't know what it was".'

One feels that someone, and probably his own mother, had said that to Gissing himself—possibly at intervals throughout his life.

When someone is a depressive the idea of suicide is likely to occur to them at intervals, more or less seriously. Suicide is certainly a theme in Gissing's novels. Apart from James Hood's ghastly suicide in *A Life's Morning*,* perhaps the most significant of Gissing's fictional suicides in the context of his own life is Arthur Golding's at the end of *Workers in the Dawn*, since there is so much of Gissing himself in Arthur, much of it apparently put there inadvertently. The young man who is presented in the early part of the book as someone of unusual vision and sense of purpose (true of his creator), gradually reveals himself as subject to periods of disorientation when his will power and his common sense both desert him (equally true of his creator). The ending of the book, when Carrie has finally been abandoned and Helen Norman has retired to die of consumption in Italy, ghosts in a fragmented way events in Gissing's own life which actually happened *before* his marriage to Nell: Arthur ships at Liverpool, crosses the Atlantic, and wanders about America just as Gissing did as a still younger man. He finally commits suicide in the Niagara Falls crying out Helen Norman's name. We know that Gissing was in a great state of tension during his own stay in America, that he disappeared suddenly from a teaching job in Boston, Massachusetts, where he had appeared to be getting on all right, and that he probably did visit the Falls. But to assume from this that he 'nearly' cast himself into them, as at least one commentator has done, is to misunderstand the essential difference between the facts of someone's life and the fiction they make of it. The salient point is not whether or not Gissing felt moved to self-destructive thoughts as he stood by the Falls, but the fact that, unlike Arthur, he did *not* do away with himself: ultimately he was stronger than Arthur Golding, just as he was stronger than all his alter-ego characters, and surfaced from troubles under which they succumbed.

By the same token the person who actually kills himself in *New Grub Street* is not Reardon, the Gissing-figure, but shabby,

* See p. 134.

gentle Biffen. The 'realist' novel, 'Mr Bailey, Grocer', on which he has pinned his hopes has failed; his decision to take his own life is born, not of despair and conflict but 'as the result of a subtle process by which his imagination had become in love with death'. He plans it with calm and care. By one of those ironies in which this novel abounds, he gets the recipe for a lethal dose of poison from a volume in the Reading Room—the one practical thing to come out of the place in the entire book. Then he walks out into the open country beyond Putney:

> Sure at length that he was remote from all observation, he pressed into a little copse, and there reclined on the grass, leaning against the stem of a tree. The moon was now hidden from him, but by looking upward he could see its light upon a long, faint cloud, and the blue of the placid sky. His mood was one of ineffable peace. Only thoughts of beautiful things came into his mind; he had reverted to an earlier period of life, when as yet no mission of literary realism had been imposed upon him, and when his passions were still soothed by natural hope. The memory of his friend Reardon was strongly present with him, but of Amy he thought only as of that star which had just come into his vision above the edge of dark foliage—beautiful, but infinitely remote.

Probably only a small minority of real suicides have this stoic, poetic, contemplative quality: certainly one cannot imagine Gissing in quite this role, though he might have played with the idea intellectually—well, he evidently *did* play with it intellectually, and Biffen's act was the result. Another quite different and very interesting fictional treatment of the theme occurs in a short story, *The Pessimist of Plato Road*—interesting because in it a depressive character is not treated sympathetically but contemptuously, with a detached irony. Dolomore, the Pessimist, is an impoverished but snobbish clerkly type, who has failed at most things, a circumstance he attributes to his superior intellect. A certain tragic air is his one claim to distinction. Because he seems so gentlemanly, his landlady forms the idea that he would be a nice match for her daughter, a gentle, feeble, trusting girl. They do indeed form a pair, but their lovers' walks on Clapham Common are characterized less by cheerful discussions about their marital future than by Dolomore instructing Evelyn on the writings of 'Shoppenhaw'. Eventually his seductive nihilism

undermines the girl and she agrees to a suicide pact with him.
The grandeur of this plan buoys them both up. But when it comes
to the appointed hour, and Evelyn faithfully swallows poison and
lies down on her bed—though not, as it turns out, quite to die—
Dolomore loses his nerve at the last moment and decamps for
another part of England.

Bearing in mind that Schopenhauer had much interested the
younger Gissing, and that Dolomore's complaint that 'intellect
is not prized in this money-grubbing world' was a consistent one
of Gissing's own throughout his life, I find this story a remarkable
one. It is as if he were recognizing his own weaknesses, and
sneering at them. One could say, in any case, that the suicides in
his novels are not people of great stature and that, however
much Gissing might have toyed with the idea himself from
time to time, he was basically someone with too much pride,
too strong a self-image and too much ambition (despite denials)
to resort easily to this 'solution'. It was as if he saw suicide as
something other people did, comprehensible but hardly admirable. He noted in his diary in September 1893 'Heard that my
successor at 7K' [The Marylebone flat] 'committed suicide—not
at home, but in the city: the atmosphere I left behind me, some
would say, overcame the poor man.' Gissing himself, of course,
was not overcome that easily.

I think that, for him, the idea of suicide was simply one form,
and not the most attractive, taken by the general theme of escape
and change that ran through his life. For instance, when in retreat
at Dorking in 1895 he wrote to Wells: 'I have a fine, lurid idea.
Could it be given out that I am dead?' Death as a metaphor for
change is familiar to dream-merchants, from fortune-tellers to
Jungian analysts. In his working life, the need tended to take
other forms, of which the retreat overseas, preferably to some
place associated with his boyhood studies, like Italy or Greece,
was his favourite. Unless, of course, you prefer to turn the
comparison round and say that his extensive trips abroad, and
escapes from one part of England to another, were a half-wish
for the ultimate 'change' of death in disguised form. If this was
so, it forms a curious commentary on the removals of his last
three years of life when, in the grip of the lung-disease that
was finally to kill him, he moved restlessly from London to
Paris, then back to England, then to the middle of France, then

farther south to Arcachon and then south again to the Pyrenees, giving every sign that Spain would have been the next stop had his life-span allowed it. (With his customary application, he taught himself Spanish during his last year.) The pretext for this odyssey was that he was trying to evade death, but his choice of places to nurse himself in was somewhat idiosyncratic and an analyst might be inclined to think that all this journeying had a more intimate and contradictory relationship with the image of his own dying, which had haunted him for years before any disease became apparent.

The theme of early death, particularly from consumption or at any rate from a respiratory condition, was one which appeared in his work from the start. In *Workers* there is a graphic account of Helen Norman discovering, in a fit of coughing, that her handkerchief is stained with blood; more than half a dozen years later, Gissing (who still showed no signs of any disease himself) recorded in his diary:

Strange how . . . I am possessed with the idea I shall not live much longer. Not a personal thought but is coloured by this conviction. I never look forward more than a year or two at the utmost, it is the habit of my mind, in utter sincerity, to expect no longer tenure of life than that. I don't know how this has come about; perhaps my absolute loneliness has something to do with it. Then I am haunted by the idea that I am consumptive; I never cough without putting a finger to my tongue, to see if there is a sign of blood.

This was in June 1888, six months after the burden of Nell's existence had finally been removed from him: it is as if he needed something else to worry about. His inability to look more than a year or two ahead was presumably a reflection of his erratic temperament, and the classic image of consumption—the painless but ominous appearance of blood—was a nineteenth-century cliché; nevertheless the fact that Gissing did eventually die of bronchitis or pneumonia on top of a lung condition—emphysema, which is a gradual and irreversible hardening of the lung-tissues— imparts to his earlier hypochondria that quality of pre-recognition[11] which is such a feature of his writings. Godwin Peak dies alone, abroad ('in exile', like Gissing in the Pyrenees) of an unspecified fever; Julian Casti dies, apparently of consumption and a broken spirit; Edwin Reardon develops a troublesome cough, finally to die, apparently of pneumonia, at Brighton. In *Jubilee* both Horace Lord and Fanny French are consumptive. Gissing's anxieties about his own health seem to have been in abeyance during his marriage with Edith: he concentrated instead on worrying lovingly each time Walter, a 'chesty' child, had bronchitis; but the moment he made the final break with Edith fears for his own health came to the fore again. The coincidence of the two events is striking, for when he communicated to Algernon in February 1897 the news that he had left home, he included, on the same brief letter-card, the information that his friend Henry Hick (a doctor) had taken him to see a specialist, and 'It appears that I have a decided weakness in my right lung, just enough to make it dangerous for me to stay here through the spring . . .'

In short, physical illness (though no doubt real enough) was also used by Gissing both as a surrogate for emotional troubles and as a pretext for escaping from them. Fourteen months earlier, on Christmas Day 1895 shortly before Alfred, the second child, was born, he described in his diary the following dream: 'Last night I had several strange dreams. I met dear old Willie somewhere [the younger brother who had died at 21, apparently of tuberculosis] and he told me he had just come from continental travels, and he had been in Rome. He looked well and cheery. Oddest of all, we conversed in German, and I remember correcting myself in a false past participle—Then I dreamt that I had cancer, though unaware of its situation. Friends gravely assured me of it, and recommended operations, and I was much perturbed.' There were also further dreams that night in which Rome was significant.

Certain aspects of this are not hard to interpret: the messenger from the distant past coming back from a 'journey' (i.e from death) is a classic dream-figure even to the alien tongue, but he takes on a particular meaning when we remember that Gissing was presently to convince himself, or be convinced by others, that his own health-situation required such a journey. In fact it was to Rome he went, in the autumn of 1897, predictably, since the Mediterranean lands had long been his favourite escape route when funds allowed: the refuge in the mythic past. (Compare Reardon in *New Grub Street*, with his plans for taking Biffen to see Greece.) As for the 'cancer' it is not hard to see this as typical Gissing-metaphor for the marriage-situation that he felt was destroying him, but, more specifically, the 'growth' may have been the second child, then visibly swelling his mother's stomach and threatening further ties and responsibilities for the overburdened father. In fact Gissing never did stay long enough after Alfred's birth to develop a full sense of parental responsibility for him as he had for Walter. Desperate to leave, he more or less abandoned the child to Edith and its fate, comforting himself with the thought that the infant seemed 'remarkably sweet-natured' and that Edith appeared to love him more than she had loved Walter, but evincing transparent guilt about the whole situation. Several years later, in December 1900, in a letter to Clara Collet mainly concerned with Walter's future schooling, he wrote 'About the lost little boy, I have no news whatever, and perhaps it is better so.'*

It seems as if, in the above dream, the dead brother Willie to some extent represented Gissing himself (and note the date of the dream—Christmas, the traditional time of family reunion). At other times it seems as if Gissing's morbid belief in his own premature death was founded on his sense of identification with his father, who had died—it is thought of pneumonia, although there may have been an associated lung-condition of longer standing as well—near Christmas-time at the age of 42. Several times in his letters and diary Gissing mentioned the time of his father's death meaningfully in relation to himself, as if comparing his own progress, spiritual as well as physical, with that of his parent. He was eventually to die himself at just forty-six, in Christmas week, after three years in which the prospect had been constantly in his mind.

As with all hypochondriacs (he once, in a letter to Algernon, described a varicose vein as 'a somewhat severe malady'!) it is hard to determine the exact moment when unjustified phobia slipped over into justified foreboding. The consensus of opinion among his friends and family was that he had started out with what that era called 'a sound constitution' and had persistently undermined it by emotional strain, by eating the wrong sort of food, by continuing to work even when exhausted or actually ill on the grounds that other people had and so could he, and

* But see p. 253.

by never, ever, taking any real rest. One might say that if he *did*
commit suicide it was by these gradual and devious means. As
Wells said (in a *Saturday Review* notice of one of Gissing's
books before the two had met) 'the *genre* of Gissing's novels
is nervous exhaustion, just as the Restoration drama is the *genre*
of witty immorality'.

Till the bitter end, medical opinions were conflicting about
the gravity of his condition and the best remedies for it; indeed
Wells, who had been hastily summoned to the Pyrenees, had a
disagreement in the very death-chamber with Gabrielle about the
respective merits of English and French methods, which did
nothing to enhance either in the other's estimation. Wells maintained that Gabrielle was useless in a sick room, had no sense
of priorities, and couldn't even provide a clean towel to wipe
Gissing's face; Gabrielle contended that Wells 'killed' Gissing
by giving him broth, wine and coffee in quick succession. At
all events he died, as he probably would have whatever had
been done for him, in a tiny French village on the fringe of the
mountains far from the scenes he had made peculiarly his own.
He lies buried in the cemetery overlooking the Bay of Biscay
at St Jean de Luz where, every ten years or so, some contemplative devotee of his descriptions of London fogs, greasy
boarding-houses, suppers of bread-and-dripping and genteel
agony, comes and pulls up the mares' tails that sprout on his
grave.

Any realistic analysis of a character as flawed as Gissing's is
bound to sound patronizing or condemnatory. There are those
among the devotees of Gissing who appear to regard such an
approach to the man as inherently unfair. They execrate Frank
Swinnerton for his book, and even object to the far more admiring tone of Morley Roberts. They will perhaps dislike this present
book too. I can only say that an approach which venerates not
only the writer but also the man to an extent at which *any*
criticism is interpreted as 'malicious' seems to me lacking both in
common sense and in historical and literary perspective. Gissing
does not belong among the select half-dozen, or even dozen, of
All-Time Great British Writers. Most of his novels have a number of things wrong with them, and appreciation of his best
books should not make us feel unable to class some of the others

as being of academic interest only. Similarly, the defects of his personality are all too apparent in his letters and diary and were quite clearly perceived by his contemporaries, including those who loved him dearly; one ought to be able to acknowledge these defects without losing sight of the admirable qualities that were also his. As Ellen Gissing wrote:

. . . in this strange, misshapen life, there was a central cord which held all the parts together; there was a principle deeply embedded in his nature which caused him to prefer that he himself should suffer rather than bring suffering upon others; and in this lay the secret of the life which to outsiders appeared only steeped in gloom, but out of which, for those who knew him, there shone a gleam of imperishable gold.

Some of this gold is more widely appreciated now than in his own day. In spite of the irrationality and passion with which he tended to attack problems in his own life, he was capable at moments of a remarkable degree of social insight, perception and long-range wisdom. Wells, who liked his books but did not rate them enormously highly, wrote in a private letter to Edmund Gosse in 1904 (when the latter was trying to get a government pension for Gissing's boys) 'Gissing was a most amiable, decent man . . .' One might add that on the occasions when this fundamental decency was united with his keen intelligence, it sometimes produced views far more genuinely advanced than those held by most people of his time. In particular, his pacifism, arising as it did from an acutely realistic perception of what war really means, makes us feel that he is one of us today rather than just another well-meaning liberal imprisoned in the outlook of his own time.

The problems he had with the idea of physical violence, his mistrust of aggressive instincts combined with the anxiety that perhaps a more openly aggressive attitude than his was proper to the male role, is something I have already touched upon. It is fortunate that he did not attend one of the traditional brutal public schools of the period; undoubtedly such an experience would have become for him a 'blacking factory', leaving behind its own mania. The school to which he was sent after his father's death, by the charity of some of his father's friends on the Wakefield Town Council, was run by a Quaker, and seems to have been quite a kindly place.[12] Even so, a passage in *The Private Papers of Henry Ryecroft* deals with his loathing for the drill they had there, supervised by an ex-military coach—and indeed this seems an oddity in such an institution. His mistrust of militarism appears quite early in his work; no doubt his friendship with Bertz, who was a refugee from Bismarck's Germany, helped to crystallize his ideas on the subject.[13] By the time he wrote *Isabel Clarendon* he was already satirizing the British ideal of the 'manly young fellow' in the persons of the odious Stratton boys, whose chief pleasure is in shooting birds with catapults and gloating over the triumphs of the British Army. (In contrast Percy Vissian, the Rector's son in the same book, is a gentle, imaginative child after Gissing's own heart.) Later, during the 1890s, his feelings on the subject grew more pronounced, no doubt in response to the incipient bellicosity which by then was widespread in England. The modern impression that no one thought of war at all until August 1914 is one of the most prevalent of twentieth-century myths about the recent past. On the contrary, 'the German menace' was specifically discussed for well over a decade beforehand, and the mindless glorification of military aggression was a characteristic of the entire late Victorian period. Gissing, like many others in the '90s, already suspected that sooner or later war was coming but, unlike many of them, he did not view the subject with any tremor of excitement, but with the sick dread of realism. In addition to the overt pacifism of *Ryecroft*, *The Whirlpool* (1897) and *The Crown of Life* (1899) contain a considerable amount of Anti-Jingo material, to an extent that might be considered irrelevant to their themes; unless one realizes that, to Gissing, this strain in the life of the period was so ominously significant that there was nothing to which it did not have relevance.

His letters of that time often contain gloomy references to the perilous state of humanity, and once he went to live in France his separation from the daily life and newspapers of his own country made him react disproportionately to such scraps of opinion and information as did come his way. While one should probably bear in mind that a great many people become pessimistic about society with the onset of middle age, and that Gissing's own failing health must have had a good deal to do with his gloomy view, some of his attitudes have been more than vindicated by events that happened long after his death. See particularly Rolfe's views in *The Whirlpool*, as ironically expressed to his friend Basil Morton:

'It's a long time since the end of the Napoleonic wars. Since then Europe has seen only the splutterings of temper. Mankind won't stand it much longer, this encroachment of the humane spirit. See the spread of athletics. We must look to our physique, and make ourselves ready. These Lancashire operatives, laming and killing each other at football, turning a game into a battle . . . We may reasonably hope, old man, to see our boys blown into small bits by the explosive that hasn't got its name yet.'

A prophetic passage indeed, and more so than Gissing, mercifully, ever knew. For Rolfe's little son in this novel clearly 'is' Walter Gissing, and Walter was to die at Gommecourt, during the second battle of the Somme on 1 July 1916. No individual grave marks his burial place: the effects of the explosives used were so devastating that only a mass memorial indicates his fate and that of numerous other officers and men of his regiment.

Gissing's tenderness towards Walter is another aspect of his almost-feminine gentleness of temperament. In an era when fathers traditionally had little intimate involvement with their young children, his portraits of Walter in *In the Year of Jubilee* and *The Whirlpool* are particularly touching, and all the more so for the fact that, like many men, Gissing had not wanted the child initially. *New Grub Street*, written a year before Walter's birth, shows no awareness of the possible relationship between a father and an infant; little Willie is merely one of several unfortunate things which, Reardon feels, take Amy away from him. In December 1891, when Walter was born, Gissing's diary first recorded relief that 'the blackguard business' was over and that 'the poor girl . . . has what she earnestly desired' (Edith then not yet figuring as a fiend). The upset in the household drove him frantic, and the baby was sent to a foster-mother for a while. But a year later the achievements of 'Little Gubsey' made an entry in the diary, and Gissing also wrote that he made him a birthday crown of laurel. From then on, the child figures rather more frequently in the diary than the mother; Gissing began taking Walter's side when Edith slapped or scolded him, in a way that was no doubt justified but could hardly have improved

matters between the couple. In October 1894, when Walter was
just under three, he chronicled a whole day spent with caring
for the child in Edith's absence, noting Walter's good memory
for books and events and his puzzled distress at the idea of
'the cow with the crumpled horn'. In January 1896, just after
Alfred's birth, Gissing was again devoting himself to Walter,
reading him Hans Andersen stories, which made him cry. This,
the father noted with a mixture of chagrin and pleasure; signs
that his son was in the same mould as himself were welcome to
him, and his opinion of Edith was now such that he had a morbid
fear of his children taking after her. Obliquely in his diary and
letters, and overtly in *The Whirlpool* where Rolfe is dissatisfied
with his own wife, though for different reasons, this risk—the
'genetic trap'—is mentioned. Gissing castigated himself for giving
his sons 'an unworthy mother'. He did not know how much
weight to give to the traditional nineteenth-century belief in the
importance of 'blood', and it was in order to avoid the trap of
environment also that in April 1896 he removed Walter to Wakefield and left him there in the care of his mother and sisters.
Visiting Wakefield a few months later, he was much upset to
find that 'the little man', once so loving, was now showing hostility
towards him. A parent of today would say this was merely a
natural reaction on the part of a child who felt that his father
had deserted him, but Gissing, who did not have the equivocal
advantage of modern textbooks on child psychology, simply
interpreted the boy's 'difficult temper' as further evidence that he
had undesirable tendencies in him which must not be allowed
to develop further. Walter never again lived with either of his
parents. Gissing was sure that he had done right, but he missed
and regretted the child. A further poignancy is added to this
passage in *The Whirlpool* when one realizes it was written when
Gissing no longer had Walter with him:

With delight he followed every step in the growth of understanding and yet it was not all pleasure to watch the mind out-
growing its simplicity . . . At four years old Hughie had forgotten
his primitive language. The farther regretted many a pretty
turn of tentative speech, which he was wont to hear with love's
merriment. If a toy were lost, a little voice might be heard
saying, 'Where has that gone now *to*?' And when it was found
again—'There is *it*!' After a tumble one day, Hughie was cautious

in running. 'I shall fall down and break myself.' Then came distinction between days of the week. 'On Sunday I do' so and so; 'on Monday days I do' something else. He said 'Do you bemember?' and what a pity it seemed when at last the dull grown-up world was substituted. Never again, when rain was falling, would Hughie turn and plead, 'Father, tell the sun to come out!' Nor, when he saw the crescent moon in daytime, would he ever grow troubled and exclaim, 'Someone has broken it!'

I have already mentioned that, when Gissing left Edith, he abandoned the younger boy, Alfred, to her, feeling that this was the price he must pay for his own escape. Eventually, however, Alfred was removed also. On 31 January 1902 Gissing was writing to Clara Collet:

> I have gloomy news from England. The other day Miss Orme had a visit from a police inspector who came to tell her that Mrs Gissing had been removed from lodgings in Brixton to the Workhouse Infirmary. It seems she had been continually beating her child, and at last the ill-usage became so serious, that her landlady called in the police. On examination, it was suspected that she was insane—hence the removal to the Infirmary . . . [Alfred] goes to a day school, and seems to be in fairly good health. But the poor little chap must have suffered much for a long time . . . Bye the bye, the police state that she has constantly threatened to kill Miss Orme and her sister . . .

Fate plays cruel tricks sometimes. While many of Gissing's misfortunes were self-provoked, it seems peculiarly hard that the girl he picked to marry should have been not merely his intellectual inferior (that he knew) but should have eventually been guilty of cruel behaviour towards her child, something Gissing's sensitivity must have found peculiarly intolerable to contemplate. He had noted in his Commonplace Book: 'A very frequent source of misery to me is the reflecting on all the frightful physical suffering through which men have gone. The martyr at the stake, the torture chamber, the arena etc. etc. These things haunt me in the night.' His chronic feeling that he was not being as efficient or effective in life as other men cannot have been helped, either, by the knowledge that he himself had let brutality happen to Alfred. That particular story has a happier ending, however, than one might expect. Alfred eventually joined his brother in Wakefield, and survived the First World War to become a particularly gentle, courteous and reserved adult, much attached to his aunts. He married, and has children of his own.

It is little wonder that Gissing, both from his own nervous dread of scenes and the varied experiences of his life, developed something of an obsession about uneducated people, particularly uneducated women, being quarrelsome. Sometimes this appears horribly, as in the verbal slanging matches between the French sisters in *In the Year of Jubilee* and in his comments, already noted, on Dickens' women, but occasionally he managed to exploit the subject in a more humorous vein. During his second marriage he wrote two short novellas, *The Town Traveller* and *The Paying Guest*, the central character of one being a commercial traveller involved with a shop-girl and the other a lower-class girl who is taken in as a lodger by a nervous middle-class couple trying to make ends meet. Gissing himself thought little of either book, but in that their form demands that material should be treated with considerable control and selectivity, as in a short-story, they are, in their way, less flawed than many of his novels. Both are, in my view, well worth an hour or two of anyone's time, particularly *The Paying Guest* where farcical accidents and idiocies follow one another at a pace which reminds the reader that, after all, in life Gissing's friends and family sometimes found him a cheerful, joke-loving person, occasionally even 'hilariously mirthful' (Ellen Gissing's phrase). Both books, too, help to convey what was becoming Gissing's decided view of urban English life and society as the century drew to its close: an environment in which new wealth, or the desire for the appurtenances of wealth, was transforming whole sections of the population, and not for the better.

Again and again, in these stories and in the later novels, one gets a sense of the gimcrack nature of Victorian society—both upper-middle and lower-middle—the fact that, though apparently so class-conscious and hierarchical, it was thickly peopled with persons whose immediate antecedents were working class or whose incomes by no means had the solid basis which you might suppose from the outward mode of life. Reardon's in-laws in *New Grub Street*, keeping up appearances in Westbourne Grove by means of a relentless meanness towards their servants, set the pattern for a number of other characters, not just in monetary matters but in their tendency to view the whole of life in terms of what people will 'think' of them. *Denzil Quarrier* is largely about keeping up appearances in more essential ways. In *The Whirlpool*, Alma's middle-class background seems solid enough, but in fact her father fails on the stock exchange and kills himself and subsequently Alma herself and other members of her circle turn out a good deal less respectable than they appear. Indeed a large part of the discussion between Alma and her husband is due to the fact that, to her, outward image is very important, while to him it counts for very little (of course it counted for Gissing himself more than it did for Rolfe, or he would not have been able to write about Alma as sensitively as he did). Her vision of life on a small income without the solace of even minor celebrity as a singer, is bleak indeed: 'As it was, a small house in Gunnersbury, a baffled ambition, a life of envy, hatred, fear, suffered in secret, hidden by base or paltry subterfuge.'

The ultimate study of social pretentiousness and secret baseness is reached in the person of Dyce Lashmar, the 'charlatan'. Lashmar's entire career, such as it is, is based on sponging, manœuvring and the assumption of 'opinions' for personal ends; though the son of a clergyman, he is in practice so socially insecure that he cannot tolerate the company of commonplace people at all unless they know 'who' he is (an aspiring MP): his only existence, like Jasper Milvain's only more so, is in other people's estimation of him, but since he never does anything estimable his precariousness is inevitable. He is a little like Rosamund Jewell in the story *The Foolish Virgin* (described in the previous chapter) wanting desperately to appear 'interesting' while yet leading a life of almost total inactivity and emptiness.

Like a number of Gissing's more memorable characters, Rosamund inhabits a boarding-house, and the boarding-house, that antithesis of the settled family home and classic refuge of the pretentious yet precarious, might be described as the archetypal Gissing setting: it provides such scope for social disorientation, guilty secrets, misleading appearances, unsuitable matches, affected conversations, emotion in a vacuum, and other staples of Gissing's repertoire. The scenes in the Naples *pensione* in *The Emancipated* are one of the brightest parts of that uneven book; there are excellent cameos—Mr Musslethwaite and his 'place' in Lincolnshire, Mrs Denyer and her 'girls, who adore Italy', Mrs Bradshawe, who secretly thinks that classical statues are indecent, but feels that she can't say so because they are Art. Another boarding-house, with less essentially amiable inhabitants, occurs in *In the Year of Jubilee*; in it is the mysterious Mrs Dameral (whose means do not live up to her conspicuous display) and the un-pleasant cypher who spirits Fanny French off to Brussels in the best late-Victorian tradition of the Wicked Seducer, an older man of military aspect. By the time he was writing *The Whirl-pool*, Gissing seems to have equated even the fact of living in a boarding-house with a degree of moral turpitude: in that book Mrs Strangeways, another in his Wade-Dameral gallery of funda-mentally evil but outwardly respectable women, lives in such a place. I do not find this type in his work particularly convincing probably because, even in his last years, Gissing knew relatively little about ordinary middle-class society. The heavy reliance which the plot of *The Whirlpool* places on the image of the Society female as a scheming viper, seems paranoid and seriously weakens a book which promises initially to be an interesting study of fundamental marital incompatibility.

In the Year of Jubilee is the book in which the make-shift nature of Victorian respectability is most convincingly suggested, though most of the characters are several cuts below those of *New Grub Street* or *The Whirlpool*. The French sisters, at heart working-class girls of no great virtue, have been left just enough money by their builder-father to be able to lead the life of 'ladies'. The jerry-built nature[14] of the villas which cover the erst-while fields of Brixton and Kennington are a symbol for the jerry-built nature of such lives. The two unmarried ones live with their married sister (Ada Peachey) in the utmost squalid disharmony; Beatrice eventually turns herself into a business woman, but Fanny's true nature is revealed when she takes off to Brussels with the boarding-house seducer. An older and better way of life is represented by stern Mr Lord, with his affection for Mary Woodruff, that decent female dodo and repository of traditional feminine virtue. Nancy Lord herself wavers for a while between various modes of life and finally finds her own salvation with Tarrant (described in Chapter 4), but among the other characters even the rather better ones, like Beatrice French and Luckworth Crewe, are totally representative of the New Order rather than the old. Beatrice becomes a business woman and (like Polly Sparkes, one of the 'new breed of shop girls' in *The Town Traveller*) leads a remarkably free life. One cannot help but feel that, at this period in time, at least two different codes of behaviour were operating, one for upper-middle-class girls and one for those slightly beneath them in the social scale who, while not working class, nevertheless derived their social habits from working-class forbears.* At any rate Beatrice French takes a flat on her own where she smokes cigarettes and entertains gentlemen friends to dinners of steak and oysters. From the description of this bachelor-girl life we are evidently meant to think that she is 'fast' (in the phrase of the period) but by no means 'beyond the pale' like her immoral sister Fanny: the point is specifically made that her bed is a single one. One senses that Gissing half-admires Beatrice, while deploring the sharp-practice that characterizes her business acumen; several times elsewhere, notably in the short story *Comrades in Arms*, Gissing drew a sympathetic picture of obviously 'emancipated' womanhood, on matey terms with men.

Luckworth Crewe in *Jubilee*, like Gammon, the central character in *The Town Traveller*, is a Spirit of the Age. One of Gissing's own particular horrors was advertisement hoardings in inappropriate places, but both men take pleasure in these and in other mindless money-spinning devices of a commercial age such as lotteries and newspaper competitions. Indeed Crewe *is* an advertising agent, one of the first, and one of his devastating but essentially innocent dreams is to turn a West Country seaside resort into an adman's paradise:

He unrolled a large design, a coloured picture of Whitsand pier as it already existed in his imagination. Not content with having the mere structure exhibited, Crewe had persuaded the draughtsman to add embellishments of a kind which, in days to come, would be his own peculiar care; from end to end, the pier glowed with the placards of advertisers. Below, on the sand, appeared bathing-machines, and these also were covered with manifold advertisements. Nay, the very pleasure-boats on the sunny waves declared the glory of somebody's soap, of somebody's purgatives.

Extra force is added to this ghastly vision by the fact that Crewe is not presented as an out-and-out villain but as a good-hearted

* See also note 6, Chapter 5.

I

fellow in his way. It is not the sturdy, plebian Crewes as such who are to blame, Gissing is saying, but the whole system in which money counts too much. Like a number of other characters in the later books, Crewe has a respect for money which outweighs his respect for many other things. It seems an ironic comment on the way both society and Gissing's own view of things had developed in the course of years, that whereas from first to last his books tend to be populated by individuals who suffer from lack of money, in the later ones the iniquity of doing everything for money alone becomes a more and more persistent theme—with Jasper Milvain, situated at the mid-point of Gissing's career, ably demonstrating both aspects of the situation. About money as about so many things, Gissing was ambivalent.

One should add that though Gissing's picture of the vulgarity and worldliness of late-Victorian society sometimes seems neurotic and unbalanced, in passages such as the one above on advertising he was merely being literal: the 1890s was the era when, for a number of years, the white cliffs of Dover were embellished by a large sign saying 'Carter's Little Liver Pills'. This was a different world from the almost-Dickensian one in which Gissing found himself in early manhood and in which his first novels were set with no apparent sense of anachronism. As he wrote to Algernon in March 1897,[15] from Budleigh Salterton whither he had fled from Edith: 'London has changed indescribably since the days when I starved and wandered about the streets in 1877. That, indeed, was just the end of an epoch.' One cannot help wondering what Gissing would have thought and written if, like most of his contemporaries, he had lived on into the twentieth century and seen the establishment of the motor-car, the telephone, the wireless, the cinema . . . Such things seem as anachronistic to Gissing's world picture as a steam engine in a medieval battle-field, yet, had he lived to a ripe old age, as Clara Collet did, he could quite well have been alive during the Second World War. If he had retained the lucidity of his better moments during the decades of the 'twenties and 'thirties his comments might have been worth having. But one is glad for his sake that he did not live to see the extensive despoliation of the English countryside which has taken place in this century—Ryecroft's cottage encroached upon by a housing estate. To him, the country remained an Eden before the Fall, symbolizing the mythic Past in all its virtues. Needless to say it is to the country (and not, like Gissing in real life, to a smoky mill-town) that Arthur Peachey flees with his young son, away from the contaminating influences of modern, urban existence.

The fact that he makes his getaway by railway underlines the ambivalence of Gissing's whole attitude to old and new. Railways, as already noted, are important in Gissing's books: key scenes take place in them; the London District Railway in particular appears as a source of incidental emancipation for Gissing's women, who are thus enabled to go about town on their own much more freely than their mothers would have. Gissing himself, on his peregrinations round England and the Continent, made extensive use of railway systems, a great number of which were built during his own lifetime. Like everyone else, he used the railways to get to out-of-the-way places that, in Dickens' heyday, were accessible only by laborious journeys under horsepower—and then complained bitterly because 'trippers', using the same railway, got there too. On balance, one may feel, Gissing, and many of his characters, should have been glad of the invention that revolutionized life far more than the coming of the car. Yet more than once the railway figures in his books as a symbol for brutal modern power. Early in *New Grub Street*, Jasper Milvain and Marian Yule stand together by a line in the country watching the London Express crash past. Their different reactions seem to exemplify Gissing's own complexity of view:

'If I were ten years younger,' said Jasper laughing, 'I should say that was jolly! It enspirits me. It makes me feel eager to go back and plunge into the fight again.'
'Upon me it has just the opposite effect,' fell from Marian, in very low tones.

A symbolic combination of advertising and railway together— this time the London Underground, with its ready associations with another underworld—is to be found in *In the Year of Jubilee*:

They descended and stood together upon the platform, among hurrying crowds, in black fumes that poisoned the palate with sulphur. This way and that sped the demon engines, whirling lighted wagons full of people. Shrill whistles, the hiss and roar of steam, the bang, clap, bang of carriage doors, the clatter of feet on wood and stone—all echoed and reverberated from a huge, cloudy vault above them. High and low, on every available yard of wall, advertisements clamoured to the eye: theatres, journals, soaps, medicines, concerts, furniture, wines, prayer-meetings—all the produce and refuse of civilization announced in staring letters, in daubed effigies, base, paltry, grotesque. A battle-ground of advertisements, fitly chosen amid subterranean din and reek; a symbol to the gaze of that relentless warfare which ceases not, night and day, in the world above.

The image is hyper-aware, slightly manic. No wonder that Gissing, with his writer's essential ignorance of commerce (all too clearly shown in *Will Warburton*) should have felt like turning from the throbbing present to the literary man's traditional retreat —the past. 'Literature', after all, is chiefly about the past, particularly that type of literature which Gissing, from his earliest years as a classical scholar, had been taught to regard as 'the best'. Nor was his acquaintance with the classical writers superficial, an educated man's affectation; like a surprising number of his generation he was really at home in Latin or Greek. On a holiday in the Channel Islands he would be reading Ovid with the gusto that most twentieth-century readers could only find in a modern tongue—while his sister Madge read 'some disgusting little pietist work' (his phrase). This aspect of his mental life is somewhat inaccessible to us today, when few of us are equipped to comment on it. It is a temptation to feel, with Wells, that the classical scholarship of which he was so proud represented a rather sterile nineteenth-century tradition more than it represented Grecian or Roman reality, and that he used it less as an enrichment to his life than, like Ryecroft, as an obscurantist retreat. Wells had had only a 'commercial' education: he could not appreciate Ovid himself, and possibly he resented the way in which Victorian snobbery turned an acquaintance with Ovid into the mark of a gentleman. He may or may not have been being fair when he remarked 'At the back of my mind I thought him horribly mis-educated' and went on to describe the sort of schooling Gissing received as 'a vast collection of monumental masonry, a pale cemetery in a twilight, through which new conceptions hurry apologetically on their way to town finding neither home nor sustenance there.'

One rather hopes that Wells kept this particular opinion to himself, in Gissing's presence, for Gissing needed his comforts, monumental or otherwise, and certainly Wells had his own limitations. Nevertheless one cannot help noticing oneself that Gissing's fossilized concept of the glory that was Greece and the grandeur that was Rome led to certain limitations in him: for example he remarked himself on his inability to get interested in the Renaissance, which is rather a large blind-spot in a man so fond of Italy. (His ignorance of the medieval world was likewise marked, except for a jejeune attachment to Charlemagne and hence to Roncevalles, near which he died.) He wrote one travel book, *By the Ionian Sea*, besides several shorter travel articles and the reason that this aspect of his work has not been mentioned till now in the present study is that his traveller's attitude seems to me so selective, and so permeated with a nineteenth-century concept of the pre-Christian Mediterranean world, that I feel what he says has little interest or relevance for the present-day reader—whether that reader is interested in the Mediterranean or in the essential quality of Gissing's life and work. By one of those ironies which characterize his life and work, Gissing considered his travel book, along with *Ryecroft*, some of the best work he had done, but this would certainly be forgotten now were it not for the novels; the only one of his novels which is really unreadable is *Veranilda*, the long-planned historical romance set in ancient Rome on which he was at work when he died. It is as if he 'used' his foreign travel, mainly if not exclusively, as a journey into a past that was more subjective than genuine. For instance he noted once in Italy in a letter to Algernon that when he heard a woman talking to her cat in Italian he felt that she was addressing it in Latin. Countries whose past did not interest him he could not 'see' properly. Although he dutifully sight-saw in Paris on earlier visits, and later lived there with Gabrielle, and although he spoke and wrote excellent French, his diaries and letters rarely have anything illuminating to say about the place. As he once remarked sadly in a letter to Clara Collet, it was a pity he wasn't more interested in French history.

His general lack of interest in the modern state of European countries, except as a basis for complaint about decadence, dirt, or militarism, is all the more surprising because, even if he could only 'see' them via the medium of books, he read extensively among nineteenth-century Continental authors also. Apparently even a familiarity with Zola could not make him feel for Paris as Dickens had made him feel for London: perhaps, for him, the basis for this emotional involvement had to be laid down in boyhood. Yet books of all kinds and periods continued to be a constant background to his life; even as a child he had been the sort of boy who took down *Nicholas Nickleby* in a friend's[16] house and read it all through between lunch and tea; evidently he was the sort of compulsive reader who goes on reading whatever else is happening in his life. Even in his darkest periods his letters are peppered with lively comments on this or that book; his unquenchable interest in what other people were writing was one of his most positive and unshakeable characteristics.

One result of his own backward-looking education was that his attitude to education for other people was extremely ambivalent, and he never seems quite to have got to grips with the fact that 'education' does not necessarily mean a familiarity with Ovid, Livy and Sophocles. On the one hand he subscribed to the theory that education was a Good Thing, particularly for women whose intellectual potential had up to then been grossly neglected. At the same time the immediate results of the nineteenth century moves toward universal education for both sexes (the Education Act of 1870 and the establishment of the Board Schools) did not meet with his approval. His unkindness toward vulgar young men on the make has already been cited, although a more traditional type of self-made man had long been a sympathetic character to him. If he was driven into a fury of irritation by the older type of semi-literate working-class woman, all superstition and lack of hygiene, the newer type of semi-educated shop-girl aroused strong antagonism in him also. The supposed scholastic achievements of the French sisters in *Jubilee* are derided; so are those of Samuel Barmby, the perfect reader for the new mass-circulation newspaper, whose head is stuffed with self-importantly useless facts and whose literary idols are 'Carlyle and Gurty'.

Gissing's contention that this level of education is useless is perhaps fair enough, particularly when he allies it to the belief that women like the French sisters have substituted a smattering of fashionable half-knowledge, and an idea that they are too ladylike to do housework, for older domestic skills. But when he complains that the new generation of shop girls are domestically useless because they have worked outside the home instead of staying within it, one feels he is on shakier ground: surely he could have realized that he could have a woman as an independent wage-earner *or* as a domestic slave, but not both virtues combined in the same woman at once? Moreover his view of women who aspire to rather higher levels of education than shop-girls or French mock-ladies, is not kind. In *Jubilee* Jessica Morgan is pilloried for an excessive concern with examinations and London University (a goal toward which Gissing of all people might have felt sympathetic). In *Our Friend the Charlatan* the literary woman is made to look ridiculous in the person of May Tomalin, with her idea about how good it would be for the working classes to read *Piers Plowman*. The Gissing 'aim in life' as expressed by Walter Allen, that 'men and women should read books together' needs a closer examination. Gissing's real aim was that he should be reading while the woman listened.

Ultimately one is left feeling that, with women, as in so many other and related aspects of his life, 'there was something he wanted and yet he didn't know what it was'. This champion of oppressed womanhood, this defender of prostitutes, who wanted woman to be paid more, to be educated more, to outgrow the 'ancient deformity' of their oppressed and tyrannized state, was yet too passionately attached to concepts of the past and hence to concepts of the traditional feminine role to take readily to the results of his propaganda. There was a gap, for him, between practice and theory, between the individual and the mass. The same thing occurred in his feeling for the working classes. He sympathized with them when they were oppressed, but as soon as their lot improved he drew aside from them, repelled by robust vulgarity. As he wrote in his Commonplace Book: 'I do not love the people. But my passion of sympathy for the suffering poor.'

Nevertheless he was in one respect, as quite often, bizarrely perceptive about changing social mores, and it seems fitting to end an account of a life so profoundly affected by women with an example of his insight in their field. Though unable properly to reconcile, in his own era, the emotionally desirable image of Ruth

Pinch, the Dickensian 'little woman', with the theoretically desirable image of Miss Rodney, the emancipated school teacher in the short story *Miss Rodney's Leisure*, he looked forward to a time when a synthesis of the two types might be achieved. Virtually alone among his generation, he seems to have perceived that the emancipation of women and the liberation of the working classes were in practice linked, and that the result of both movements would be a sharp decline in the numbers of people available to form a feminine servant class. In fact in the 1890s this decline—spoken of as 'the servant problem'—was already beginning, but its significance seems to have gone largely unrecognized. Surprising as it seems to us now, the militant women of the 1900s had a considerable blind-spot about the rights of *lower-class* women; it never seems to have occurred to them that the right to live and work as men did depended, to some extent, on there being a plentiful supply of *un*emancipated women to cook, wash and child-mind. Gissing's irreconcilable distinction between the 'little woman' and the New Woman was borne out in practice.

Yet Gissing seems to have recognized that this should not, and could not, last. Towards the end of his chapter on Dickens' women, much of which is short-sighted and subjective, there occurs a remarkable piece of prophecy, forecasting a time when the two types of women may be synthesized into one:

There are those who surmise that in the far-off time when girls are universally well-taught, when it is the exception to meet, in any class, with the maiden who deems herself the natural inferior of brother, lover, husband, the homely virtues of Ruth Pinch will be even more highly rated than in the stupid old world. There are those who suspect that our *servant-question* foretells a radical change in ways of thinking about the life of home; that the lady of a hundred years hence will be much more competent and active in cares domestic than the average shopkeeper's wife today: that it may not be found impossible to turn from a page of Sophocles to the boiling of a potato, or even the scrubbing of a floor.

Some seventy-five years have passed, and we are not all there yet, but it seems to me that we have come quite a lot of the way. Both the sexual structure of society and the class structure have been greatly modified. Perhaps the fact that we have abandoned the idea that true education equals Sophocles has also helped—but, substituting a modern alternative to Sophocles, I recognize myself in the above passage. In the course of writing this book I have stopped to boil many a potato. I like to think that Gissing, if he knew, might in his rueful, 'if only' way be pleased at the thought.

Appendix

List of Gissing's
published works

Books by Gissing
currently in print

Acknowledgements

References

Index

Appendix

The three-volume novel and the role of Mr Mudie

To understand the reason why so much of Gissing's fiction took the form it did, you have to understand the economic stranglehold which the three-volume novel had over the greater part of his working life and the reasons for this situation. In the eighteenth century novels were as long as a piece of string; two volumes was a common pattern, but quite often there were four or five. It was Scott who did much to further the fashion for the standard three volumes and by the year of his death (1832) the price had likewise been standardized at ten shillings and sixpence per volume, or thirty-one-and-six for a set of three. That this price remained static for the next fifty years may be a tribute to the stability of the pound in the reign of Queen Victoria, but it acted as a brake on the free evolution of the fictional form. The point is, for all but the very rich, thirty-one-and-six (£1.57 in modern style) was then a substantial sum of money: perhaps its equivalent in modern purchasing power would be more like £10 or £12. This meant that the initial edition of any novel (not counting the magazine serial form in which the books of particularly successful writers first appeared) was almost exclusively a library edition, and lavishly bound accordingly. Few people expected to read new novels except by borrowing them—the heroine of *Denzil Quarrier*, who is supposed to have spent a year or two abroad, inadvertently reveals the fact that she has been in England all the time by a reference to a recently published novel. After a year or more a one-volume reprint edition would sometimes appear, paper-bound at six shillings, and frequently in a cut or revised version. But such a reprint

would hardly appear if there had been little demand for the
three-decker edition—and the demand was not only reflected
by the subscription libraries, it was also manipulated by them.
An established and popular author might confidently expect the
libraries to order hundreds or even thousands of copies of his
book on the very day of publication, knowing that they had a
captive market for it. Even an unknown author who wrote to
the popular bland formula might expect that the libraries would
risk taking a fair number of copies of such a recognizable,
approved commodity, with probably more to follow so long as
none of their subscribers complained that the book was 'outspoken' or 'distasteful'.

But the author who wrote on an apparently daring subject (as
Gissing did in *Workers in the Dawn*) or one whose novel contained expressions, or single passages, which might 'offend the
daughters of Mrs Grundy', was likely to find his work totally
boycotted by the libraries, with the result that, unless he were
very well known indeed, the whole of the first edition became
virtually unsaleable. *Workers in the Dawn*, whose publication
Gissing paid for himself, sold, all-in-all, twenty-nine copies when
it appeared in 1880. The library owners became, therefore, not
merely the arbiters of popular taste, but—since their prejudices
were well known to publishers—the persons who decreed whether
a book were publishable at all. The fate of Gissing's *Mrs Grundy's
Enemies*, which Smith and Elder would not publish because the
libraries would never take it, is a case in point. Other books, in
deference to librarians' sensibilities, were deformed out of all
reality. The bowdlerized version of Ida Starr's occupation which
is given in *The Unclassed* is doubtless due to this, for Gissing
had now learnt that he must hope to please the libraries or
flounder. When his third published book, *Demos*, appeared, we
find him writing to his sister wondering if the Church Institute
in Wakefield had a copy, since 'It is a branch of Mudie's, and
nothing but persistence is wanted'.

Charles Edward Mudie was by far the most important and
famous of the subscription library kings. Throughout most of the
reign of Victoria his rates were a guinea a year for one volume
at a time, with bulk rates for country houses. Many people took
out more than one subscription. He had opened a library section
in his stationery shop in Southampton Row, Bloomsbury, in 1842.

Ten years later he moved to larger premises in New Oxford Street and delivered books by cart all over London. In 1860, having swallowed several smaller competitors, he moved to a palatial hall in Oxford Street itself (it is described in *New Grub Street*) and his books were sent daily to branches all over Great Britain. You could even have them shipped to 'the colonies' by special arrangement. Like some towering totem-figure who both bestows goods on his subjects and oppresses them, he stands above the Victorian literary scene, the first era in history of mass-literacy and a substantial middle class. On the one hand it must be admitted that he was supplying the newly-literate and leisured classes with an ever-changing (if little varied) supply of reading matter. He undoubtedly saw himself as a benefactor. But on the other hand he, his sensibilities and his system, undoubtedly helped to foster the mediocre and imitative by providing a guaranteed sale, while it discouraged original and experimental work, and this charge was increasingly levelled at him by writers as the century went on. As he turned down Meredith's *Richard Feverel*, a work of full-blown romanticism (and, bizarrely, Gissing's favourite novel) it may be seen that the threshold of the 'shocking' was, for him, soon reached. Mudie himself always maintained, as many another organization has since in various contexts, that he was simply following the prevailing public opinion in these matters, but some people felt that he was also trying to shape it, and that a certain amount of the mealy-mouthedness of the Victorian era could actually be laid at Mr Mudie's lavish portals. What is perhaps hard for the modern reader to grasp is the extent to which, at that period, 'refinement' was associated with 'culture' in a way that it certainly is not now by the educated classes. The self-made provincial industrialist with a house full of women living in consciously ladylike idleness, who was Mudie's ideal subscriber, undoubtedly made an equation in his mind between what was 'proper', 'decent' or 'genteel' and what was upper class. Anything too reminiscent of what was 'sordid' or even merely proletarian was to be avoided in the interests of the newly-won class-image. No doubt Mudie himself, who had started as a seller of paper and pens but rose to have power over the users of such things, understood his clients' tastes and prejudices very well. So did his son, who inherited and carried on the business in an identical manner, as if the original Mudie was surviving, godlike, forever.

It is not hard, therefore, to see why the library system was in practice a form of literary censorship. What, however, is less immediately obvious is why Mudie's supported the three-volume novel for so long and what the unnatural results of this were. A concise explanation of the situation is to be found in Gissing's *New Grub Street*, in a conversation between Reardon and Milvain:

'For anyone in my position,' said Reardon, 'how is it possible to abandon the three volumes? It is a question of payment. An author of moderate repute may live on a yearly three-volume novel—I mean the man who is obliged to sell his book out and out, and who gets from one hundred to two hundred pounds for it. But he would have to produce four one-volume novels to obtain the same income; and I doubt whether he could get so many published within the twelve months. And here comes the benefit of the libraries; from the commercial point of view the libraries are indispensable. Do you suppose the public would support the present number of novelists if each book had to be purchased? A sudden change to that system would throw three-fourths of the novelists out of work.'
'But there's no reason why the libraries shouldn't circulate novels in one volume.'
'Profits would be less, I suppose. People would take the minimum subscription.'

There, in a nutshell, is the dilemma, and the reason that the system was allowed to endure for so long. Once the production-costs of a three-decker had been covered, its high price ensured that it made money quickly. Many authors, though they might chafe against the domination of Mudie, were uneasily aware that they owed him their livelihood and that they would never make the same amount of money from one-volume novels at six shillings a time, even if the libraries were prepared to stock them—and even if the authors could think up three or four separate plots and settings a year, which most could not. In fact many Victorian three-volume novels, including some of Gissing's own, are all too clearly good ideas for one or at most two volumes, which had been stretched and padded to fill the statutory three. This is doubtless why authors were, after all, reluctant to take the plunge and try their luck with single volumes; Gissing himself was exactly the type of writer, good but not to everyone's taste, who scraped a kind of living from the traditional novel but who would undoubtedly not have been able to live just on the proceeds of shorter ones, of which he would have had to sell enormously more copies to achieve the same result. His brave and premature remark in a letter to his brother (in the mid-1880s) that 'the old three-volume tradition is being broken down. One volume is becoming the commonest of all', was not, fortunately for him, true. Indeed, though during the 1890s he published several deliberately brief one-volume novels, these tend to be skeletal or designedly 'light'; he continued to write three-deckers, or potential three-deckers, till the end of his life. *The Crown of Life* would have been long enough for the old pattern, also *The Whirlpool*, and *Veranilda* (never finished) was planned in volumes. It was as if, despite his protests and the pains which writing cost him, he felt at home with the form.

Meanwhile the form obviously suited the libraries. The sheer expensiveness of the books, even taken volume by volume, made the subscriptions of Mudie and others a good bargain. And the separation into volumes meant that three subscribers could all, in theory, be reading the same book at the same time. When various well-known writers began to campaign in earnest against the three-decker, Mudie for quite a long time turned a deaf ear. George Moore, whose books had not on the whole found favour with the librarian, was a leading campaigner; so was Henry Vizetelly who had been in trouble over his translations of Zola's works and who had his own *A Mummer's Wife* issued in one volume in 1885. So was Rider Haggard, the popular author of *She*. But the book which probably turned the scales was Hall Caine's *The Manxman*, published by Heinemann in 1894 in one volume. It was a runaway best seller, and perhaps it was this that made Mudie listen at last. Publication figures tell the tale. In 1884 the number of three-deckers published was 193. In the nineties the figures began to fluctuate somewhat, but in 1894 they were back at 184.* That year too came *The Manxman* and Mudie made a sudden about-turn, altering his purchasing terms in such a way as to make the three-decker an uneconomic proposition. He claimed that he had 'no wish to dictate to the publishers' but inevitably that was what he was doing. The following

* For these figures, and for some of the facts in this Appendix, I am indebted to *Mudie's Circulating Library & the Victorian Novel* by Guinevere L. Griest, David & Charles, 1970.

year only fifty-two three-deckers were published, and by 1897 there were only four. A whole dominating tradition had come abruptly to an end and, with it, there quietly died the Victorian gentleman-writer, neither best-seller nor failure, who could actually hope to live from the novel alone.

It seems ironic, though fitting, that it was Mudie who had sustained the three-volume novel so long, Mudie who finally killed it off—and Mudie's Library, also, which was ultimately killed by its demise, though the Library's death was far more lingering. It continued to thrive through Edwardian days and even afterwards, but, in that people now could afford to buy their favourite writers outright, writers were no longer dependent on the Mudie seal of approval and its position of power was gone. The directors' faithful preoccupation with the shocking rapidly became outmoded, and by the inter-war period the once-dominating literary influence had become a declining business supplying old-fashioned romances for nervous old ladies of both sexes. It finally closed its doors in 1937; the big Oxford Street building remained empty for several years until destroyed by a German bomb.

List of Gissing's
published works

Two other collections of short stories previously published in
magazines were later issued, in 1927 *A Victim of Circumstances*

(Constable & Co.) and, in 1938 *Stories & Sketches* (Michael Joseph). Nine of the Prefaces Gissing wrote for the Rochester edition of Dickens' works were published in 1925 under the title *The Immortal Dickens* (Cecil Palmer).

Books by Gissing
currently in print

Of the above books some, such as *The Private Papers of Henry Ryecroft*, went into numerous editions in the two decades following the author's death and are therefore readily available second-hand—and in fact that particular book exists in a 1966 bilingual edition (French–English) published by Aubier-Montaigne of Paris. Others, such as *Workers in the Dawn*, are rare items in a bookseller's catalogue, never having been reprinted in England since the 1880s—though the position is different in America (see below). Novels that have been reprinted in England in the last few years are:

Demos, Harvester Press (facsimile), 1971
Isabel Clarendon, Harvester Press (facsimile), 1969.
The Nether World, projected by Harvester Press for 1974
New Grub Street, Bodley Head, 1967. Also available in Penguin, 1968
Born in Exile, Gollancz Classics series, 1970
The Odd Women, Blond, Doughty Library series, 1968
The Paying Guest, Japanese (yes!) reading edition in English with notes in Japanese. Recent. Kinseido, Tokyo.

Most of the other books, and also the volumes of short stories, are fairly readily available from dealers, in odd editions dating from the 1920s or late 1940s.

In America rather more is immediately available:
New Grub Street, Houghton Mifflin, 1962
The Odd Women, Stein & Day, 1968, and Norton, 1971
The Private Papers of Henry Ryecroft, New American Library, 1961
A Victim of Circumstances, Books for Libraries Press, 1971

In addition a number of novels now exist in reprint-facsimile editions issued by Abrahams' Magazine Services, New York, in 1968 and 1969. The edition used for these reprints is not always, however, the original one and omissions may be noted. The books are: *Workers in the Dawn, The Unclassed, A Life's Morning, Thyrza, The Emancipated, Born in Exile, Denzil Quarrier, The Crown of Life, Eve's Ransom. In the Year of Jubilee, The Odd Women, Our Friend the Charlatan, The Paying Guest, The Town Traveller, The Whirlpool, Will Warburton, Veranilda.*

Acknowledgements

Grateful acknowledgements are due to the Curator of the Henry W. and Albert A. Berg Collection, New York Public Library, Astor, Lenox and Tilden Foundations, and to that of the Beinecke Library, Yale, for making unpublished material available to me, and for the helpfulness of their staffs in doing so in a limited space of time. My grateful thanks are also due to George Gissing's son, Mr Alfred Gissing, for allowing me to make use of this material. It was also very kind of him to allow me to meet him.

I am also particularly grateful to Mr Robert Collet for allowing me to quote from the letters of George Gissing to Clara Collet, which are in his possession, have never been published, and have been seen by few Gissing scholars. His information to me on the subject both of his aunt, Clara Collet, and of Gabrielle Fleury, has also been extremely useful.

I am also somewhat more than indebted to Professor Pierre Coustillas of Lille University, who not only made available to me copies of letters written by George Gissing to Edith Sichel, and others written by John George Black to Gissing, but has been impressively generous with his time, advice and personal knowledge. We are all of us familiar with the academic researcher who sits on 'his' material like a jealous squirrel: Professor Coustillas has been a shining exception to this.

My thanks are also due to Mr Norman Willox, the Librarian of Wakefield City Library, who pointed out various Gissing 'sites' to me and lent me a book on the town. Also to Professor Francis Noel Lees of Manchester for advice on the whereabouts of various letters. Also to Alan Clodd of the Enitharmon Press for lending me the galley-proofs of *Henry Hick's Recollections of George Gissing*. Also to Chris Kohler, bookseller, who, with an amazing degree of altruism, actually lent me a copy of *Workers in the Dawn*, the rarest of Gissing's novels and one virtually unobtainable through most library channels. He has also been extremely helpful in supplying me with photos, addresses, introductions, and general information.

I believe it is customary to end any such list of acknowledgements with some such remarks as 'last but not least, thanks to my husband/wife without whose help and support I could never have completed this work . . .' However such a remark always strikes me as a little absurd: are the writers of biographical studies supposed to be so feeble that they really wouldn't have got their own work done without being propped up by someone else? (And what of the unmarried researcher?) In any case, my husband suggests that I ought to write instead: 'This book has been completed despite the mounting opposition of my family, who got sick of the sound of the word "Gissing".' I will simply, therefore, confine myself to saying that, despite their most understandable lack of profound interest in the subject, both husband and son did accompany me manfully to Gissing's places of birth and death, and that my husband took a number of photographs of intermediary stations on Gissing's life odyssey, some of which appear in this book.

The illustrations

The author would like to thank the following for permission to reproduce the illustrations: Professor Pierre Coustillas for 1 and 5; the *Radio Times* Hulton Picture Library for 2 and 3; Madame Denise le Mallier for 4; her husband for 6, 7, and 8; and Mr C. C. Kohler for 9 and 10.

References

Sources

The letters written by George Gissing to his family, and particularly to his brother Algernon, are mainly to be found in two places, in the Berg Collection of the New York Public Library and in the Beinecke Rare Book and Manuscript Library at Yale University, Mass. Some of the letters, including a few that I have quoted, are also to be found in *The Collected Letters of George Gissing to his Family* arranged by Algernon and Ellen Gissing and published by Constable in 1927, but this collection has for so long been more famous for what it leaves out than for what it includes, that it is only of limited value to the serious student. I understand that a complete edition, including the hitherto unpublished letters, is currently being prepared by Arthur J. Young.

The Diary of George Gissing is in the Berg Collection of the New York Public Library and has never been published. This source is not reiterated in a note each time the diary is quoted. Professor P. Coustillas is working on an edition of the diary for publication.

In general, where a reference is given in a note, it is not repeated next time the same source (e.g. Commonplace Book) is quoted, unless the next quotation comes very much later in the book.

Introduction

1 Morley Roberts, *The Private Life of Henry Maitland*, first published by Eveleigh Nash, 1912.

1 The Born Exile

1 Quoted by Morley Roberts, op. cit. It is interesting that, in a late novel, *Our Friend the Charlatan*, Gissing made a character re-

mark on the widespread phenomenon of the successful writer or
scientist sprung from a commonplace background, but I think
one may fairly assume that Gissing himself had then only just
noticed the fact.
2   *Walks about Wakefield*, S. W. Banks.
3   It is still there, with a railway bridge in front of it, a traffic
roundabout beyond and electric cables overhead.
4   See also Sidney Kirkwood's attitude to the country in *The
Nether World*. The descriptive terms—'tilth', 'mantled pool'—
are Chaucerian or Shakespearian rather than real.
5   *The Immortal Dickens: Prefaces*, Cecil Palmer, 1925. Originally written by Gissing in the late 1890s for the Rochester edition
of Dickens' works.
6   Letter in the Berg Collection dated 1885 (no month).
7   To Clara Collet, November 1895.
8   Frederic Harrison was a successful journalist and the leader
of the London Positivists, whom Gissing briefly joined.
9   All three, he claimed later, were written within seven months,
but the order of writing was not the order of publication.
10   In addition his brother Algernon displayed the same tendency: writing books about the English countryside, in a vein
of determined rusticity, became his speciality.
11   Published by the New York Public Library, 1962, edited by
Korg.
12   Touchingly preserved in the Berg Collection and at Yale.
13   In an article in *Nineteenth Century Fiction*, 1927.
14   See footnote on page 53.
15   'Reminiscences of my Father', unpublished manuscript at
Yale.
16   Clara Collet.
17   Letter to Algernon in the Berg Collection.
18   Mabel Collins Donnelly, *George Gissing: Grave Comedian*,
Harvard University Press, 1954.
19   Unpublished. In the Berg Collection.
20   Gissing attempted to tell Gabrielle this, in a letter written to
her in 1898 shortly after they had met, but Gabrielle, who was
totally attached to her own mother, does not seem to have believed
him. Profoundly French, she seems in any case to have misread
many of Gissing's relationships in his own land, whether with
family or with friends—a circumstance in which she was abetted
by Gissing himself, who, in his new-found emotion for her, was
not always strictly accurate to her about past events and relationships in his life.
21   In an article in *Nineteenth Century Fiction*, 1927.
22   Henry Hick.
23   Quoted in the *Bulletin of the Boston Library*, December
1947.
24   In point of fact, within a year Algernon, who shared his

brother's tendency to change his mind, was talking of giving up housekeeping.

25 The novel was actually written while Gissing himself was oppressed by an 'exile' of another kind—his lonely and circumscribed life within the confines of his ill-advised second marriage.

26 Far from keeping his second wife away from them as he had done with Nell, he hoped that she would become friends with them—hopes which she failed to gratify.

27 In the article in *Nineteenth Century Fiction*, already cited.

28 Letter at Yale, written in 1897 when Gissing, Edith and the children were on an abortive holiday together immediately before the final break.

29 He thought of calling an early (unpublished) novel this.

2   The Escape Downwards

1 *The Immortal Dickens: Prefaces*, op. cit.

2 Black. See further in chapter.

3 *Munby, Man of Two Worlds—the Life and Diaries of Arthur Munby*, edited by D. Hudson, John Murray, 1972.

4 From *The Private Life of Henry Maitland*.

5 I am indebted to Professor Pierre Coustillas for access to copies of these documents.

6 The idea of saving a 'fallen woman' was not, of course, peculiar to Gissing: it was a standard nineteenth-century dream, shared by persons as diverse as Hazlitt, Gladstone and Dante Gabriel Rossetti. Indeed Rossetti seems to have nursed the idea for many years, rather as Gissing did. His never-finished picture, *'Found'*, for which he made numerous studies shows a young countryman who has driven into London with a netted heifer in a cart finding his old love turned prostitute, collapsed against a wall. In multiple ways—the theme of country-health as opposed to town-sickness, the theme of the 'clean' man's indirect guilt for woman's plight as exemplified by the heifer—this picture reflects ideas which were also part of Gissing's own mental landscape.

7 Now at Yale.

8 Both letters at Yale.

9 Letter at Yale.

10 Letter at Yale.

11 Two quotations from *Thyrza* seem significant here. The first concerns Walter Egremont and the second Luke Ackroyd, both of whom are partial alter-egos of Gissing himself (Gilbert Grail is a third):

> (i) '. . . He would have said that there lay in him a great faculty of love which Annabel, if she willed it, could at a moment bring into life . . . It was not passion, and the consciousness that it was not often depressed him. One of his ideals was that of a passion nurtured to be the crowning glory of life. He did

not love Annabel in that way; would that he could have done!'

(ii) 'Essentially his nature was very gentle and ductile, and he had strong affections. Probably he could not have told you, with any approach to accuracy, how often he had been in love, or fancied himself so, and for Ackroyd being in love was, to tell the truth, a matter of vastly more importance than all the political and social and religious questions in the world.'

12 *The Working Classes in Victorian Fiction*, Routledge & Kegan Paul, 1971.

13 See Godwin Peak in *Born in Exile*: 'I was born in exile. It took a long time before I had taught myself how to move and speak like one of the class to which I belonged by right of intellect.'

14 *Experiment in Autobiography*, Gollancz, 1934.

15 See Godwin Peak in *Born in Exile*: 'I can't pretend to care for anything but individuals. The few whom I know and love are of more importance to me than all the blind multitude rushing to destruction.'

16 Mrs Frederic Harrison.

17 The phrase is Orwell's.

18 Quoted in the published edition of Gissing's *Letters* edited by Alfred and Ellen Gissing, Constable, 1927.

19 For an informed discussion of the various different *kinds* of Socialism surveyed in *Demos* see Professor Coustillas' Introduction to *Demos*, Harvester Press edition, 1972.

20 See Diary, 1888.

21 Letter quoted in published *Letters*.

3 The Guilty Secret

1 Letter at Yale.

2 Published in 1913.

3 This view of petty theft is actually expressed—though slightly mocked—in *In the Year of Jubilee* (1894).

4 The value of this sum at the period was, of course, enormously greater than it is today.

5 In an article originally published in *The Times Literary Supplement* and included in *Katherine Mansfield and Other Literary Studies*, Constable, 1959.

6 *George Gissing*, Methuen, 1965.

7 See Gissing's own comment on Arthur Golding, the first of his alter-egos, near the end of *Workers in the Dawn*: 'The secret of his life lay in the fact that his was an ill-balanced nature, lacking the element of a firm and independent will.'

8 Nor did he make any of his characters a Jew. Surprisingly for one so concerned with exile and with the person subtly set apart

from society, he writes as though the existence of English Jews was unknown to him.

9 In *New Grub Street* the successful young journalist Jasper Milvain is rumoured—quite wrongly—to be 'somebody's illegitimate son', as if such a background were an advantage rather than otherwise.

10 Letter dated 26 March 1876.

11 Letter at Yale.

12 Letter at Yale.

13 Letter in *Henry Hick's Recollections of George Gissing*, edited by Pierre Coustillas, Enitharmon Press, 1973.

14 Frank Swinnerton, *George Gissing*, Martin Secker, 1912.

15 In January 1898 Gissing wrote to Clara Collet: 'A woman must always more or less despise a man, who in his relations with women, has shown himself lacking in sense, lacking in self respect, lacking in delicacy, lacking in ambition.'

16 When Frederic Harrison wrote a letter of condolence on Gissing's death to the woman he supposed was Edith and whom Gissing had told him was a 'farm girl', he was somewhat surprised to received an acknowledgement in French from Gabrielle.

4 The Woman-Question

1 The few letters from Edith which have survived are in a clerkish, not illiterate hand, with a few minor spelling mistakes. They are in the possession of Robert Collet.

2 Although the hypothesis that she could herself have been syphilitic (see previous chapter) should not perhaps be totally discounted.

3 Diary for 1890.

4 She wrote to ask if she might translate *New Grub Street* and he asked her to visit him in Dorking.

5 Letter to Wells, January 1901, in R. A. Gettmann's *George Gissing and H. G. Wells*, University of Illinois, 1961.

6 Unpublished letter to Clara Collet for same period.

7 Letter of June 1901.

8 Edited by Pierre Coustillas, published by the New York Public Library, 1964.

9 Letter dated 11 September 1898.

10 Letter dated 1 April 1899.

11 See *George Gissing and H. G. Wells*, op. cit.

12 Many unpublished letters in the Berg Collection.

13 Gollancz, 1934. This book also gives a graphic account of Gissing's death.

14 Robert Collet, Clara Collet's nephew.

15 This lady, then a widow, considered but rejected Gissing's offer of a free union. She subsequently married again and became

the mother of Kitty Dobbs, who was to marry Malcolm Muggeridge.

16   A couple of years later he planned a short story with this title, but apparently did not finish it.

17   Andrew Long in the *Author*. Quoted by Mabel Collins Donnelly, op. cit.

18   Letter dated 15 August 1890. *Letters of George Gissing to Edward Bertz*, edited by Arthur Young, Rutgers, 1961.

19   Diary, December 1890.

20   In an article already cited.

21   See Lionel Tarrant who, in *In the Year of Jubilee* (1894) reflects on his marriage: 'in acting honourably, it seemed probable that he had spoilt his life'.

22   Introduction to *New Grub Street*, published by Bodley Head, 1967.

23   Letter to Bertz, 23 January 1891. In subsequent letters to this correspondent he never referred to his marriage till it was all over.

24   In an unpublished letter to Edith Sichel.

25   Walter T. Spencer, author of *Forty Years in my Bookshop*, Constable, 1923.

26   During the previous year he visited Thomas Hardy and recorded in his Diary the view that it would have been much better had Hardy married 'an honest homely woman who would have been impossible in fashionable society'. Diary, September 1895.

5   Studies in Conflict

1   Douglas Goldring, *Reputations: Essays in Criticism*, Chapman & Hall, 1920.

2   Mallard.

3   Roberts had travelled widely in Africa and the South Seas. This, his considerable physical vitality and his determinedly extrovert public persona, apparently concealed deeper levels of neurosis and sensibility. See Morchard Bishop's introduction to the edition of *The Private Life of Henry Maitland*, Richards Press, 1958.

4   Gissing was an unfailingly generous friend to Roberts, who was one of the two people—Wells was the other—whom Gabrielle sent for when Gissing was dying. But Gissing once recorded disgustedly in his Diary (October 1893): 'Roberts *boasts* that he spent weeks in Paris without so much as entering the Louvre.'

5   Barbara Hardy, *The Appropriate Form*, Athlone Press, 1964.

6   This comment possibly belongs in the department of changing social mores rather than Author's Neuroses, but for an

apparent Gissing prejudice couched in the form of an objective social comment, see his remark on Irene's first engagement in *The Crown of Life*: 'For caresses, for endearments, the time was not yet; that kind of thing, among self-respecting people of a certain class, came only with the honeymoon.' While this may have been the outward convention of the period, did Gissing really believe it represented reality? It is just possible, however, that the remark is intended ironically, since Irene is engaged to Arnold Jacks whose cold-blooded view of such matters is that 'Women have "hearts"; they really do grow fond of the men they admire; a singular provision of nature.' Anyway the pair sit in a railway carriage alone for some time with complete propriety. Compare and contrast (as exam papers say) the squalid association in *The Odd Women* between Everard Barfoot and Amy Drake, which takes place *because* the two are alone in the same situation—this unfairly proving that Amy Drake was no lady. Compare also the part which a chance encounter between Monica Madden and Barfoot on the District Line plays in leading Rhoda (who catches sight of them) to believe that there might be something 'between' them. Clearly technological changes in themselves were, in Gissing's day, forcing modifications in accepted social conventions about what a nice woman should or should not do if she wishes to avoid finding herself in a position in which she might be tempted to behave in a Nancy Lord-like manner. But in any case the idea that ladies had more power of resistance than working girls seems rather illogical, since for the whole of the nineteenth century it was the lower-class girls who enjoyed a relatively free, unchaperoned existence without exciting adverse comment, while gently-reared girls led, at least in theory, a far more circumscribed existence. You would think from this that the working girl might be supposed to be better used to looking after herself.

7 He apparently planned to in *The Whirlpool* (see letter to Bertz dated 9 May 1896) but the concept of the book changed in the writing.

8 Letter to Algernon dated 23 January 1896. At Yale.

9 See his letter to Bertz dated 2 June 1893: 'My demand for female "equality" simply means that I am convinced there will be no social peace until women are intellectually trained very much as men are. More than half the misery of life is due to the ignorance and childishness of women.'

10 To be found in the collection called *A Victim of Circumstances*, Constable, 1927.

6 The Man and his World

1 Morley Roberts regarded him as 'a natural bookworm, compelled to spin fiction'. Although Gissing frequently recorded in

his diary times when he was unable to write, or wrote very slowly with many set-backs, making holocausts of many weeks' work when he suddenly lost confidence in an idea or a theme, there were other times when he wrote extremely quickly and with that intense absorption peculiar to the person whose writing is an integral part of his thought-processes. For instance, when he finished *Isabel Clarendon* (August 1885) he wrote to Algernon: 'Yesterday I wrote for nine hours, and at last in that peculiar excitement in which one cannot see the paper and pen, but only the words . . .' Elsewhere he spoke of his pleasure in 'moulding' and arranging words. Needless to say, however, he hoped that his sons would not take after him; in fact his faintly sentimental hopes for Walter, as expressed to Clara Collet in a letter in 1899, are worth quoting, they are so typical of him: '. . . heaven forbid that he should want to write! Your suggestion about rose-growing was not at all bad. I should be delighted if he took to anything of that sort—a quiet, healthy life in old England.'

(Neither son did take to writing to any great extent. Walter worked for the National Trust till his death in 1916 at the age of twenty-five. Alfred, the younger, became an architect specializing in church architecture, something about which his father would have had mixed feelings. In later life he ran first a school and then a hotel in Switzerland. At the time of writing (April 1973) he is still there, living in an idyllic village of the Valais not far from Trient, where George Gissing and Gabrielle Fleury spent a happy holiday in July 1899.)

2 Letter at Yale.

3 Letter dated February 1880 at Yale.

4 Quoted in *Times Literary Supplement* article 'The Permanent Stranger', 14 February 1948.

5 Brian Boru' Dunne. Quoted by R. A. Gettmann in *George Gissing and H. G. Wells*, op. cit.

6 *Experiment in Autobiography*, op. cit.

7 Edward Clodd, *Memories*, Chapman & Hall, 1916.

8 Both letters in the Berg Collection.

9 In 1927 article already cited.

10 See *George Gissing and H. G. Wells*, op. cit.

11 In fact he first found himself coughing blood in September 1897. See letter to Wells.

12 See Pierre Coustillas, *George Gissing at Alderley Edge*, Enitharmon Press, 1969.

13 See his portrait of the Germanophile, culture-despising John Yule in *New Grub Street*.

14 See also the description near the end of *The Nether World* of the damp new villa in Crouch End where the doors don't fit properly, and even so the Hewett-Kirkwood family who inhabit it can hardly afford the rent. It is memorably described as being in an area which is a new 'dark patch' on the map, as

if the very spread of London at that period were akin to the spread of rot in a house—which it was, but few people other than Gissing saw it that way: even intelligent, thoughtful persons of the period, while they might object to certain things, seem to have been largely mesmerized by belief that Progress equals Good.

15 At Yale.
16 Cited by Pierre Coustillas in *George Gissing at Alderley Edge*, op. cit.

Index

m_3